SACRED SITES, SACRED PLACES

ONE WORLD ARCHAEOLOGY
Series Editor: P. J. Ucko

SACRED SITES, SACRED PLACES

Edited by

David L. Carmichael
Department of Sociology and Anthropology, University of Texas at El Paso, USA

Jane Hubert
Department of Psychology, University of Southampton, UK

Brian Reeves
Department of Archaeology, University of Calgary, Alberta, Canada

Audhild Schanche
Institute for Samfunnsvitenskap, University of Tromsø, Norway

London and New York

First published 1994
by Routledge
11 New Fetter Lane, London EC4P 4EE

Simultaneously published in the USA and Canada
by Routledge
29 West 35th Street, New York, NY 10001

Typeset in 10 on 12pt Bembo by Florencetype Ltd, Kewstoke, Avon
Printed and bound in Great Britain by Butler & Tanner Ltd, London and Frome

Printed on acid free paper

British Library Cataloguing in Publication Data
A catalogue record for this book is available from the British Library

Library of Congress Cataloging in Publication Data
Sacred sites, sacred places / edited by David L. Carmichael . . . [et al.].
    p.   cm. — (One world archaeology ; 23)
Includes bibliographical references and index.
1. Sacred space.   2. Religion, Prehistoric.   3. Historic sites.
4. Indians — Religion and mythology.   I. Carmichael, David L.
II. Series.
BL580.S24 1994
291.3'5 — dc20 93–33400

ISBN 0–415–09603–0

Contents

List of contributors

George H. Okello Abungu, Department of Coastal Archaeology, Fort Jesus Museum, Mombasa, Kenya.

Pamela A. Bunte, Department of Anthropology, California State University, Long Beach, USA.

David L. Carmichael, Department of Sociology and Anthropology, The University of Texas at El Paso, USA.

Gabriel Cooney, Department of Archaeology, University College, Dublin, Ireland.

Robert J. Franklin, Department of Anthropology, University of California, Dominguez Hills, USA.

Jane Hubert, Department of Psychology, University of Southampton, UK.

John F. C. Johnson, Chugach Alaska Corporation, Anchorage, Alaska, USA.

Frank LaPena, Wintu Tribe, California, USA.

Katarzyna Marciniak, Institute of Prehistory, Adam Mickiewicz University, Poznań, Poland.

Hirini Matunga, Centre for Maori Studies and Research, Lincoln University, Canterbury, New Zealand.

Gordon Mohs, Stalo Mission, British Columbia, Canada.

Inga-Maria Mulk, Svenskt Fjall Och, Samemuseum, Jokkmokk, Sweden.

Mary Maimo Mumah, Association for Creative Teaching, Bamenda, North West Province, Cameroon.

Henry Mutoro, Department of History, University of Nairobi, Kenya.

O. V. Ovsyannikov, Institute of the History of Material Culture, St Petersburg, Russia.

Nicole Price, Medicine Wheel Alliance, Lame Deer, Montana, USA.

Chantal Radimilahy, Museum of Art and Archaeology, University of Madagascar, Antananarivo, Madagascar.

Brian Reeves, Department of Archaeology, University of Calgary, Alberta, Canada.

David Ritchie, Aboriginal Areas Protection Authority, Darwin, NT, Australia.

Inés Sanmiguel, Chiapas, Mexico.

Nicholas J. Saunders, Department of History, University of the West Indies, Jamaica.

Audhild Schanche, Institute for Samfunnsvitenskap, University of Tromsø, Norway.

N. M. Terebikhin, Cultural Department of the Archangel Region, Archangel, Russia.

Dorothea J. Theodoratus, Department of Anthropology, California State University, Sacramento, California, USA.

Simiyu Wandibba, Institute of African Studies, University of Nairobi, Kenya.

Foreword

This book is the third in the *One World Archaeology* (OWA) series to derive from the Second World Archaeological Congress (WAC 2), held in Barquisimeto, Venezuela, in September 1990. Despite many organizational problems (Fforde 1991a, p. 6), over 600 people attended the Inaugural Session of WAC 2, with more than 450 participants from 35 countries taking part in academic sessions, and additional contributions being read on behalf of many others who were unable to attend in person.

True to the aims and spirit of WAC 1, over three-quarters of the participants came from the so-called Third and Fourth Worlds (see Fforde 1991a, p. 7 for details) and the academics came not only from archaeology and anthropology but from a host of related disciplines.

WAC 2 continued the tradition of effectively addressing world archaeology in its widest sense. Central to a world archaeological approach is the investigation not only of how people lived in the past but also how and why those changes took place which resulted in the forms of society and culture which exist today. Contrary to popular belief, and the archaeology of some twenty-five years ago, world archaeology is much more than the mere recording of specific historical events, embracing as it does the study of social and cultural change in its entirety.

Like its predecessor, this Congress was organized around major themes. Several of these themes were based on the discussion of full-length papers which had been circulated previously – or were available to be read at the Congress itself – to all those who had indicated a special interest in them. Other sessions, such as the thematic one from which this book derives, were based on three days of discussion of a combination of fifty precirculated papers, lectures and 'councils' (Reeves 1991, p. 14).

The main aim of the theme, and of the resultant *Sacred Sites, Sacred Places*, was to focus attention on the nature and special features of one category of site with which archaeologists, anthropologists and heritage managers have to deal: sites of especial significance to the peoples who created them, and/or to those who now 'own', investigate or protect them.

This overall theme has a special historical place in the development of the
World Archaeological Congress (WAC). It has been claimed that perhaps one
of the most significant features of its First Congress (Hubert 1987, p. 163) was
the active participation of indigenous peoples from many parts of the world in
the discussions hitherto considered to be the exclusive domain of archaeologists. Certainly, this participation led on to the choice of the theme of WAC's
First Inter-Congress, held in South Dakota, USA, in August 1989 (Hubert
1989) on 'Archaeological ethics and the treatment of the dead'. WAC had
therefore already by then recognized the centrality of sites of special significance to future relationships between archaeologists or anthropologists and
indigenous peoples or ethnic groups in various parts of the world. Indeed, as a
result of the 1990 WAC 2 meeting in Barquisimeto on 'Sacred sites/sacred
places and "sites of significance"' (and see Preface), the WAC Plenary Session
and Council adopted the following resolution:

> That WAC acknowledges that the identification and conservation
> of sacred sites are of major concern to all the peoples of the world,
> and that a meeting be organized under the auspices of WAC to
> explore the issues involved, with a view to drawing up an inter-
> national accord on sacred sites, sacred places, sacred spaces and sites
> of significance.

A planned seminar for 1991/2 specifically to discuss legislation in relation
to sacred sites, and to formulate details of future WAC meetings (possibly
to form the theme of a future WAC Inter-Congress) on the subject of sacred
sites, unfortunately never eventuated (Fforde 1991b, p. 20; *WAC News*
1992, p. 7), nor, as a result, did an expected report from Professor B. O. K.
Reeves, detailing the results of the WAC 2 meeting. To some extent,
therefore, this book, *Sacred Sites, Sacred Places*, must form the charter
for future WAC activities in this vital area of archaeological action and
enquiry.

Perhaps the first striking revelation of this book is how very little serious,
analytical attention archaeologists have paid, until recently, to such important
records of the past. Even this recent work reveals a sad situation, emphasizing
that 'the extraordinary neglect of ritual and religion in archaeological theory is
a weakness which must be addressed' (Garwood, Jennings, Skeates & Toms
1991, p. v), and concluding that 'the current conceptual and methodological
situation with respect to the study of ritual and religion in archaeology . . .
seems to be characterized by a very wide range of interpretative and analytical
approaches, and few threads of consistency in specific theoretical terms'
(Garwood, Jennings, Skeates & Toms 1991, p. vi). It is within the context of
this vacuum that *Sacred Sites, Sacred Places* also documents, almost incidentally,
the consequent heavy-handedness of the legal and social treatment of many
such special places. This lack of considered concern regarding the nature of this
category of site (or, as many chapters point out, the several categories of site)
has been accompanied by lack of discussion about the nature of any special

consideration which should be afforded them, whether in reports about their existence, or in legislation and subsequent attempts to preserve them.

Meanwhile, however, social anthropologists (e.g. Bowman 1993, pp. 431–3) have recently returned to a framework deriving from the writing of Hertz (1913) in order to place the analysis of sacred places within their considerations of boundary-drawing between the 'us' and the 'other'. Bowman (1993, p. 433) concludes (in the context of current Palestinian and Israeli attitudes and practices) that 'holy sites serve as monuments to imaginings of community and . . . such monuments prove to be as labile as are those communities themselves'.

For archaeologists, such shifts in meaning according to social context and in response to particular circumstance have recently been appreciated in their analyses of works of art (*Animals into Art*, edited by Howard Morphy), and in their discussions about the nature and genesis of ethnicity (*Archaeological Approaches to Cultural Identity*, edited by Stephen Shennan) but the present book is the first to examine the problems involved in such a changing conception of 'significance' specifically in the context of site classification, site recording and registration, and subsequent site management.

Sacred Sites, Sacred Places shows how far ahead in its thinking Australia was, and possibly still is, in this regard, and in its attempts at application in actual research contexts, in comparison with other parts of the world. Whereas a general recognition of the existence of Aboriginal sacred sites was evident in discussions at a National Seminar held in 1972 (see chapters in Edwards 1975), some Australian academics have attempted to draw distinctions between 'sacred' and 'secret-sacred' materials and information, at least since the early 1970s (partly as a result of the publication of photographs which have caused grave offence to Aborigines). Although never published, a discussion document which I commissioned in 1974, to be written jointly by an Aboriginal site recorder and a professor of anthropology, appears sophisticated in its awareness of the fluid nature of the categories which were being considered.

> We are concerned, in this context, with living situations, where Aborigines themselves take a vital interest in secret-sacred aspects of their society and culture, and regard information about its content as being in various ways and in various circumstances restricted, closed to certain categories of persons – Aboriginal, as well as non-Aboriginal. . . .
>
> The area or dimension which is called, for convenience, 'secret-sacred' is not always easy to stipulate in broad terms, in such a way that it has a general significance which can be applied in all or nearly all situations. . . . One point, however, is clear – the idea of 'secret-sacred' needs to be separated from the generalized concept of sacred. . . .
>
> However, it is important to remember that Aboriginal religious systems varied considerably, and we must look to the local in

specific circumstances. In other words, what is secret–sacred in one Aboriginal society is not necessarily secret–sacred in another.

Moreover, what is categorized as secret–sacred at one period of time may not necessarily be so at another period of time – in other words, classification of this dimension may change over time. There are several outstanding examples of this. . . . The issues, then, are not clear-cut, and must inevitably take into account local communities and individual persons as well as more general considerations.

Who decides on what is secret-sacred: Quite obviously, the principal persons here are those Aborigines who are most intimately concerned with maintaining the concept of secret–sacred in relation to some aspects of their actively functioning religious life. In an ultimate sense, the real control of this must rest with such Aborigines themselves – in withholding such information as they consider necessary from specific categories of persons, including non–Aborigines (anthropologists included), and controlling access to, and distribution of what they may regard as 'restricted' or 'dangerous' material within the communities of which they are members.

(Berndt & Roughsey 1975, pp. 3–5)

By 1977, the Australian Institute of Aboriginal Studies had taken the major policy decision only to record sites of significance to Aboriginal people *where the Aboriginal custodians wish such sites to be recorded*; by 1978, it had formulated its Sites of Significance recording policy which it did

particularly conscious of the fact that its concerns are directly those of the Aboriginal people throughout Australia, arising from their aspirations and needs, and therefore recognized as its priorities those programs and proposals which will encourage and enhance Aboriginal identification or re-identification with land and sites in the areas of: identification and location of sites; studies of the nature of Aboriginal land tenure and relationships to sites or spectrums of sites; methods of conservation and physical protection of sites; education and public information which aims to expand the awareness and understanding of this identification or which facilitates such Aboriginal identification. In implementing such priorities it was concerned to ensure that there is (a) maximum involvement and training of Aboriginal people; (b) support for appropriately qualified researchers in the field; (c) appropriate high standards of research and reporting; (d) priority for threatened areas or endangered sites.

(Ucko 1979, p. 14)

In the context of such early discussions it is fascinating to read in this book how the problems involved in accepting the notion of a 'secret' category of information, in some sense 'owned' by the indigenous peoples of Australia, have to some extent at least been accommodated in subsequent, and current, site registration practice and in site legislation in Australia. In the Berndt & Roughsey document of 1975, archaeologists and anthropologists were exhorted to make Aborigines aware of the fragility and transitory nature of oral tradition in what now seems to us to be a somewhat patronizing way (presumably reflecting the social anthropologists' continuing unease with regard to the handling of the evidence of 'social change' within the then available structural and functional models of social dynamics):

> It is vitally important that traditionally-oriented Aborigines be made aware of the fragile nature of secret-sacred material – the degree to which it can change over a period of time; and the hazards of passing on such knowledge orally. Large areas of such knowledge have been changing radically, and within the last few years . . . a great deal of such belief and action is being telescoped, modified, and discarded. We can provide numerous examples of this. Also, there is the question of passing on such knowledge to on-coming generations. Again, this is not functioning as smoothly as it did in the immediate past. . . .
>
> It is true that some Aborigines have reacted in a parochial and ethnocentric fashion: 'if we cannot possess that cultural heritage, no one else should'. And some have been content to let that knowledge die with themselves; or because of lack of receptivity on the part of the younger generation, they have refused to pass on that knowledge. Others have taken a contrary stand . . . where they have realized that it is important that the knowledge they hold should not be lost. It is undoubtedly a dilemma, and one with no easy or simple solutions.
>
> (Berndt & Roughsey 1975, p. 6)

However patronizing such views may, or may not, appear to be, many, if not all, of these same attitudes and dilemmas are examined in *Sacred Sites, Sacred Places* in the context of experiences from many parts of the world. In Australia itself, there continues to be debate about the role and training of Aborigines in managing the sites, some now contained within parks, and others both in, and off, Aboriginal land (and see Australian Heritage Commission 1989). In the USA, legal and ethical considerations regarding sacred sites and land ownership are bedevilled by the competing claims of different groupings of Native peoples. Behind all such examples throughout the world lies the apparent problem, facing those responsible for managing the past, in accepting that the ascription of what is, or is not, of *special* value about a particular site or area of land is not only outside their own control, but may not even be commensurate with the classifications of archaeologists or ecologists.

In other words, what still lies behind many of the current debates is a conflict between the 'freezing' of the record of the past and the contemporary attitudes and beliefs and 'new' mythology relating to the sites concerned (and see Ucko 1994 for a discussion of how these apparently opposing interests also reflect the kind of archaeology which is made available, for a variety of political reasons, in any particular country). There is also potential conflict between the creation of (more or less) immutable legislation and measures to protect sites, and the needs of those with continuing interests in the sites of the past to be able to exploit their potential multivalency. Archaeologists and heritage managers in particular also need to draw a line between what is seen as 'traditional' and the – supposedly less important, and certainly not 'pristine' – present. In Brazil (Guidon 1992), recognition of the importance of archaeological sites of special significance in the State of Piaui has recently led to the creation of a National Park (as well as inscription on the World Heritage Register), with the result that all 'traditional' use of materials (hunting, collection of foods or wood, etc.) within the Park has now been banned; little chance here, therefore, for any reassertion of 'ownership' through the sorts of 'troublesome' activities recently undertaken by Australian Aborigines in repainting their rock art sites (Ucko 1990, p. 18).

Sacred Sites, Sacred Places is a powerful book, dealing with powerful matters. Whether or not concepts of the 'sacred' remain unchanging, wherever sacredness is ascribed at any particular moment, powerful emotions and attitudes are involved. There is no point in anyone denying the importance of special locations to those actively, and believingly, involved in their appropriate ('correct') management ('treatment') at any given time, simply by arguing that their meaning may have been different in the past, or may shift again in the future. At any particular moment such places are vested with identity, an identity which involves both the supernatural sphere and the power of social self-definition and personal self-identity. Sometimes the supernatural power of such localized sacred sites may become inter-cultural, even international:

> the number of rocks being returned to Ayers Rock [Australia] after tourists blamed the souvenirs for bad luck has become a virtual avalanche. For the past month or so, the park headquarters near the world famous monolith has received up to 20 rocks a day from as far afield as Hawaii, England and the United States.
> (*The Evening Post, Wellington*, 11 May 1993)

In other cases, and often dependent on the nature of the sites concerned, appropriate behaviour is more personal and digressions lead to localized, rather than widespread, negative results.

Sites of significance form part of the landscape; landscape everywhere in the world is a construct of human beings – whether through human ascription to it of mythological creation, or through physical actions by the humans themselves. All the chapters in *Sacred Sites, Sacred Places* accept it as axiomatic that – whatever the difficulties of recognizing such special sites from the archaeological record – all societies in the past would have recognized, as do all societies in the present, some features of their landscapes (if not all the earth) as special. Most of the authors take it for granted that what would have been classified as special within the same landscape may well have varied at different times during the past. Archaeologically, therefore, the challenge is to recognize how such special features of a particular time in the past may have been incorporated into the concepts and activities of a subsequent period of the past. Similarly, *Sacred Sites, Sacred Places* emphasizes, in many of its chapters, the way that such subsequent incorporation of significant sites into the meaning of cultural activity may have been on quite different grounds, and accompanied by quite different rationales, from preceding attitudes and associated practices.

This book therefore poses some difficult questions of its own. What hope can there be for archaeologists and others to be able to obtain a satisfactory feeling for the sacredness of past surroundings? In one sense, the answer is discouraging. Chapter after chapter reveals that many of the sites and areas regarded as significant by living peoples are not marked by any human construction or other human activity which would be recognized through archaeological investigation. In another sense, *Sacred Sites, Sacred Places* should serve to force an awareness of this missing dimension from most archaeological site and area reports; even the mention of such an assumed missing dimension to archaeological reports would be a positive result of this publication.

The reader is confronted with another of the dilemmas currently preoccupying archaeologists, legislators and heritage managers. If the physical characteristics of many of the sacred sites and sacred places of a past culture do not incorporate elements which are currently ascribed significance by archaeologists, or tourists – i.e. the evidence of human skills and ingenuities – how can they be catered for in any acts of preservation?[1] And, on the other hand, what criteria of a humanly derived site should form the basis of deciding their worth in the context of preservation of a site for posterity? In Australia (as in many other countries) such questions revealed conceptual differences between those who were anxious to construct a Heritage Commission's Register of the National Estate, with inclusion only of 'sites which were the most outstanding Aboriginal places deserving of national recognition' (Ucko 1979, p. 15), archaeologists who claimed that all sites were, by definition, of equal academic worth, and Aboriginal people who were often loath to enter into an argument which started from the assumption that gradings of value should be made within the overall concept of the sanctity of the entire earth. In countries such as Zimbabwe such questions, and potentially conflicting interests in the designation of sites, threaten to determine the nature of future archaeological investigations in that country, if not even the nature of archaeology as a discipline of the elite for the elite, almost entirely divorced from the interests and concerns of local communities (Ucko 1994). In countries such as the UK, many of the judgements regarding the preservation of sites are now overtly couched in terms which include concepts such as the sites' archaeological 'rarity' value and their state of preservation.

Unesco's World Heritage Convention allows whole areas of land to be recognized as a site (e.g., in the UK, 'the joint site of Stonehenge, Avebury, and their associated sites') (Ucko, Hunter, Clark & David 1991, pp. 1, 255). Complementary national legislations could lead to the acceptance of protective measures for whole 'cultural areas' and 'cultural landscapes', in effect serving to preserve sites of past significance which are not evident *per se* from archaeological enquiry. Legislation which includes the possibility of preservation of *areas* of land does exist in some countries (such as Zimbabwe and Kenya), but has so far not been applied to the preservation of the past. In most countries (such as the UK), however, legislation is still single site-specific, and no complementary national legislation accompanies acceptance of the World Heritage Convention.

Another challenge to emerge from *Sacred Sites, Sacred Places* demands renewed consideration of the vexed debate between those who assume that all attempts at empathy with another culture (perhaps particularly with cultures of the past) are not only dangerous but also methodologically unsound and doomed to failure, and those who see the vesting of emotion in the evidence of the past – whatever the paucity of archaeological evidence to support the existence of such emotions – as part and parcel of studying the past. A good example concerns the evidence presented in this book about attitudes to, and practices associated with, caves. Several chapters document the special significance of these (and other) 'natural' sites to cultures widely separate in distance and in time. Given the widespread ascription of special meaning to caves, would it be legitimate to assume special meaning in other cultures too, even when no evidence of special activity exists? Alternatively (e.g. Ucko & Rosenfeld 1967, pp. 101–15), is it sounder methodological practice to continue to draw attention to the existence within one and the same culture of caves which are decorated and those which are not, to the contemporaneous existence of caves with evidence of habitation and those without? Is it merely pedantic (e.g. Ucko 1989, pp. 331–7) to continue to stress that other cultures may not share with many from the western world of the 1990s their assumption that dark caves are fearsome, and that clambering around in them may not have been thought to be dangerous? Instead, would it be more useful to stress that, whatever the feelings of members of a past culture which were associated with the physical character of cave usage, there is the likelihood that such cave sites were incorporated within the belief systems of the cultures concerned? Several chapters in this book encourage consideration of such often neglected (but see Skeates 1991) areas of investigation.

The final point which I choose to highlight about the contents of *Sacred Sites, Sacred Places* concerns the messages, in several chapters, about the respective roles of men and women in the domain of sacred sites and any practices associated with them. Whereas it may suit the liberal tendencies of the past twenty or so years in the western world to stress that women have their own ritual and sacred domain which is complementary to that of men (e.g. see Brock 1989), and whereas much recent archaeological and anthropological writing about gender studies has cogently emphasized the under-representation of female researchers in both disciplines, most of the discussion in this book lays emphasis on the land and sacred sites as of primarily masculine concern. Indeed, still today, it may be difficult for a female researcher to penetrate the mysteries and secrecy of myth and ritual controlled by men (just as, presumably, the contrary may equally apply).

Even such exclusive gender domains may also be at risk from the changing ascriptions of value which I have mentioned above. Thus, for example, by the late 1970s in Western Australia 'prehistoric' rock engravings located in association with grinding hollows (long accepted to be the preserve of female domestic mundane activities) were being appropriated by male Aborigines who were attempting to ban Aboriginal women and non-Aboriginal female researchers from access to the art sites. There is little doubt that such changes formed part of a growing movement, in various parts of Australia in the 1980s, to give ongoing living significance to many ancient Aboriginal sites. Ascription of value to remains of the past is often a political decision, whether such a decision is taken by the descendants of those who were originally responsible for the construction of the surviving artefact, or a decision by those with vested responsibility for the current management of the past. In both cases, as many chapters in this book demonstrate, how to value which aspects of the past is often as much to do with the exercise of political power as it is to do with the intrinsic value of the sacred nature of a particular location. However, it is crucial to recognize that there is no reason to suppose that both sets of values are necessarily mutually exclusive; herein rests the dilemma for both students of the past and those involved in the practices of the present. *Sacred Sites, Sacred Places* forces the reader to consider – immediately in its very first chapter – the meaning of respect for others' beliefs and practices. It demands reflection about what we *really* mean when we claim to give equal respect to the beliefs of all peoples, when we recognize the legitimacy of demands for the freedom of all to be allowed to practise their religions without interference. As I have already pointed out, this book is concerned with weighty matters and the implications of much of its content are profound – and badly in need of further discussion.

P. J. Ucko
Southampton

Note

1 As this book goes to press the World Heritage Committee (meeting in Cartagena, Colombia, 6–11 December 1993), has announced further details of its new policy of recognizing 'Associative landscapes' within its category of 'Cultural landscapes'. Associative landscapes are those with powerful religious, artistic or cultural associations, with or without any material cultural evidence.

On 9 December 1993 the Committee reconsidered 'the most difficult of all the sites . . . one that was already on the World Heritage list, Tongariro National Park in New Zealand [which] had been listed as a "natural" site since 1990. As a natural landscape of deep religious significance to the native Maori, New Zealand [submitted] a nomination which would add cultural criteria to the natural criteria for which it was already inscribed. However, as the first "cultural landscape" to be added to the world list, it evoked extensive debate . . . over how to apply the cultural criteria to a natural area that had no physical cultural evidence on it. The redefinition of the New Zealand park as a "mixed" site of natural and cultural values was ultimately accepted.'

On the last day of its meeting, the Committee received a report stressing the need for 'more work . . . particularly in the study of living continuing landscapes still inhabited by indigenous peoples . . . and [urging] that more attention should be given to the continuing values of living indigenous peoples'.

References

Australian Heritage Commission 1989. *A Sense of Place*. Canberra: Australian Heritage Commission.

Berndt, R. M. & D. Roughsey 1975. On the question of the secret-sacred dimension *vis-à-vis* traditional Australian Aboriginal life. Unpublished report to Council of the AIAS, 18 September 1975.

Bowman, G. 1993. Nationalizing the sacred: shrines and shifting identities in the Israeli-occupied territories. *Man* 28, 431–60.

Brock, P. (ed.) 1989. *Women, Rites and Sites: Aboriginal women's cultural knowledge*. Sydney: Allen & Unwin.

Edwards, R. (ed.) 1975. *The Preservation of Australia's Aboriginal Heritage: report of National Seminar on Aboriginal Antiquities in Australia May 1972*. Canberra: Australian Institute of Aboriginal Studies.

Fforde, C. 1991a. The Second World Archaeological Congress (WAC 2). *World Archaeological Bulletin* 5, 6–10.

Fforde, C. 1991b. WAC Executive and Council Meetings. *World Archaeological Bulletin* 5, 17–21.

Garwood, P., D. Jennings, R. Skeates & J. Toms (eds) 1991. *Sacred and Profane: proceedings of a conference on archaeology, ritual and religion, Oxford, 1989*. Oxford: Oxford University Committee for Archaeology.

Guidon, N. 1992. Manejo del Parque Nacional da Sierra da Capivara, Brasil. Paper presented to the IVth Congresso Mundial de Parques Nacionales y Areas Protegidas, Caracas, Venezuela, 10–12 February 1992.

Hertz, R. 1913 (1983). Saint Besse: a study of an Alpine cult. In *Saints and their Cults: studies in religious sociology*, S. Wilson (ed.), 55–100. Cambridge: Cambridge University Press.

Hubert, J. 1987. In *Academic Freedom and Apartheid: the story of the World Archaeological Congress*, P. J. Ucko, 161–6. London: Duckworth.

Hubert, J. 1989. First World Archaeological Congress Inter-Congress, Vermillion, South Dakota, USA. *World Archaeological Bulletin* 4, 14–19.

Reeves, B. O. K. 1991. Sacred places, sacred spaces and 'sites of significance'. *World Archaeological Bulletin* 5, 14–15.

Skeates, R. 1991. Caves, cult and children in neolithic Abruzzo, central Italy. In *Sacred and Profane: proceedings of a conference on archaeology, ritual and religion, Oxford, 1989*, P. Garwood, D. Jennings, R. Skeates & J. Toms (eds), 122–34. Oxford: Oxford University Committee for Archaeology.

Ucko, P. J. 1979. Review of AIAS activities 1978. *Australian Institute of Aboriginal Studies Newsletter* 11, 6–26.

Ucko, P. J. 1989. La subjetividad y el estudio del arte parietal paleolitico. In *Cien Años Después de Sautuola*, M. R. Morales (ed.), 284–358. Santander: Disputación Regional de Cantabria y Universidad de Cantabria.

Ucko, P. J. 1990. Foreword. In *The Politics of the Past*, P. Gathercole & D. Lowenthal (eds), ix–xxi. London: Unwin Hyman; Routledge pbk 1994.

Ucko, P. J. 1994. Museums and sites: cultures of the past within education – Zimbabwe, some ten years on. In *The Presented Past*, P. Stone & B. Molyneaux, chapter X. London: Routledge.

Ucko, P. J., M. Hunter, A. J. Clark & A. David 1991. *Avebury Reconsidered: from the 1660s to the 1990s*. London: Unwin Hyman.

Ucko, P. J. & A. Rosenfeld 1967. *Palaeolithic Cave Art*. London: Weidenfeld & Nicolson.

WAC News 1992. WAC officers meet, *WAC News* 1, 7–8.

Preface

The theme at the World Archaeological Congress (WAC) 2 in Barquisimeto, Venezuela, 1990, on *Sacred sites, sacred places and 'sites of significance'* focused on the issues surrounding the identification, preservation and interpretation of sacred sites. Over thirty papers were presented by archaeologists, anthropologists and scholars from related disciplines from many different parts of the world, as well as representatives of indigenous peoples, including Inuit, Maori, Saami and Native Americans. The theme ran for three days, and was divided into six sessions: recognition, archaeological recognition, practice, legislation, management and ownership of sacred sites. The Maori contribution was a particularly moving experience, combining traditional prayers, songs and dance with the presentation of papers. The concluding session was organized and held as a traditional Native American council. Resolutions were forwarded to the Plenary Session of the Congress, and on to the WAC Council and Executive, with regard to specific sacred sites, and also regarding the urgent need to move towards the goal of a United Nations resolution for the conservation of sacred sites of all peoples.

We are grateful to all those who helped to organize the theme, and to all those who agreed to chair the sessions.

Thirty-three papers prepared for, presented at, or arising out of the Congress were submitted to the *One World Archaeology* series by Carmichael, Reeves and Schanche. Upon review by the Series Editor, 15 of the submitted papers were excluded, some of the remaining were extensively revised and 3 further chapters were added to give the book thematic balance, conveying a series of significant messages in keeping with the aims and standards of the *One World Archaeology* series. This final and detailed editing was undertaken by Jane Hubert in consultation with the Series Editor, Reeves and Carmichael.

We are very grateful to Hirini Matunga, David Ritchie and Nicholas Saunders for the great efforts that they made to produce manuscripts in record time. We would also like to thank Ben Alberti for his assistance with several Spanish translations and Peter Ucko and Pierre Vérin for their translation and editing of the chapter by Chantal Radimilahy.

Brian Reeves   Jane Hubert
Calgary   Southampton

Introduction

DAVID CARMICHAEL, JANE HUBERT
& BRIAN REEVES

Native peoples throughout the world are becoming increasingly vocal about who has the responsibility for the interpretation of their cultural heritage, and in the management of their sites and artefacts, which represent that heritage (Layton 1989a, 1989b). Archaeologists are observing this trend with interest. Some, like the contributors to this book, are supportive of native peoples' desire to have greater involvement in the presentation of their own heritage and, indeed, seek to incorporate such concerns within protective heritage and site management (and see Cleere 1989). Others, for the first time, are addressing the heritage of native peoples as a contemporary phenomenon rather than simply as something that existed in the past. Most archaeologists are now well aware that many native peoples are deeply concerned about burial sites and the treatment of human remains (Hubert 1989, 1992). In general, though, there is still a lack of understanding and appreciation of the importance of other kinds of sacred sites to native peoples. One goal of this book, therefore, is to broaden the perspectives of archaeologists, and others, to include a better understanding of what kinds of places are important to people of different cultures, and why.

It has become clear, in the process of preparing this book, that there are broad similarities between peoples from various parts of the world, both in the nature of their sacred sites, and in their heritage concerns. The authors involved have not compared notes in order to present a united front. Rather, they are people whose individual accounts demonstrate that they share similar relationships with the land as a whole, and with certain parts of the land, their sacred places, in particular. Over and over again these sacred places are connected with, or are, what the western world classes as 'natural' features of the 'landscape', such as mountain peaks, springs, rivers, woods and caves.

Sacred places, in almost every case, demand offerings, and these are similar not only in terms of their functions – mainly appeasement, supplication and thanksgiving – but also in the nature of the materials and objects that are used. Furthermore, the symbolic aspects of the environment often coincide; colour symbolism, for example, is found in many cultures, and even the same group of colours may be considered sacred in parts of the world as far from each other as the Arctic tundra (Ovsyannikov & Terebikhin, Ch. 4) and the coast of Kenya (Mutoro, Ch. 10).

Many of the peoples represented in this book have shared the experience of colonial control and interference, and the concomitant pressures at least of religious acculturation. These pressures are not only in the past, though they may be less explicit today, and manifested in different ways, for example in the threats that accompany modern trade and technological development.

Although there are these similarities, it is important to remember that there are many discrete indigenous voices, not a single voice. The richness and diversity of indigenous cultures would be diminished by any suggestion that there is true pan-tribal unanimity. For political purposes, however, it can be useful to raise many voices together, to be better heard by those who threaten the safety of sacred sites in many parts of the world, through economic and commercial development such as the building of roads and bridges, shopping centres or houses; through the development of tourism (Reeves, Ch. 21; Price, Ch. 20); as a result of 'accidents' that pollute the land (Johnson, Ch. 16); and, in some areas, through the practice of archaeology.

Despite the similarities, in the context of sacred sites it is apparent that even within a single group, and certainly between groups, there are often considerable differences of attitude and opinion regarding the importance and appropriate treatment of specific sites (Carmichael 1989). The chapters in this book reflect the diverse interests and priorities expressed by native groups concerning the treatment of those places that have particular cultural significance, usually referred to as sacred sites.

The nature of sacred places

In her introductory chapter to this book Hubert (Ch. 1) discusses many of the issues surrounding sacred beliefs and beliefs of sacredness, issues that are dealt with in varying detail in the following chapters. Among the critical issues she examines are the universal aspects of the sacred, as well as cross-cultural variations. These, as she points out, have very important implications for the understanding and management of sacred sites, and there are various fundamental questions that must be faced in dealing with these issues.

The question of how people define and perceive sacred sites is an integral part of every chapter in this book. Some authors (e.g. Price, Ch. 20, Johnson, Ch. 16, Sanmiguel Ch. 13) concentrate on individual sites, others discuss the range and diversity of sites within one culture (e.g. Mohs, Ch. 15, Mumah, Ch. 7, Matunga, Ch. 17). In some cases the focus is on the past, even the very distant past (e.g. Cooney, Ch. 3, Sanmiguel, Ch. 13), in some cases tracing connections up to the present, to contemporary beliefs and practices, but in others showing how, in contemporary perceptions, the landscape has been frozen at some specific period in the past (e.g. Marciniak, Ch. 11).

To say that a specific place is a sacred place is not simply to describe a piece of land, or just locate it in a certain position in the landscape. What is known as a sacred site carries with it a whole range of rules and regulations regarding people's behaviour in relation to it, and implies a set of beliefs to do with the non-empirical world, often in relation to the spirits of the ancestors, as well as more remote or powerful gods or spirits.

Most chapters are concerned with changes over time. Mulk's account (Ch. 9) is mainly concerned with Saami sites as described by seventeenth- and eighteenth-century churchmen, though she stresses that these 'natural' sites are still significant to Saami people today. Many authors demonstrate that the significance of sacred sites can transcend cultural changes and assimilations, and even religious conversions. Sanmiguel (Ch. 13), writing about one specific cave site in Chiapas, Mexico, relates how some of the rituals connected with the 'master of the earth', who lives in the cave, have been transferred to the Catholic church, whereas others are still carried out in the cave, and many traditional beliefs and practices continue in spite of the domination of Catholicism in the area. The Christianization of many countries of the world has often resulted in the existence of a dual system of beliefs. On the coast of Kenya it is Islam that has become intertwined with traditional customs and beliefs. Abungu (Ch. 12) records that many of the people who are involved in spirit propitiation nevertheless see themselves as Muslims, although this is a very un-Islamic practice, since Allah must only be approached directly. At Mbaraki, traditional rituals are still carried out next to the new mosque, and are grudgingly tolerated by the Imam.

In some areas there is no observable continuity between the sacred sites of the past and the present – and yet these ancient sites are still recognized, and to some extent treated as special places. Cooney (Ch. 3) describes the neolithic tombs still to be found in the Irish landscape. Although the neolithic landscape has changed over the centuries, some of these sacred places have continued to be the focus of burials; they have become incorporated in folk beliefs, and although there is no evidence of continuity of the use of such sites, some sort of renegotiation of the past has occurred which reaffirms their cultural significance.

Some sites that have religious significance may also assume historical or political importance. Religious sanctuaries in Poland, for example, are said by Marciniak (Ch. 11) to have been used as sanctuaries by people fleeing from political persecution. Her chapter on Christian and pre-Christian sacred sites provides a useful contrast to the majority of chapters in this book, which focus on sites associated with native cultures. She draws attention to the existence of sacred sites among contemporary and historic urban cultures, and also to the bitter ongoing conflicts between the religious groups surrounding these sites and the sacred landscapes of which they are a part. The use of sacred sites as sanctuaries is also described by Theodoratus & LaPena (Ch. 2) regarding a specific sacred site said to have been used by Wintu people hiding from American troops.

Sacred sites are intimately linked to gender, status and role. The importance of age is demonstrated in Mutoro's account (Ch. 10) of Mijikenda sacred sites, and in Mumah's study (Ch. 7) of sites in the Bamenda Grassfields of Cameroon. The Bamenda sites reveal an intricate system of spiritual power and sacred space, tied to status and rank, within a traditional kingdom which does not differentiate between religious and secular power. As a woman, Mumah had difficulty obtaining information about some of the most sacred sites of Nso'. The Nso' attitude to women is also demonstrated by the fact that no woman (except the High Priestess) is allowed to see, approach or even speak about the sacred grave of the *Fon*, or ruler.

The inferior status of women is also pointed out by Wandibba (Ch. 8) in connection with the differing status of various Babukusu shrines, and also in relation to Babukusu burial sites in Kenya. All Babukusu graves are venerated, but men's graves are revered more than those of women, as demonstrated by the number of ceremonies carried out after the initial burial ceremony. Ovsyannikov & Terebikhin (Ch. 4), writing about the Arctic tundra, describe a rather different situation, although again emphasizing the importance of gender in relation to sacred sites and knowledge. As in many traditional cultures (and see Mumah, Ch. 7), women were believed to be impure, but at the same time were also believed to have enormous capacities for creation and destruction, and thus were subject to a wide range of taboos restricting their behaviour. In this Arctic culture male and female were symbolically polarized – north/female, south/male. Thus, when the reindeer breeders migrated to the south in the spring, the women had to carry out extensive cleansing rituals at the sacred site at the dividing-line between the north and the south, and on the way back to the north in the autumn, the men would have to do the same. Ovsyannikov & Terebikhin's discussion of this Arctic (Nenets or Samoyed) sacred space also reveals the interconnectedness of the symbolic classification of sacred space in dwellings, migratory routes, resource areas, topography, burials and sanctuaries, as well as the structuring principles – including gender, directions and colours. Their chapter, one of the very few to appear in English from the former Soviet Union on this subject, combines the region's archaeology, history and ethnography in a structuralist perspective, including the impact of Christianization and the resulting dualism of religious practice. Comparing this chapter with Marciniak (Ch. 11) and with those from North America one is struck by the remarkable circumpolar congruence in sacred sites and beliefs of northern traditional peoples.

The sacred sites described in this book are either male sites, or undifferentiated, although in many cultures women also have their own sites, which may be forbidden to men (Brock 1989). Apart from gender specification, sacred sites may also have specific functions, and within one culture there may be a wide range of site types. Mohs (Ch. 15) reports that the Sto:lo Indians of British Columbia have no word to cover all sites of spiritual significance, and that there are many different types of site: transformer sites, spirit residences, ceremonial areas, traditional landmarks, questing sites, legendary and mythological places, burial sites and traditional resource areas. Many of these site types can be found in other cultures described in this book. Matunga (Ch. 17), for example, documents a range of *waahi tapu* among the Maori. Carmichael (Ch. 6) and Reeves (Ch. 21) also discuss a variety of sacred site types recognized by the Apache and Blackfoot Indians respectively. These sites are places of power, areas that derive significance from their place in native cosmology and ceremonial practice; these chapters thus illustrate the importance of the concept of sacred geography.

The question of what is a sacred site is addressed by Radimilahy (Ch. 5) in her review of sites in Madagascar. Johnson (Ch. 16), writing about the destruction of sites in Alaska, stresses the special importance of burial sites, a theme echoed throughout the book.

Ownership and management of sacred places

The question of ownership of sacred sites arises in the context of intrusion by other peoples or individuals. Franklin & Bunte describe the clashes that have arisen between the Navajo, Paiute and Hopi, as a consequence of the redefinition of the boundaries of their respective lands. The loss of a piece of land is perceived not only as a material loss, but as a spiritual deprivation, inasmuch as Indian religion and cosmology are intimately connected with the land. As with other Native American groups (and also Australian Aboriginal groups) the land is made sacred by events that took place in the mythical past.

In other areas sacred sites are situated on public lands. Price (Ch. 20) and Reeves (Ch. 21) consider the problems relating to recreational use of Native sites. They raise questions about the appropriateness and effectiveness of a multiple-use management strategy for protecting the sacred and heritage values of such sites.

Mohs (Ch. 15) addresses the difficulties of managing sacred sites that are located outside reservation lands. For the Sto:lo tribe, much of the problem stems from being left out of the non-Indian planning and decision-making processes. The problems involved in the management of sites on non-Aboriginal land are also addressed by Ritchie (Ch. 18).

Sacred landscapes

Several authors, for example Carmichael (Ch. 6), Theodoratus & LaPena (Ch. 2) and Cooney (Ch. 3), consider sacred places and places of significance in the broad sense of sacred landscapes. Cooney's chapter (Ch. 3) on neolithic sacred and secular landscapes of Ireland illustrates the value of combined archaeological, historical and related studies in revealing the sacred landscapes created by ancient cultures, the transformations they have undergone, and the relevance they still have to Irish society today.

As noted by a number of authors, many native peoples' religions are cosmotheistic; they believe that all natural parts of the world have a human-like life force. In such a belief system, plants, animals, rocks, etc. are conscious and wilful; they must be treated with proper respect. The source areas for plants, animals and earth materials may be considered powerful or sacred, as they are by the Mescalero Apache (Carmichael, Ch. 6).

Wandibba (Ch. 8) and Ovsyannikov & Terebikhin (Ch. 4), among others, make the point that western scholars have misinterpreted what is commonly referred to as 'ancestor worship' in a typically Eurocentric manner, suggesting that the ancestors are the objects of worship, when in fact they are merely intercessors between the supernatural and the people. Misinterpretations of this kind are rife in anthropological and religious literature, including the common tendency by scholars to substitute animalism for animism in the study of tribal religions (Hultkrantz 1981; Willis 1990), which confuses the intermediary with the source of sacred power. These Eurocentric perceptions are still widely held among western European and Christianized peoples, and are still promoted by some Christian churches, particularly of the funda-mentalist kind, to whom the only true sacred sites are those associated with the foundations of Christian belief. These attitudes work against the understand-ing and conservation of sacred sites of other cultures and indigenous peoples.

Although especially important places may be identified as sacred sites, it is often the case, as with the Wintu, for example, documented by Theodoratus & LaPena (Ch. 2), that such sites are parts of a network of powerful places that encompass entire landscapes (and see also Ritchie, Ch. 18). Clay sources, spruce forests, raptor eyries, piñon groves and stands of agave can be cultur-ally sensitive. Maintaining the productivity of such resources, and native access to them, may require the preservation of relatively large areas of natural habitat, a goal compatible with much current thinking in ecology.

Prospects for progress

Protection of sacred places may be seen as one part of a larger issue of environmental preservation. Modern science may, to a large extent, be inap-propriate as a model, reducing nature to quantifiable and measurable elements, rather than focusing on the holistic, and the interconnectedness of all of creation, which is the essence of the cosmotheistic religions of many peoples.

It is possible to protect some sites, individually or in groups, at the local or regional level. But it is unrealistic to expect to halt population growth or technological development in the near future. It is unfortunate and ironic that indigenous peoples may stand to make economic and political gains from resource development while sacred and heritage values of the land are degraded (and see Ucko 1983).

Johnson's discussion (Ch. 16) of the Exxon Valdez oil spill clean-up is a case in point. Although Native corporations in Alaska may benefit from oil

industry employment, the benefits are accompanied by the risk of environmental damage resulting from spills. The National Park Service reported
(Gleeson 1989) that archaeological and historic sites were being protected, yet
Chugach burial sites were desecrated during the clean-up operation following
the oil spill.

Ultimately, proper treatment of sacred places will be a matter of respect.
Respect, as defined by Harjo (1992), Native American poet and activist, means
the recognition of the inherent right of others to be here. Unlike many others
in the world, native peoples have respect for the earth; not only humans, but
also plants, animals, rocks, burials, and other sacred places all have a right to
be here. It is this reverence for the earth (Berry 1988) that is embodied in
concepts of sacred geography (Lovelock 1988), and there is now a growing
realization among scholars that sacred sites are indeed very special places (e.g.
Swan 1990).

Archaeologists, indigenous peoples and sacred sites

Archaeologists are sometimes concerned that discussions of indigenous
attitudes and beliefs have a palpable anti-science, anti-history undercurrent,
and may express direct criticisms against their investigators. In essence,
some feel that they, as archaeologists, are often personally blamed for the
current problems in the treatment of sacred places. Frustrations about the
many ways that technological development has affected some sacred sites are
understandable, but archaeologists already familiar with the problems,
and intending to contribute to a solution, do not welcome becoming
targets.

A landscape is sacred because humans perceive it as sacred (Saunders
Ch. 14). There are different ways of knowing about the earth, about sacred
places, and about archaeological sites. Some of the ways are scientific and some
are spiritual. One way of knowing does not negate the validity of another.
Although the world-views and goals of indigenous peoples and archaeologists
will not always correspond, the protection of cultural sites should be an
instance where they can. Anti-science and anti-spiritual sentiments are both
counter-productive.

It is essential that scientific knowledge and influence are accepted, but at the
same time the legitimacy of traditional indigenous ways of knowing must also
be recognized. People from all spheres and with widely diverging interests
must therefore work together to reach a situation in which everyone will
respect and protect sacred sites, regardless of whose they are. To this end, it is
important to continue building co-operative relationships between archaeologists and native peoples, both to protect specific sites and to educate others
about the importance of sacred places. Anthropologists and archaeologists
who respect native views of earth spirituality are well suited to transmit that
sensitivity to others in non-indigenous societies. This book is intended to

contribute to a better understanding and more effective protection of sacred places throughout the world.

References

Bean, L. J. (ed.) 1992. *California Indian Shamanism*. Menlo Park, Calif.: Ballena Press.

Berry, T. 1988. *The Dream of the Earth*. San Francisco: Sierra Club Books.

Brock, P. (ed.) 1989. *Women, Rites and Sites*. Sydney: Allen & Unwin.

Carmichael, D. L. 1989. Native American consultation in the context of Air Force program planning. Paper presented at the World Archaeological Congress First Inter-congress on Archaeological Ethics and Treatment of the Dead, Vermillion, South Dakota.

Cleere, H. F. (ed.) 1989. Introduction: the rationale of archaeological heritage management. In *Archaeological Heritage Management in the Modern World*, H. F. Cleere (ed.), 1–9. London: Unwin Hyman.

Gleeson, P. 1989. Exxon oil spill response. *Federal Archaeology Report* vol. 2, no. 3: 3–4. National Park Service, Washington, D.C.

Harjo, S. S. 1992. The story of indigenous women through the perspective of Suzan Harjo. Lecture presented at the University of Texas at El Paso, 15 September 1992.

Hubert, J. 1989. A proper place for the dead: a critical review of the 'reburial issue'. In *Conflict in the Archaeology of Living Traditions*, Robert Layton (ed.), 131–66. London: Unwin Hyman; Routledge pbk 1994. Reprinted in *Journal of Indigenous Studies* 1, 1990.

Hubert, J. 1992. Dry bones or living ancestors? Conflicting perceptions of life, death and the universe. *International Journal of Cultural Property* 1, 105–27.

Hultkrantz, A. 1981. *Belief and Worship in Native North America*. Syracuse: Syracuse University Press.

Layton, R. (ed.) 1989a. *Who Needs the Past? Indigenous values and archaeology*. London: Unwin Hyman; Routledge pbk 1994.

Layton, R. 1989b. *Conflict in the Archaeology of Living Traditions*. London: Unwin Hyman; Routledge pbk 1994.

Lovelock, J. 1988. *The Ages of Gaia*. London: W. W. Norton & Co.

Swan, J. A. 1990. *Sacred Places: how the living earth seeks our friendship*. Santa Fe: Bear & Co.

Ucko, P. J. 1983. The politics of the indigenous minority. *Journal of Biosocial Science, Supplement* 8, 25–40.

Willis, R. 1990. Introduction. In *Signifying Animals: human meaning in the natural world*, R. Willis (ed.), 1–24. London: Unwin Hyman; Routledge pbk 1994.

1   Sacred beliefs and beliefs of sacredness

JANE HUBERT

The limitations of my land are clear to me. The area of my existence, where I derive my existence from, is clear to me and clear to those who belong in my group. Land provides for my physical needs and my spiritual needs. New stories are sung from contemplation of the land. Stories are handed down from spirit men of the past who have deposited the riches at various places, the sacred places. These places are not simply geographically beautiful: they are holy places, places that are even more holy than shrines. They are not commercialised, they are sacred. The greatest respect is shown to them. They are used for the regeneration of our people, the continuation of our life: because that's where we begin and that's where we return.

(Father Pat Dodson n.p.)

The discussion of sacred sites can take many forms. It may concern specific sites – how they are defined or how they can be recognized; who owns them and who has rights of access to them; what they mean to individuals and to communities, and what their relation is to both the living and the dead. Such questions are central to the discussion of the management of sites and how they can be protected, both physically and legally, from those people and processes that threaten them.

The Aboriginal people of Australia, Native Americans, Maori, Saami, Inuit and other peoples from countries all over the world, are deeply concerned about the threats – and actualities – of intrusion into their sacred sites, and of their destruction, whether they be 'living sites' in contemporary use, or sites that are no longer used, but remain important symbols of a distant past. There is no doubt that many sites, throughout the world, are currently under threat from many sources. One major threat is from commercial developments such as the construction of roads and bridges, shopping centres, housing and industries. Sites are also threatened by tourism, an increasing source of valuable currency, but potentially damaging to sites in both physical and spiritual terms.

In some areas the work of archaeologists may also be a threat to sacred sites. Apart from the intrusiveness, and physical damage that excavation involves, archaeologists have often added insult to injury by claiming to have 'discovered' sites which the indigenous people have known to exist for centuries, and which are their sacred sites. Such disregard for the indigenous population is widespread. Condori, with regard to the Aymara Indians of Bolivia, writes: 'The Portugals . . . take no notice of the original cultural context of our archaeological sites, and simply rename places whose names a long oral tradition has preserved, as if this was enough to credit them with their discovery' (Condori 1989, p. 48). He describes how the site of Tiwanaku has been plundered, and monoliths taken away to decorate private houses; most distressing of all, however, is the total appropriation of the site:

> They have built earthworks round the ruins so that today we can no longer get in to Tiwanaku. The Aymara people have to pay an entrance fee to visit the ruins as tourists where they listen to invented accounts of the meaning of our history. The archaeologists completely ignore the fact that for our culture the site is sacred. It is a *wak'a*, a place where our ancestors lived and through which they communicate with us in various ways.
>
> (Condori 1989, pp. 48–9)

What is it that Condori means when he says that Tiwanaku is a sacred site? What does the term 'sacred site' actually mean – to the Aymara and to other peoples in countries throughout the world? The members of one cultural group may – though not necessarily – know what they mean when they talk about their own places and sites, but can people of one cultural group know what other people in other cultures mean when they talk about their sacred sites?

What does the word 'sacred' mean, anyway? Even if we can define it in our own language, to what extent is the word an adequate translation of the word or words that denote unfamiliar concepts in other cultures and religions? All concepts expressed in a specific language are necessarily limited by that language. How far is it possible to translate, from one language into another, words that denote concepts that do not precisely – or even imprecisely – match? Furthermore, if such concepts *are* dissimilar, how can such a disparity be discovered? In the worldwide discussion of 'sacred sites' the English word 'sacred' has become the accepted term. However, it is quite clear that there are wide variations in the concept that the word denotes, and in what it includes or excludes.

The Maori people of New Zealand, for example, classify their cultural sites into 'everyday' sites and *waahi tapu* (and see Matunga 1994). According to Sole & Woods: 'The literal translation of wahi tapu is "sacred place", but the modern translation of tapu as "sacred" fails to capture its true essence, for the deep spiritual value of wahi tapu transcends mere sacredness' (Sole & Woods 1992, p. 342).

There are even greater complications, for even within Maori society there are said to be different definitions and classifications:

> The hierarchy and complexity of wahi tapu classification is compounded by the people of each iwi, hapu or whanau (tribe, subtribe or extended family) having their own definition which is valid only to them. No iwi, hapu or whanau would be so presumptuous as to define wahi tapu for another group.
>
> (Sole & Woods 1992, p. 342)

There may also be a wide variety of different kinds of sacred sites, with quite different forms and functions, within one culture.

The English word 'sacredness' is derived from Latin, and is defined as restriction through pertaining to the gods. The concept of sacred implies restrictions and prohibitions on human behaviour – if something is sacred then certain rules must be observed in relation to it, and this generally means that something that is said to be sacred, whether it be an object or site (or person), must be placed apart from everyday things or places, so that its special significance can be recognized, and rules regarding it obeyed.

Although the translation of words and concepts in other cultures may be inexact, the concomitant concepts of separateness, respect and rules of behaviour seem to be common to sacred sites in different cultures. But the nature of the sacred sites themselves may be very different, and thus difficult for those outside the culture to recognize, except by observation of the rules of behaviour that pertain to them. There may be no other way to recognize a sacred site, and this is of central importance, for the clash of interests between the people who are responsible for disturbing sacred sites – for whatever reason – and those whose sites they are often arises because outsiders are unable to recognize the sacredness of the sites they are disturbing. It is only comparatively recently that archaeologists, for example, have come to understand that what makes something sacred to people of a different culture may have none of the characteristics or trappings of those things or places they consider sacred in their own society.

To complicate the issue further, it is often the case that the names that are used for individual sites may also be applied to wider areas of land. In Australia, for example:

> White people generally would think of sites as things that can be pinpointed on a map. A site can be distinguished from its surroundings, just as the eyes of a potato can be distinguished from the rest of the vegetable. Laws to protect sacred sites seem to assume this characteristic. Yet Aboriginal usage is often less exact. The same word, for example, may function as the name of a clearly identifiable feature of the landscape and of a more or less extensive area in which that feature is located.
>
> (Maddock 1983, p. 131)

It may be possible for archaeologists and other outsiders to come to recognize the characteristics of sacred sites in cultures other than their own, and to treat them with due respect. But does this imply a fundamental acceptance of the sacredness of the site, or is it merely the adoption, without conviction, of appropriate behaviour? Is it, in fact, possible for people who have different religious beliefs really to believe in the sacredness of the sites or objects that are part of another religion? What do we mean when we say that we believe in the sacredness of someone else's site? How far can we really believe in the sacredness of sites which relate to beliefs that we do not share? If we *treat* something as sacred, is that enough? Is it enough if we follow the rules set down by those whose sacred site it is – or is this merely paying lip service to their belief that it is sacred, rather than really believing it to be sacred ourselves? Can we say that something is sacred to someone else but not to us? Is that not the same as saying that it is not sacred? Could it be, on the other hand, that what is sacred to one person is in essence sacred?

In England, which is predominantly Christian, the concept of sacredness is very specialized, and tends to be restricted to one area of life, religious activity. Religion is, for most people, in a compartment all of its own. It tends not to be part of daily life, and has little connection with family relationships or with the economic or political activities of the community (except in some notable cases).

In a country such as England the concept of the sacredness of the land as a whole is largely lost. So too are the sacred sites that serve to bind together the past, present and future of living communities. Environmental groups may struggle to prevent the destruction of specific sites, whether archaeological sites, areas of outstanding natural beauty, or bird and animal sanctuaries; but such threats to the environment are just that, and are not usually seen as having any deeper significance.

There are some sites in England, however, which are widely believed to have been sacred sites in the past, such as the ancient stone circles to be found in various parts of the British Isles. These are not treated as sacred sites by the majority of the population today, although religious significance is claimed for some sites – Stonehenge for example – by a minority (Fig. 1.1). As in many other parts of the world, the beliefs of this minority are dismissed, and their practices in the neighbourhood of the monument disallowed, even to the extent of persecution by the law of the land.

As far as the 'Church of England' and other Christian denominations are concerned (quite apart from other major religions that exist in England), the associated sacred places are usually very recognizable, at least to those who live in the community. They mainly consist of buildings, such as churches, chapels and cathedrals (Fig. 1.2). Today, even the churches are treated less and less as sacred places. The rules of dress that used to apply are no longer adhered to, and women may now enter bareheaded. There are still some rules that are usually followed, even by 'non-believers' – people tend not to shout or play games or run about in a church. Certain areas within the building are treated

Figure 1.1 Stonehenge, England. The stones are fenced off to prevent damage by visitors to the site. Photo: G. Gardiner.

with particular respect, such as the altar; Christians may genuflect as they pass or approach it, and will tend not to draw too near.

In the context of sacred sites and sacred places the prohibitions on behaviour that exist define the relationship between the god or gods and the people. Gods can protect and assist, but they can also punish and destroy, and therefore there is always some degree of danger involved in offending a deity, who must be placated and assuaged.

In many Christian societies, however, the prohibitions on behaviour that exist to maintain the fragile relationship between the people and their god tend to be restricted only to those activities that we call religious activities. Beyond these narrow confines the prohibitions do not exist, and daily life is relatively free from such restrictions.

In many other societies the concept of 'sacred' is not confined to one small area of life, but is manifested much more widely, and permeates all areas of life. For those people whose religion is confined to one small section of their lives it may be difficult to understand the concepts that underlie these different cultures, or to realize that what is believed to be sacred may not be confined to easily recognizable buildings or objects, but may consist of an apparently unmarked piece of earth or a rock, or a ledge on a mountainside. Perhaps one of the reasons why archaeologists and developers find it so hard to understand the reactions of indigenous peoples to the desecration of their sacred sites is because within the Christian religion it is possible to *deconsecrate* sacred sites. A church, for example, can be deconsecrated, by the carrying out of rituals, so that it becomes a secular site, an ordinary building that can then be used

Figure 1.2   Canterbury Cathedral, England. Now as much a tourist attraction as a place of worship? Photo: D. Hinton.

for any purpose. Thus the sacredness of the church is not something that is inherent in the place itself. Ritual leaders can create a sacred place, and uncreate it.

Can sacred sites become secular sites in other societies, such as Native American or Australian Aboriginal communities? In Australia the sacred sites originate from the Dreamtime, when the ancestors created the land – and are said to be still there in the form of 'natural' phenomena such as rocks and rivers. Is it possible, in these circumstances, for a sacred site to cease to be one, if ritual elders decide to change its status? Or does it belong only to the ancestors and thus will remain a sacred site for ever, just as it has already been a sacred site for ever? Perhaps this difference between the nature of the sacred sites of indigenous peoples and the sacred sites of most of the people who wish to disturb them contributes towards the confusion and disagreement between the two groups.

There are many different kinds of sacred sites, but it is burial sites, perhaps, that have become one of the major causes of controversy in many parts of the world. What has come to be called the 'reburial issue' has focused attention on a wide range of issues concerning attitudes to burial sites, the relationship between the living and the dead, and – in particular – the question of who has prior rights to burial sites, the people whose ancestors are buried there, or archaeologists and others who wish to disturb or destroy the sites for various purposes.

Burial sites often become sacred places in themselves (Fig. 1.3). What happens to these, and to other sacred sites, when the rules of behaviour that surround them are disregarded? Among the Suba people of Kenya the most important shrines, or sacred sites, are ancestral burial grounds. According to Odak (1989), a sacred site is desecrated if someone other than a ritual leader visits it. When the taboos surrounding a site are broken in this way, not only is its sacredness eroded, but an essential part of the traditional culture of the people is also lost.

Payne also points out, with regard to Australian Aboriginal sites, that the well-being of the people is dependent on the maintenance of their sites:

Figure 1.3 The creation of a sacred site: a reburial ceremony at Wounded Knee, South Dakota, USA in 1989. The bones, which had been disturbed by road construction, were reburied under the direction of Sioux and Seminole ritual leaders. Photo: Lydia Maher.

The maintenance of a site requires both physical caring – for example the rubbing of rocks or clearing of debris – and the performance of items aimed at caring for the spirit housed at it. Without these maintenance processes the site remains, but it is said to lose the spirit held within it. It is then said to die and all those who share physical features and spiritual connections with it are then also thought to die. Thus, to ensure the well-being of life, sites must be cared for and rites performed to keep alive the dreaming powers entrapped within them.

(Payne 1988, p. 72)

This concept is also acknowledged by Jo Mangi, from Papua New Guinea, who has had to confront the problems inherent in the situation of being a Papuan archaeologist working within his own culture. Faced with the dilemma of whether or not to excavate a site which, to him, has no special significance, he accepts the voice of the local cultural group to whom the site belongs, because of the effect his interference would have on the status of the site:

If it's sacred to them I would rather leave it, even if I know I *can* excavate – if I go to the trouble of negotiating it. I'd leave it. I'd rather take their account of it, the oral accounts of it . . . the minute you tamper with it they lose their respect they had for it.

(Mangi 1986, interview)

Many indigenous peoples would extend the concept of sacredness to the whole of their land. This is a very important point, and to some extent indicates a different understanding of sacred and sacredness. The focus on sacred sites and sites of special significance, in the controversy between indigenous peoples and those who threaten them from outside, has been a necessary focus. But it should not obscure the fact that in some cultures the very land itself is sacred. In North America, for example, Chief Seattle (quoted in Turner 1989), on the signing of the Treaty of Medicine Creek in 1854, said: 'Every part of this country is sacred to my people. Every hillside, every valley, every plain and grove has been hallowed by some fond memory or some sad experience of my tribe' (Turner 1989, p. 192).

In many countries there are people of different cultures, or even groups within the same culture, who have differing attitudes towards the earth, and opposing interests regarding the use of the land. In particular, perhaps, where indigenous people and colonizing Europeans co-exist, the difference in beliefs about the nature of the earth lies at the very heart of the controversy about who owns the land, who has rights over it and how it should be protected.

The belief that all the land is sacred is also held by the Aborigines of Australia. Tunbridge, writing about the Adnyamathanha people of the Flinders Ranges in South Australia, demonstrates this, saying that there are many signs in the landscape which indicate the presence or the passing of the spiritual ancestors:

> The visitor to the Flinders Ranges may see a hill, a rock, a water-hole or copper where traditionally an Adnyamathanha person would have seen that and more: the huge serpent Akurra, a Dreamtime Spirit's head, a Dreamtime Spirit's urine, and emu meat thrown by two Dreamtime Spirits passing by . . . it is quite common for Dreamtime Spirits to leave behind them their faeces and urine, the former generally in the form of rock, the latter in the form of waterholes. Blood is left behind in the form of red ground. When both the birds Marnbi and Yuduyudulya leave their feathers behind, it is in the form of white quartz, and when the eagle leaves his feathers behind, it is in the form of flintstone.
>
> (Tunbridge 1988, p. xxxiv)

This does not mean that the Adnyamathanha do not have special places, especially sacred places, which are set apart, and which carry their own prohibitions and rules of behaviour for those who come into contact with them. But the rest of the land is *also* sacred in a way that it is hard for people from other cultures to understand.

In Australia, some Aboriginal groups who have long been alienated from their land, and know little about the individual sites and stories connected with them, have come to consider all of it to be 'sacred', though in a different sense from those Aborigines who know wherein the significance lies.

> A new kind of 'sites of significance' has been developing in the recent past. To some people of Aboriginal descent who were not reared in a living-traditional Aboriginal culture, almost everything of that culture which they hear about or read about now is, by definition, sacred, or almost so. And that applies to 'country' as well: all sites in Australia are 'sites of significance' because they are, or were, *Aboriginal* sites.
>
> (Berndt 1989, p. 17)

In some places sacred sites are now protected from intrusion or destruction by law. Thus Maddock asks whether all of Australia could be called a sacred site, and then continues:

> This is not a facetious question. In the flurry of attention to sacred sites in recent years some striking assertions have been made by Aborigines and others. As with statements about land rights generally, these assertions are aimed at affecting the use and control of land. A sacred site – by definition almost – should be respected and left alone.
>
> (Maddock 1983, p. 131)

It may be that to some urbanized groups who have lost their link with their original homeland anything connected with the traditional past has become 'sacred' to them; others may use the word deliberately, because of its power as a deterrent to those who wish to destroy the land.

For the majority of people, however, who talk of the sacredness of their land, there is no desire to manipulate, only a desire to ensure that the land is preserved. Leonard Bastien of the Peigan Nation in Alberta, Canada, talking about the threatened destruction of part of the Oldman River Valley, writes:

> Napi created the animals, birds and people and could talk with them. If Napi could talk with animals, plants, birds and rocks, seeking their power to help him, it follows they must have spirits and must be sacred. From this the Indian believes that nothing is inanimate and therefore all is sacred. Rocks are sacred as a human life is sacred. It then follows that the Oldman River Valley, home for many of these birds, rocks, plants and animals is sacred as well.
> (Bastien 1989, p. A5)

Echoing Odak (above), Bastien also points out that the destruction of the land is also the destruction of traditional culture:

> Without the valley as it is, existing medicine bundles would become vestiges of a dead culture, since input for change would not be possible. For the Peigan the river, the valley, the plants and the animals allow for the self-perpetuation of their culture.
> (Bastien 1989, p. A5)

Although the whole landscape may be considered sacred, there are differences between this and the sacredness of sites that have particular significance. Not every stone or plot of earth can be treated with the same degree of respect. Does this mean that there are *degrees* of sacredness? Or is it, again, merely limitations in the understanding of the cultures and languages concerned?

It may be difficult to define what is meant by 'sacred' among different peoples and in varying contexts, but when the land comes under threat then the sacred sites, sacred places and sites of special significance become identifiable, even to outsiders, by the extent to which the communities concerned will fight to preserve and protect them from disturbance, interference or destruction.

References

Bastien, L. 1989. Oldman dam's cultural impact a major concern for Peigans. *The Lethbridge Herald*, 8 July 1989.

Berndt, C. H. 1989. Retrospect and prospect: looking back over 50 years. In *Women, Rites and Sites: Aboriginal women's cultural knowledge*, Peggy Brock (ed.), 1–20. Sydney: Allen & Unwin.

Condori, C. M. 1989. History and prehistory in Bolivia: what about the Indians? In *Conflict in the Archaeology of Living Traditions*, R. Layton (ed.), 46–59. London: Unwin Hyman; Routledge pbk 1994.

Dodson, P. n.d. *Aborigines – a Statement of Concern*. Australia: Catholic Commission for Justice and Peace.

Maddock, K. 1983. *Your Land is our Land: Aboriginal land rights*. Harmondsworth: Penguin Books.

Mangi, J. 1986. Interview. WAC1, September 1986, Southampton.

Matunga, H. 1994. *Waahi tapu*: Maori sacred sites. In *Sacred Sites, Sacred Places*, D. L. Carmichael, J. Hubert, B. Reeves & A. Schanche (eds), 217–26. London: Routledge.

Odak, O. 1989. Shrines: ancestral burial sites among the Suba of Kenya (unpublished MS). Paper given at the WAC Inter-Congress on Archaeological Ethics and the Treatment of the Dead, Vermillion, USA.

Payne, H. 1988. Singing a sister's sites: women's rites in the Musgrave Ranges. Ph.D. Thesis, University of Queensland.

Sole, T. & K. Woods 1992. Protection of indigenous sacred sites: the New Zealand experience. In *Aboriginal Involvement in Parks and Protected Areas*, J. Birckhead, T. de Lacey and L. Smith (eds), 339–51. Canberra: Aboriginal Studies Press.

Tunbridge, D. 1988. *Flinders Ranges Dreaming*. Canberra: Aboriginal Studies Press.

Turner, E. 1989. The souls of my dead brothers. In *Conflict in the Archaeology of Living Traditions*, R. Layton (ed.), 189–94. London: Unwin Hyman; Routledge pbk 1994.

2 Wintu sacred geography of northern California

DOROTHEA J. THEODORATUS &
FRANK LaPENA

> The world is a gift from our old ones. This sacred gift was created
> through love and respect by those elders who understood the
> beauty of their surroundings. . . . The evidence for the represen-
> tation of the earth as a mystical and magical place was given
> embodiment through the experiences of those who made visits to
> sacred places. . . . We respect those thoughts and teachings; when
> we are forgetful and need reminding of those teachings they are
> given back to us in our dreams.
>
> (LaPena 1987, n.p.)

Introduction

This chapter is about Wintu sacred geography, specifically those topographical
features which give meaning and distinction to people and place and are apart
from villages and daily home life. It is about topographical features which are
the embodiment of Wintu expression of an ordinary and non-ordinary world,
and about a concept of land and interpretations of that natural universe which
translate into a coherent world. We are concerned here with a physical
geography – an ethnogeography which, as a whole, forms a complex unit of
sacred domain.

The Wintu or Northern Wintun were (and remain) a comparatively large
and widespread Native American group occupying the present-day Shasta and
Trinity counties, and parts of Tehama and Siskiyou counties in California.
Wintu territory includes an extensive range of environmental topography,
from a relatively flat terrain to rugged canyons and mountains, all of which
provided a diverse subsistence base for the benefit and maximization of the
Wintu lifestyle. The Wintu held portions of the Trinity, Sacramento and
McCloud rivers, as well as a network of creeks. Within this domain, they
recognized a number of geographically based population divisions, but the
exact social boundaries are not precisely known today. Currently, there are

several Wintu organizations or groups, but no single one is representative of all Wintu. After contact, the Wintu suffered substantial destruction of their habitat and native economy as non-Indians expanded into their territory, destroying traditional economic conditions and developing a new, non-Indian land base (mining, logging, transportation routes and towns).

The data used here come from a cultural inventory of religious places on federal lands which was compiled to meet the requirements of the American Indian Religious Freedom Act (Theodoratus Cultural Research 1981). The approach was to review past anthropological and historical data and to consult with Wintu traditionalists.[1]

The study resulted in a recording of places and regions of religious signifi-cance to the Wintu. These places and regions are a major aspect of Wintu identity. As the study progressed, it became clear that topography is essential for the maintenance of Wintu identity and cultural continuity. Cultural and personal loss occurs when locales are altered, destroyed or placed off-limits. It is clear that significant alterations have taken place in the Wintu domain due to non-Indian development of artificial lakes, railroads, highways and habitation areas, and through economic ventures such as mining, ranching, deforestation and recreation.

The study also aimed to translate Indian realities into concepts understand-able and useful to government officials in designing meaningful strategies for site protection. Federal land management policies and their burdensome, often ethnocentric interpretations sometimes serve to polarize the assessment of Indian claims as unusual and illogical. In other words, the qualities of a place or a region which make them sacred, as well as the concomitant reverence and spiritual activities of the native practitioners, are profoundly different from mainstream perceptions of these places, attitudes and actions. This is, of course, the problem in converting Native American site realities into 'under-standable' non-Indian categories. The intention here is to present a perception of some of the structures and characteristics of the Wintu universe which will provide a clearer conception of Wintu ethnogeography. The requirements for the development of a methodology of sacred geography have been usefully discussed by Nabokov (1986, p. 486).

Power of place

LaPena writes:

> As the secrets of an esoteric world became known to seekers of knowledge and told to the people, never again was it possible to take for granted or approach the earth in a thoughtless fashion. . . .
> The earth is alive and exists as a series of interconnected systems where contradictions as well as confirmations are valid expressions of wholeness.
>
> (LaPena 1987, n.p.)

Religious cosmology, often related through myth, defines power and directs human action and interactions so that dangers may be minimized and success maximized. At the centre of the Native American religious system is the affirmation that spiritual power is infused throughout the environment in general, as well as at interconnected special places, and that knowledgeable people are participants in that power. Thus some special locations are imbued with benevolent sacred qualities which assist people in having good health, good luck and good energy. Other localities are imbued with malevolent forces capable of aiding in injurious acts. LaPena reminds us that such 'poison places' are warnings that:

> Caution and preparation must be used in order to maintain a proper respect for life and the unexpected. With things of power and life everything is possible. Our actions determine both good and bad. There are new things to learn, which can enlighten us or confuse us by their challenge.
>
> (LaPena 1987, n.p.)

Specific types of features, such as mountains, rock outcroppings, caves and pools, possess qualities important for Wintu spiritual experience or veneration. These form the sacred domain which is integral to the maintenance of Wintu cultural tradition. Humans relate to topographical features (i.e. sacred sites) and these features, in turn, give expression to conceptual life and cultural identity. The landscape provides images whose meaning has influence on daily activities, spiritual life and ethical considerations. This is perhaps what Nabokov means when he discusses the 'inner landscape', which he defines as the 'soul behind the surface that our eyes pick up' (Nabokov 1981, n.p.). For Wintu people, these localities are not discrete elements or cultural sherds. They are combined and bonded into cultural domains and sacred realms which provide essential meaning to life. As a Wintu travels through the countryside, he/she is aware of this sacred dimension that is 'power of place', and of its interconnectedness in Wintu sacred cosmology (note especially, Towendolly's stories of travel in Wintu country (Masson 1966)).

Wintu mythology

Wintu mythology provides an insight into their concept of the universe and a cultural map for their relationship with the environment (DuBois & Demetracopoulou 1935; Masson 1966). Myths often explain natural phenomena and set models for behaviour within the context of the geography; all have meaning as part of Wintu cosmology. Mythology helps keep the balance of spirit and body, and gives direction to Wintu life. It paints a philosophical portrait for those beings – human, animal and spiritual – which inhabit the earth, providing an ongoing process and meaning to life (LaPena 1987). Mythology, then, is intricately entwined with the environment. Features of nature are imbued with various powers and levels of sacred importance. Wintu people understand their own humanity in relation to the perception of this universe. Wintu poet Tauhindalí (1979, p. a3) writes,

> I am related
> in a universe
> bigger than
> my mind . . .
>
> I travel
> both earth and heaven
> trails
>
> lost in reference
> to other lives
>
> to other stars
> and songs
> of other constellations

Familiarity with the way the environment 'should be' is related to the Wintu sense of well-being, and thus reality. LaPena (1987) sees the subjective spirit world and the objective physical world as giving vision and meaning to life, and thus the world is, in a conceptual sense, both real and symbolic. Myth and its embodiment in geographical reflections enhance the Wintu sense of consciousness. Geographical formations remind Wintu that a great range of possibilities exists, and that a person must be open to reality if he/she is to be enlightened about the world. LaPena reminds us that the essence of the living Wintu world is meaningful and not to be taken for granted (LaPena 1987).

Geographical features

Localities of unusual configuration, such as distinctive rock outcrops (often in human or animal shapes), caves, knolls, whirlpools in a river, and seepage holes, often house spirits – especially those of coyote, deer and sucker. The spirit often makes its presence known through an audible buzzing. Such places are visited chiefly by men – often shamans – seeking transcendence in order to achieve another level of jurisdiction over a domain more potent and supreme in its influence than that found in the everyday world. Such locales are generally avoided by women, and they are especially dangerous to unmarried or menstruating women. Only places inhabited by the coyote spirit are used by women (DuBois 1935, pp. 79–81). A person in quest at these locations might travel from one sacred locality to another in search of dreams and spiritual influence. Different locales possess different degrees of sanctity; some are sources for shamanistic power while others are primarily used for special skills such as gambling or hunting or, in the case of women, for basket-making. Many such places are recognized by Wintu people (DuBois 1935, p. 81).

Shamans seek sacred energy at locations where they can acquire the skills necessary to serve as practitioners in the medical and religious aspects of Wintu life. A candidate visits a sacred place and invokes the spirits associated with that esoteric domicile. The Wintu revere a creator or omnipotent spirit, Olelbis, who plays an integral role in the mythology, and to whom prayers are addressed. Prayers are a part of daily life, associated with sojourns in sacred places. Topographical features such as caves, springs and rock outcroppings serve as settings for these functions.

Tauhindalí (1979, p. 24) writes about the power of caves in the poem 'Power Waits':

> The cave has power
> whirlwind dances
> on the valley floor
>
> sometimes people
> come to watch
> not all of them can see

Caves are used for gaining skills or for achieving success in secular endeavours, and some offer enrichment in a full range of activities. These may be used by any person who seeks the ends for which the cave is known. Some caves, known as *sauwel*, have to be approached in a specific manner. A *sauwel* has been specified by Wintu consultants as a place for religious people to acquire special power and spiritual guidance (e.g. Samwell Cave).

Springs are important for numerous reasons. They are often a component in healing practices, and as such are related to activities such as mud bathing, herbal treatment, or use of water in some other physical manner. The healing properties of some water are such that in some springs the water is used directly for healing physical ailments and treating open wounds, as well as in cleansing and purifying the body of poisons. At other springs, which offer spiritual energy, prayers are made to attain the guidance of the specific spirit-beings found in such places. Of particular importance are springs found inside caves, especially *sauwel*. These springs are instrumental in the acquisition of spiritual prowess and other favours. Springs are also used for bathing and swimming.

Springs might also be created for specific purposes. For example, one particular basin or spring of water, occurring in a basaltic formation (Fig. 2.1), was created by a shaman to supply water to a group of Wintu who were hiding out from vigilantes and American troops (Theodoratus Cultural Research Field Data 1979–91). Vernal pools or seasonal rain ponds might also have significance. One seasonal rain pond used by doctors as a source for power takes on the 'look of blood' when filled.

Figure 2.1   Sacred spring in rock formation adjacent to modern road.

Indwelling spirits are attributed to rock features of unusual configuration (Figs 2.2, 2.3). Numerous places that are considered sacred are mentioned in the literature, particularly in the mythology, and are said to resemble a spirit, a heart or a salmon (Bag of Bones, Lake of the Bleeding Heart). Present-day consultants discuss the importance of these formations to modern Wintu. Tauhindalí (1979) writes in 'A rock, a stone':

> I can't pass a rock
> like you
> without being mystified
> or hypnotized
>
> I have heard stories
> of rocks
> and have known some
> rocks personally

Figure 2.2   Rock formation referred to as Bag of Bones. Photo: Frank LaPena.

> They represent the
> world by their presence
> wisdom has no
> relationship to size
>
> One time, perhaps many times
> a man became a rock
> thinking that a fine way
> to gain immortality

A 'guide rock' was one particular kind of formation used to show directions to particular places, some of which were sacred (Fig. 2.4). One type of guide rock, for example, a split rock on the side of a hill, was visible from a distance, and was used to direct travellers to both ordinary and non-ordinary places. Many guide rocks were pointed out by a Wintu consultant who had travelled extensively by foot through a Wintu area. The guide rocks are interconnected, and a traveller can understand the direction to proceed to the next guidance point.

Streams and rivers are often used to determine cardinal orientations, and are

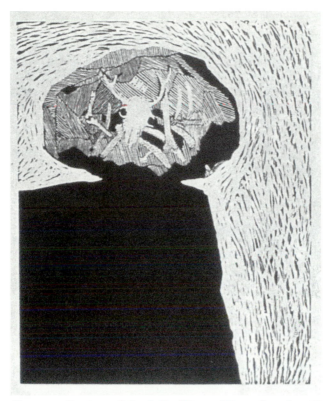

Figure 2.3 Conceptualization of the indwelling spirit attributed to Bag of Bones. Drawing: Frank LaPena.

thus part of a configuration of the Wintu world-view. Rivers are sometimes named in a manner which includes direction of flow. Pools or holes which form along a watercourse are frequently assigned spiritual significance. Other topographic features – such as special rock formations, natural bridges, and caves associated with watercourses – are thought to contain spiritual beings within their confines. Wintu myths often detail the creation of streams and numerous references to streams in the mythology reveal them as significant elements of Wintu life. Streams are generally avoided by menstruating women; however, some streams present such spiritual danger that women avoid them at all times.

Mountains house supernatural animal beings (such as werebeasts, mountain lions, mountain boys and bush boys) which can transform themselves into human form. Werebeasts are associated with evil or malevolent influences, so areas inhabited by these creatures are avoided (DuBois 1935, pp. 84–5). Mountains also possess benevolent spiritual power, and a number of such peaks were named by consultants – Mount Shasta being the main one (Fig. 2.5). LaPena reminds us that mountains (along with rocks) have slow

Figure 2.4 Guide rock known as Old Man Rock (Washington Rock), believed by Wintu to have been carved by lightning.

deliberate ways about them (1987, n.p.). *Sanchaluli*, a sacred place, is described as 'constant and patient in its teaching' (LaPena 1987, n.p.). Tauhindalí (1979, p. 22) tells us about a mountain in 'Bird healer':

> Yolla Bolli
> holds the imprints
> of mud tracks
> showing mother
> father
> and the children . . .
>
> One of each
> covered with
> feathers and wings

Figure 2.5   Mount Shasta, in the Cascade Range of northern California, is regarded as the main Wintu sacred mountain.

suitable for
this mountain

Suitable for
a spirit responsible
for the beginning
of the world

Spirits of the living and the dead could also be manifest in the environment. The spirits of the dead might manifest themselves in whirlwinds of dust or as ghosts. The soul of the newly deceased could linger a few days before travelling northward, where it would go to Mount Shasta or to a spring known only to souls; it would then rise to the Milky Way, where it would travel south to a fork in the spirit trail, and then east to a grassy plain where Indians 'are always having a big time' (DuBois 1935, p. 79). Generally, at death, the body would be oriented towards the north, the direction the ghost must travel to drink from the spring of life before starting the journey to the next world (DuBois 1935, p. 65). Different soul-travel orientations might be used for a person buried outside the Wintu area; then the spirit would be released in the direction of Mount Shasta, but funeral oratory would always direct the soul on its celestial journey.

Many Wintu today are particularly synchronized with, engaged in, and committed to their landscape. One consultant said that, in order to record the Bald Hills area properly, we would have to be content to cover less than a mile each day. Other Wintu have similarly detailed knowledge of the network in their landscape, showing intense regard for their physical environment even though the order of the Wintu world has been broken by development and western disorder. For many, there has been a perpetuation of the meaning of landscape – that is, the relation of geographical features to life in general. LaPena (1987, n.p.) reminds us that 'we are all connected because time has no boundary and space is of one continuity'. Clearly, Wintu perceive the sacredness of features and the power of place in their environment, but also resplendent in this wide-angle vision is the interconnectedness of these features into a broader cosmology, or a complex sacred geography.

Again, according to Tauhindalí (1979), in his poem 'I am related':

> I am related
> in a universe
> bigger than
> my mind
>
> I am connected
> to the stars
>
> and sing to
> chosen star groups
>
> I travel
> both earth and heaven
> trails
>
> to other stars
> and songs
> of other constellations.

Note

1 The field research was carried out in 1983 by Dorothea Theodoratus, with native anthropologist, scholar, poet, artist and Wintu traditionalist, Frank LaPena.

References

DuBois, C. 1935. Wintu ethnography. *University of California Publications in American Archaeology and Ethnology* 36 (1), 1–148.
DuBois, C. & D. Demetracopoulou 1935. Wintu myths. *University of California Publications in American Archaeology and Ethnology* 28 (5), 279–403.
LaPena, F. 1987. *The World is a Gift*. San Francisco: Limestone Press.
Masson, M. 1966. *A Bag of Bones, Legends of the Wintu Indians of Northern California*. Happy Camp, Calif.: Naturegraph.

Nabokov, P. 1981. Land as symbol. Speech recorded in the American Indian Option Series at Ames, Iowa. National Public Radio, Washington, D.C.

Nabokov, P. 1986. Unto these mountains: toward the study of sacred geography. In *Voices of the First America: text and context in the New World*, G. Brotherston (ed.), Special issue of *New Scholar* 10, 1–3, 479–89.

Tauhindalí 1979. *Sanusa Stopped the Rain*. Carmichael, Calif.: Chalatien Press.

Theodoratus Cultural Research 1979–91. Field Data. Fair Oaks, Calif.: Theodoratus Cultural Research.

Theodoratus Cultural Research 1981. Native American cultural overview, Shasta-Trinity National Forest. Principal, Dorothea Theodoratus. Report, US Department of Agriculture, Forest Service, Shasta-Trinity National Forest, Redding, CA. Fair Oaks, Calif.: Theodoratus Cultural Research.

3 Sacred and secular neolithic landscapes in Ireland

GABRIEL COONEY

Introduction

A landscape has been recently defined as 'a cultural image, a pictorial way of representing, structuring or symbolising surroundings' (Daniels & Cosgrove 1988, p. 1). The image of depiction suggests an ability to stand back from the landscape and examine it. In fact the word 'landscape' was introduced into English as a painter's technical term in the early seventeenth century (Tunnard 1978). However, both in the case of those from a variety of disciplines who are attempting to analyse the meaning of landscape and for the people actually occupying landscapes, their views and understanding of the landscape are conditioned by their culture. A person's perception or mental map of a place is what underpins his/her actions rather than the objective reality of that place (e.g. Abler, Adams & Gould 1972; Lynch 1972). Because landscape is an integral part of a person's life, it is impossible for him or her to step outside it. As Smyth (1984, pp. 29–30) put it, society can be seen as structured in a spiralling series of territorial networks which on the one hand embrace the earth with its economic, socio-political and ideological systems and, on the other, reverberate to impinge on the actions and mentalities of each individual.

Looked at from different sides of a cultural frontier, the same landscape may be viewed in a totally different way. Concentrating on the Ireland of the eighteenth century AD, Corkery (1924) outlined the traditional Gaelic perception of the landscape, in which different family names were associated with physical districts, and where the recollection of place-names in certain regions was the remembrance of the ancient tribes and their deeds. He contrasted this with the perception of the settlers coming into Ireland from Britain as part of the colonizing and land redistribution process; the landscape they looked upon was nothing but rock and trees and stones. But they had an obsession with putting their mark on this landscape through building houses, estates and villages, and in the artistic depiction of themselves with and in the landscape (Foster 1988, p. 192). We can see this as the contrast between an oral and a cartographic perception of landscape (Andrews 1985; Harley 1988).

The relevance of considering neolithic landscapes in Ireland, from 4000 to 2500 BC, in a wider context is that they form the visible foundation of all subsequent cultural landscapes in Ireland. The mesolithic fisher-gatherer-hunters who were Ireland's first inhabitants, coming into the country in the postglacial period (e.g. Woodman 1986), may have imbued places in their surroundings with special meaning, but they apparently left the environment largely unaltered. What made the activities of early farmers different is that they deliberately altered the landscape for socio-economic reasons, and that human adaptation and alteration, incorporating cultural elements already in the landscape, continues to the present day. Over the course of time some of the major areas of activity during the Neolithic have continued to be perceived as important symbolic landscapes, while others have become marginalized and have only been rediscovered through archaeological research.

In the dimensions of time and space there are a number of issues that can be explored. How does landscape evolve over time? Was there a divide between what have been termed sacred and secular landscapes? If landscapes are symbolic images, were they used in an active way to express social power? Is there a link between the long-term occupation of landscapes and the way in which they come to be viewed and used in oral and written history?

Sacred and secular

In a real, human sense these are not separate but interwoven aspects of life. A better view might be to suggest that the sacred is a current underlying all aspects of everyday life (Barrett 1989) and that there are specific times, places and events when the sacred comes to the fore, as for example in mortuary practices. For people in a social group the nature of participation in a sacred activity will depend on what that activity is. There may be certain people who are deliberately excluded, and control of sacred action may be a key component of social power.

In landscape terms what could be defined as a secular landscape is one concerned with everyday life – home, field and farm – while the sacred would be identifiable as containing special places – for example sites for ceremony and ritual, including tombs. In a spatial sense these sacred sites could be integrated with or separate from the secular ones (e.g. Renfrew 1981), although for the people who identified with them the sites would in either case have been seen as part of their world-view or mental map. Links between the sacred and the secular would have been reiterated in everyday life, for example by the use of objects such as stone axes, which could also turn up in special places, either deliberately deposited in a tomb, or in a place of special significance in the landscape such as a bog or river (e.g. Cooney 1989).

Another useful way to look at the sacred and secular is in terms of Braudel's (1980) distinction between the *longue durée* – the underlying structure that marks the routine of everyday life – and *events* – which on the one hand may be short-term, but on the other may mark turning points in the way people live their lives and how society is organized. Alternatively, historical events can be seen as having only a peripheral impact on an everyday continuity in life which may extend over several millennia. Thus Evans (1981, p. 62) held that in Ireland there were aspects of life, such as agricultural practice, settlement form and organization and folk customs, which showed 'a continuity from early times, indeed from the very beginning of agriculture'. What is interesting in terms of landscape is that some areas that had already become 'special' in the Neolithic were to be the scene of continuing attention in archaeology, history and mythology, as people referred back to the past and as social leaders sought to incorporate the past as part of the legitimization process of their authority.

Secular landscapes in the Irish Neolithic

Research programmes approaching this issue from a number of different perspectives are showing up an increasingly diverse and complex picture of the Irish landscape in the period 4000–2500 BC. The classic view of forest clearance, temporary settlement, abandonment and forest renewal (e.g. Pilcher, Smith, Pearson & Crowder 1971) has been convincingly challenged by Edwards (1985) on palynological grounds. The result of survey work on field systems subsequently covered by the growth of blanket bog peat, especially in northwest Mayo (Caulfield 1978, 1983, 1988), shows a variety of layouts, from individual farmsteads to large-scale farmed landscapes, the latter laid out and maintained on a communal basis over several hundred years. Other evidence suggests that there were instances of shorter-term clearance (Molloy & O'Connell 1987). Field survey and museum research are showing that the distribution of lithic scatters of neolithic date is much more widespread than had previously been suggested (e.g. Woodman 1983; Zvelebil, Moore, Green & Henson 1987). It is clear, for example, that settlement was not confined to those areas where megalithic tombs were constructed. Settlement involved both individual, apparently isolated, houses and groups/clusters of houses, such as that at Lough Gur (Ó Ríordáin 1954; Grogan & Eogan 1987) and the recently discovered houses at Tankardstown, Co. Limerick (Gowen 1988; Gowen & Tarbett 1988). Around the houses it appears that a system of mixed farming was carried out in an organized manner. Beyond this home world would have been places visited more occasionally but still with a central position in people's lives: places where raw materials were obtained, other settlements, places where particular events took place such as burial and commemoration. The concept of a spiralling series of networks linked by human activities illustrates how all these places could have been linked in the mind's eye.

How important was the perception of landscape in the neolithic world? It could be said that the creation of field boundaries, as well as being of practical benefit, was a deliberate statement of a different view of the land and its ownership from that of the hunter-gatherer (Cooney 1991), the construction of a clear perceptual frontier. The creation of large field systems, as at Céide in Co. Mayo, is indicative of both social cohesion and the organization of dispersed families together to create a communal landscape which may itself have been seen as symbolizing and articulating this community (Fleming 1987, 1988).

At Lough Gur there are indications that social ranking within the settlement was built into the landscape. Not only were there differences in the degree to which people had access to non-local artefacts, but these differences could also be correlated with the location of the houses within the settlement cluster and the presence or absence of an enclosing wall (Grogan & Eogan 1987).

Because of their visibility in the landscape, and survival in large numbers, much attention has been focused on the role of megalithic tombs in the landscape of early farming communities. It is clear that their siting was very frequently deliberate, often incorporating a topographical location shared by tombs of the same type (e.g. Ó Nualláin 1983) and in some areas a placement close to areas potentially attractive for early farming and settlement (Cooney 1979, 1983). It has become an orthodoxy to speak of such tombs as territorial markers (Renfrew 1976). This can be taken to mean many different things, but what is most relevant here is to consider the tombs as a link between everyday life, ever visible in the landscape, and the sacred, marked by ceremonies at the sites which emphasized the continued link between the past and present, between the ancestors, the dead and the living community (Bloch 1971; Connerton 1989).

Sacred places, sacred landscapes

Places recognized as sacred can be made permanent by monument building. The introduction of a monument into the 'natural' environment can signify that the human institutions that created the monument are taking on the permanence of nature: architecture and nature ideally united as one (Oechslin 1984), as exemplified in the use of nature's resources in the monument. As Bradley (1984) has shown, monuments become a permanent fixture and they influence subsequent activity. In the context of the Irish Neolithic the most visible sacred places, as introduced above, are the megalithic tombs. As the name suggests, their most archaeologically detectable function was to contain deliberate, often selective, deposits of human remains. Different types of tombs have in the past been seen as representing different cultures or peoples (e.g. Herity & Eogan 1977; Harbison 1988). But this view overlooks significant spatial, cultural, morphological and chronological overlaps between the tombs. What is of particular interest here is a supposed dichotomy separating one of the four tomb types – passage tombs – from the other three well-known Irish types. Passage tombs are seen to be different in that they stand spatially apart from the secular landscape and are grouped into cemeteries, i.e. they

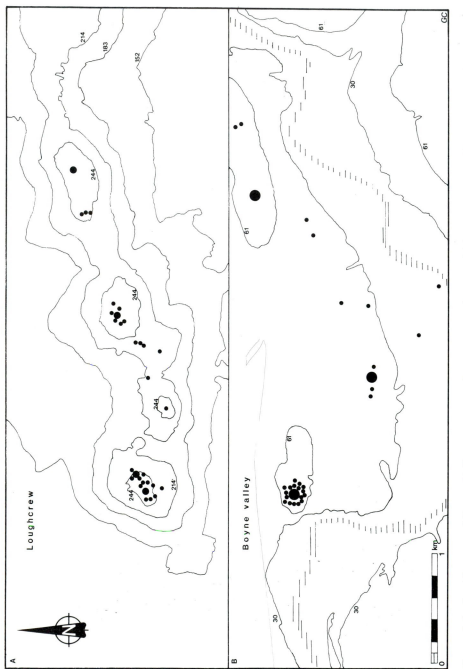

Figure 3.1 Loughcrew and Boyne Valley passage-tomb cemeteries, showing deliberate patterns of location of small (satellite) tombs around large (focal) ones. Both circular and linear patterns can be identified.

form a sacred/ritual landscape. The other tombs have been regarded as dispersed within the secular landscape, each tomb acting as a local communal focus point (Herity 1974; Darvill 1979; O'Kelly 1981; Eogan 1986). I have argued elsewhere (Cooney 1990) that the situation is not as straightforward as this and that there are examples of clusters of tombs other than passage tombs that should be regarded as cemeteries, where the repetition of the siting of tombs in a spatially limited area created a special place. There was, in this context, a range of perceptions of the link between sacred and secular landscapes, varying on a continuum from integration to complete separation and influencing how these sacred places were used. (This applies not only to megalithic tombs but other places where possible periodic, repeated actions and events of a special nature took place.)

In terms of special places there is no doubt that the four large cemeteries of passage tombs in Ireland, including the Boyne Valley and Loughcrew (Fig. 3.1), both in Co. Meath, are very distinctive in terms of the scale of building and activity that went on within them over several hundred years. The clearest sequence in the development of these cemeteries can be seen in the Boyne Valley where excavations at Knowth (e.g. Eogan 1984) and Newgrange (O'Kelly 1982; O'Kelly, Lynch & O'Kelly 1978; O'Kelly, Cleary & Lehane 1983) have shown that settlement activity preceded and possibly interdigitated with the construction and use of the tombs. It has been suggested that these increased in scale and complexity over time as the dead were used by their descendants in competitive emulation to increase power and status (Sheridan 1985/6). The construction of the tombs involved a large number of people and presumably an area larger than the cemetery itself. It can be argued that the high fertility and 'island'-like topography of the Boyne Valley made it an important settlement area, and this fertility took on a special character as the wealth was expressed in the construction and use of the tombs, perhaps with settlement becoming restricted in area and with the elite directing the cemetery project.

Much emphasis has been placed on the complexity of building and the events surrounding the tombs. This was taken to greater lengths in the Boyne Valley than in the other three large passage tomb cemeteries. There are contrasts between the interior and exterior of the tombs and between the size of different tombs. A vital element, however, which has been little discussed, is that the location of the tombs appears to take cognizance of the siting of existing tombs. There are deliberate patterns of tomb siting recognizable within the cemeteries, and the tombs are located with reference to others (Cooney 1990). As McCullough & Mulvin (1987) put it, the landscape became part of the architecture of the tombs. It appears that the landscape was being remodelled and transformed through the addition of new monuments and layers of cultural activity. An interesting change occurs in the Boyne Valley towards the end of the Neolithic, where it appears that the ideology of a landscape dominated by respect for the ancestors was transformed (Fig. 3.2). There was continued respect for the old locations but there was also a return to more extensive settlement, by people using Beaker pottery around the edges of the large tomb mounds at Newgrange and Knowth (Eogan 1984; O'Kelly, Cleary & Lehane 1983). Now an emphasis was put on the provision of open-air earthen enclosures where a variety of activities took place, apparently of a formalized, repetitive nature (Sweetman 1976, 1985), suggesting that they were central to the way in which power was exercised within society. There may have been deliberate destruction of the past at this time to reaffirm the new order, for example in damage to megalithic tombs (including Newgrange?) and the insertion of a burial into the collapsed passage of a tomb at Knowth (Eogan 1984). A similar sequence of events appears to have occurred in the Orkney Islands off the northern coast of Scotland (e.g. Simpson 1988) with which people in the Boyne Valley were in contact.

Post-neolithic use of landscapes

It is clear, then, that neolithic landscapes were not static, but that, over time, they underwent changes in both appearance and meaning to their occupants. However, because they fit into one of our major time/cultural blocks there is a tendency to conceptualize neolithic landscapes as a single entity, something that can be viewed in a unitary, synchronic sense, whereas in fact they may be the result of over a thousand years' activity. Even in the case of apparently synchronic landscapes, such as the coaxial field system, tombs and settlement enclosures at Céide in Co. Mayo, it can be suggested that some elements may not be contemporary, such as the court tombs (S. Caulfield *pers. comm.* 1990). When we recognize changes occurring within the period of the Neolithic we tend to set them apart from later developments, although some of these may have been closer to each other in time than the changes that occurred during the lengthy course of the Neolithic.

Writing about the concept of place in time, Gregotti (1984) observed that the concepts of environment and site contain a great quantity of physical and historical debris which must be taken into account on new projects. He suggests that there are two ways of doing this – by imitation, assimilation and the creation of a conspicuous complexity or, second, by measurement, distance, definition, change and, specifically, through a lack of coincidence with what has gone before. While this embodies an architectural concept of environment and the distinction between a postmodernist and modernist perspective, it is an interesting perspective from which to study the way in which neolithic landscapes were transformed over time (and also to think about the way landscapes changed during the course of the Neolithic period itself).

Neolithic places and landscapes were altered in many ways. Large parts of the secular landscape changed as agricultural methods and technology altered. In other cases environmental changes marginalized areas that had earlier been of significance, for example the growth of blanket bog over upland areas (e.g. Edwards 1985) that had previously been farmed sealed them from further change. However, in some instances sacred places such as tombs continued as a focus of burial and other activity. It was where there were such visible remains in the landscape, and in those areas where there was prolonged continuous or episodic activity, that the transformation of greatest significance took place. These areas took on a mythic quality which has endured down to the present day, and this still dominates many people's perception of land-scapes such as the Boyne Valley and Tara. This is also true in Co. Meath, where the earliest visible element in what was to become a complex prehistoric and early historic landscape and royal site was a passage tomb.

Looking at traditional Gaelic culture, Foster (1988, p. 5) has observed that:

> the literal representation of the country was less important than its poetic dimension . . . the terrain was studied, discussed and referenced. Every place had its own identity and legend. *Dindsenchas*, the celebration of place-names, was a feature of this poetic topography, what endured was the mythic landscape.

This mythic landscape also provided an ideal medium for symbolism, manipulation and transformation of the past. In myth and folklore neolithic sites are presented in different ways. What these presentations have in common is that they were part of a complex system of folk belief into which places were incorporated and explained in a way that had continuing meaning for people. This meaning was orally transferred from generation to generation; in this sense we can see landscape as 'territories of the voice that intimated across death and generation how a secret was imparted' (Cannon 1990, frontispiece). For example, one of the common folk-names for a megalithic tomb is 'Diar-muid and Grainne's Bed'. This is after the lovers in the *Fianniocht* cycle of stories, who eloped to escape the attentions of the ageing hero Fionn Mac Cumhaill, who pursued them throughout Ireland. The lovers made a fresh bed in a different place every night, hence the megalithic tombs (Fig. 3.2). On his death Diarmuid was said to have been brought to Brugh na Bóinne, identified either as Newgrange specifically, or as the Boyne Valley passage-tomb ceme-tery in general. In mythology the Brugh was said to have been the home of the *Tuatha De*, supernatural beings from a remote past but who lived on in another world – a fairy world. This is a very strong component in Irish folk-belief and a range of archaeological sites of different types and dates were explained in the folk-mind as the homes of the fairy folk or the *sidhe*.

The political value of an association with this mythic world is demonstrated by the fact that in the first millennium AD members of the ruling dynasty at the royal site of Tara appear to have attempted to aggrandize themselves by associating their ancestors with the Brugh, by suggesting that it was the burial-place of the pagan kings of Tara (O'Kelly 1982). It is interesting to note that other royal sites of this period have evidence of neolithic activity on them. Is this also a conscious attempt to create a link with the antique? Or is it a sign

Figure 3.2 Portal tomb at Gaulstown, Co. Waterford. This is the type of Irish megalithic tomb most commonly referred to in folklore as Diarmuid and Grainne's Bed because of the characteristic large capstone. Photo courtesy of the Office of Public Works, Dublin.

of the continuing importance of certain landscapes throughout prehistory?

In a modern political sense the mythological view of neolithic remains was associated with the image of Celtic Ireland which has been portrayed, in nineteenth- and twentieth-century nationalist politics, as the ideal Ireland. Thus a megalithic tomb, particularly of the portal tomb type, was constantly in the background in illustrations of folk-tales. The portal tomb became one of the national icons along with the early medieval round towers and high crosses. The appeal of the past was deliberately manipulated on important occasions, such as when Daniel O'Connell, the great nineteenth-century nationalist politician, held a huge meeting at Tara, which attracted over half a million people, one of a series of meetings aimed at repealing the 1800 Act of Union between Ireland and Britain.

In relation to everyday life the appeal of the past has been seen in a different light. The continuity seen by Evans (1981) and others in the patterns of everyday life, stretching from the Neolithic to the present day, relies on an assumption of the strength of oral tradition in transferring the knowledge and rituals of everyday life. Fleming (1988) has discussed this problem in the context of the organization of farmed landscapes. But this continuity can be overstressed and it must be set alongside cultural and historical discontinuities. It is clear, for example, that the search for continuity in settlement organiz- ation has not adequately taken into account regional and chronological vari- ations (e.g. see Burtchaell 1988). In many ways this search for continuity is futile, since change in traditional societies can equally be justified with regard to the past in what Glassie (1982, p. 436) termed 'conservative extension'. In this sense we are brought back to the integration of the sacred and profane, because central to the operation of the everyday landscape is the belief that it is founded on the sacred, on permanency. That permanency can be renegotiated by social leaders/elites, incorporating the old into a new version of reality that suits their purposes, and by the socially impotent to create a vision of the past in which they shared the spoils. It would appear that in Ireland this process has been going on since neolithic times.

Acknowledgements

My thanks to Eoin Grogan and Richard Bradley for their valuable comments on an earlier draft of this chapter; also to the participants in both the Landscape and Heritage Management and the Sacred Sites sessions at WAC 2, in Barquisimeto, Venezuela, for much discussion and inspiration. In particular I would like to thank Bassey W. Andah for his encouragement and comments.

References

Abler, R., J. S. Adams and P. Gould 1972. *Spatial Organisation: the geographer's view of the world*. London: Prentice-Hall International.

Andrews, J. H. 1985. *Plantation Acres: an historical study of the Irish land surveyor and his maps*. Belfast: Institute of Irish Studies.

Barrett, J. 1989. Time and tradition: the rituals of everyday life. In *Bronze Age Studies*, H.-A. & A. Knape (eds), 113–26. Stockholm: Statens Historika Museum.

Bloch, M. 1971. *Placing the Dead: tombs, ancestral villages and kinship organisation in Madagascar*. London: Seminar Press.

Bradley, R. 1984. *The Social Foundations of Prehistoric Britain*. London: Longman.

Braudel, F. 1980. *On History*. London: Weidenfeld & Nicolson.

Burtchaell, J. 1988. The south Kilkenny farm villages. In *Common Ground: essays on the historical geography of Ireland*, W. J. Smyth & K. Whelan (eds), 110–23. Cork: Cork University Press.

Cannon, M. 1990. Taom. In *Territories of the Voice: contemporary stories by Irish women writers*, L. A. De Salvo, K. W. D'Arcy & C. Hogan (eds), frontispiece. London: Virago Press.

Caulfield, S. 1978. Neolithic fields: the Irish evidence. In *Early Land Allotment*, H. C. Bowen & P. J. Fowler (eds), 137–44. Oxford: British Archaeological Reports.

Caulfield, S. 1983. The neolithic settlement of north Connaught. In *Landscape*

Archaeology in Ireland, T. Reeves-Smyth & F. Hamond (eds), 195–215. Oxford: British Archaeological Reports.

Caulfield, S. 1988. *Céide Fields and Belderrig: a guide to two prehistoric farms in north Mayo*. Killala: Morrigan Book Co.

Connerton, P. 1989. *How Societies Remember*. Cambridge: Cambridge University Press.

Cooney, G. 1979. Some aspects of the siting of megalithic tombs in County Leitrim. *Journal of the Royal Society of Antiquaries of Ireland* 109, 74–91.

Cooney, G. 1983. Megalithic tombs in their environmental setting, a settlement perspective. In *Landscape Archaeology in Ireland*, T. Reeves-Smyth & F. Hamond (eds), 179–94. Oxford: British Archaeological Reports.

Cooney, G. 1989. Stone axes from north Leinster. *Oxford Journal of Archaeology* 8, 145–57.

Cooney, G. 1990. The place of megalithic tomb cemeteries in Ireland. *Antiquity* 64, 741–53.

Cooney, G. 1991. Irish neolithic landscapes and land use systems: the implications of field systems. *Rural History* 2, 123–39.

Corkery, D. 1924. *The Hidden Ireland*. Dublin: Gill and Son.

Daniels, S. & D. Cosgrove 1988. Introduction: iconography and landscape. In *The Iconography of Landscape*, D. Cosgrove & S. Daniels (eds), 1–10. Cambridge: Cambridge University Press.

Darvill, T. 1979. Court cairns, passage graves and social change in Ireland. *Man* 14, 311–27.

Edwards, K. J. 1985. The anthropogenic factor in vegetational history. In *The Quaternary History of Ireland*, K. J. Edwards & W. P. Warren (eds), 187–220. London: Academic Press.

Eogan, G. 1984. *Excavations at Knowth*. Dublin: Royal Irish Academy.

Eogan, G. 1986. *Knowth and the Passage Tombs of Ireland*. London: Thames & Hudson.

Evans, E. E. 1981. *The Personality of Ireland: habitat, heritage and history*. Belfast: Blackstaff Press.

Fleming, A. 1987. Coaxial field systems: some questions of time and space. *Antiquity* 61, 188–202.

Fleming, A. 1988. *The Dartmoor Reaves*. London: Batsford.

Foster, R. F. 1988. *Modern Ireland: 1600–1972*. London: Allen Lane.

Glassie, H. 1982. *Passing the Time: folklore and history of an Ulster community*. Dublin: O'Brien Press.

Gowen, M. 1988. *Three Irish Gas Pipelines: new archaeological evidence in Munster*. Dublin: Wordwell.

Gowen, M. & C. Tarbett 1988. A third season at Tankardstown. *Archaeology Ireland* 2, 156.

Gregotti, V. 1984. The place in time. *Daidalos* 15, 66–7.

Grogan, E. & G. Eogan 1987. Lough Gur excavations by S. P. Ó Ríordáin: further neolithic and Beaker habitations on Knockadoon. *Proceedings of the Royal Irish Academy* 87C, 299–506.

Harbison, P. 1988, *Pre-Christian Ireland*. London: Thames & Hudson.

Harley, J. B. 1988. Maps, knowledge and power. In *The Iconography of Landscape*, D. Cosgrove & S. Daniels (eds), 277–312. Cambridge: Cambridge University Press.

Herity, M. 1974. *Irish Passage Graves*. Dublin: Irish University Press.

Herity, M. & G. Eogan 1977. *Ireland in Prehistory*. London: Routledge & Kegan Paul.

Lynch, K. 1972. *What Time is this Place?* Cambridge, Mass.: MIT Press.

McCullough, N. & V. Mulvin 1987. *A Lost Tradition: the nature of architecture in Ireland*. Dublin: Gandon Editions.

Molloy, K. & M. O'Connell 1987. The nature of the vegetational changes at about 5000 BP with particular reference to the elm decline: fresh evidence from Connemara, western Ireland. *New Phytologist* 107, 203–20.

Oechslin, W. 1984. Nature and its reduction to architecture. *Daidalos* 15, 44–53.

O'Kelly, M. J. 1981. The megalithic tombs of Ireland. In *Antiquity and Man*, J. D. Evans, B. Cunliffe & C. Renfrew (eds), 177–90. London: Thames & Hudson.

O'Kelly, M. J. 1982. *Newgrange: archaeology, art and legend*. London: Thames & Hudson.

O'Kelly, M. J., R. M. Cleary and D. Lehane 1983. *Newgrange, Co. Meath, Ireland: the late neolithic/Beaker period settlement*. Oxford: British Archaeological Reports.

O'Kelly, M. J., F. Lynch & C. O'Kelly 1978. Three passage-graves at Newgrange, Co. Meath. *Proceedings of the Royal Irish Academy* 78C, 249–552.

Ó Nualláin, S. 1983. Irish portal tombs: topography, siting and distribution. *Journal of the Royal Society of Antiquaries of Ireland* 113, 75–105.

Ó Ríordáin, S. P. 1954. The Lough Gur excavations: neolithic and bronze age houses on Knockadoon. *Proceedings of the Royal Irish Academy* 56C, 297–459.

Pilcher, J. R., A. G. Smith, G. W. Pearson & A. Crowder 1971. Land clearance in the Irish Neolithic: new evidence and interpretation. *Science* 172, 560–2.

Renfrew, C. 1976. Megaliths, territories and populations. In *Acculturation and Continuity in Atlantic Europe*, S. de Laet (ed.), 198–220. Bruges: de Tempel.

Renfrew, C. 1981. The megalith builders of western Europe. In *Antiquity and Man*, J. D. Evans, B. Cunliffe & C. Renfrew (eds), 72–81. London: Thames & Hudson.

Sheridan, A. 1985/6. Megaliths and megalomania: an account and interpretation of the development of passage tombs in Ireland. *Journal of Irish Archaeology* 3, 17–30.

Simpson, D. D. A. 1988. The stone maceheads of Ireland. *Journal of the Royal Society of Antiquaries of Ireland* 118, 7–52.

Smyth, W. J. 1984. Social geography of rural Ireland: inventory and prospect. In *Irish Geography 1934–84*, G. L. Herries Davies (ed.), 204–36. Dublin: Geographical Society of Ireland.

Sweetman, P. D. 1976. An earthen enclosure at Monknewtown, Slane, Co. Meath. *Proceedings of the Royal Irish Academy* 76C, 25–73.

Sweetman, P. D. 1985. A late neolithic/early bronze age pit circle at Newgrange, Co. Meath. *Proceedings of the Royal Irish Academy* 85C, 195–221.

Tunnard, C. 1978. *A World with a View: an inquiry into the nature of scenic values*. New Haven: Yale University Press.

Woodman, P. C. 1983. The Glencloy project in perspective. In *Landscape Archaeology in Ireland*, T. Reeves-Smyth & F. Hamond (eds), 25–34. Oxford: British Archaeological Reports.

Woodman, P. C. 1986. Problems in the colonisation of Ireland. *Ulster Journal of Archaeology* 49, 7–17.

Zvelebil, M., J. A. Moore, S. W. Green & D. Henson 1987. Regional survey and analysis: a case study from southeast Ireland. In *Mesolithic Northwest Europe: recent trends*, P. Rowley-Conwy, M. Zvelebil & H. P. Blankholm (eds), 9–32. Sheffield: University of Sheffield Department of Archaeology and Prehistory.

4   Sacred space in the culture of the Arctic regions

O. V. Ovsyannikov & N. M. Terebikhin

Translated from the Russian by Katharine Judelson[1]

Introduction

This chapter concerns questions relating to the organization of sacred space in the culture of the Arctic regions (Fig. 4.1, I–IV). The cultures of this region are polyethnic; the diverse peoples who, at various times in the past settled on territory in the northern latitudes, have played their part in the evolution of the culture of the region, each bringing to the Arctic their own culture and methods of harnessing the environment. An early culture of hunters of wild reindeer, identified in the archaeological record, gave way to a culture of reindeer breeders and fishermen. The cultural experience which Russian hunting groups, peasants and seafarers brought with them was of quite a different kind. Yet, although the external, superficial aspects of these cultural traditions carried different implications, the essential mechanisms for settling new territories were similar. So, too, was the symbolic classification of space into two categories: sacred and profane, and the demarcation of sacred space with specially produced religious objects that sanctified humans' ordering of their life and environment, and gave meaning to that activity.

Archaeological evidence

Archaeological research in recent years has made it possible to single out, in broad outline, a whole ethnocultural level dating from the sixth to the thirteenth centuries, represented in the main by sacrificial sites in the mainland tundra (Chernov 1951; Khlobytsin 1986; Murygin 1984; Ovsyannikov 1985; Rybatseva & Semyonov 1990). It has been established that the earliest historical level in these sites dates from the sixth to the tenth century. During that time contacts with 'Rus' cannot be traced, since they had not yet been established. Material from this period closely resembles that from the ethno-

---

[1] 14 Thornhill Road, Southampton SO1 7AT

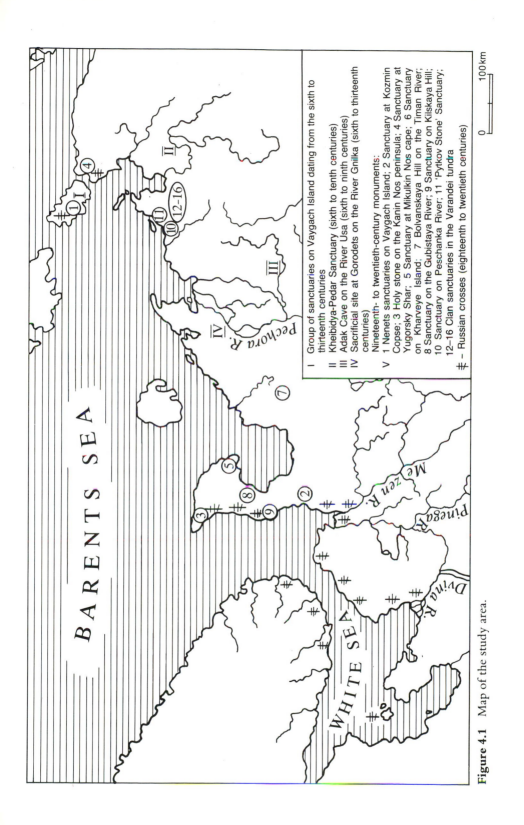

Figure 4.1 Map of the study area.

cultures of the second to fourth centuries traced in the area, stretching from the lower reaches of the Ob to the range of sites distinguished by artefacts in the so-called 'animal' style of the Perm region dating from the sixth to tenth centuries (Oborin 1971). All these sacred sites are characterized by a profusion of sacrificial objects, including silver, bronze and glass ornaments, as well as deliberately broken and bent iron axes and cauldrons made from copper, which was believed to have purifying properties (Figs 4.2–4.4) (Yevsyugin 1979). The remains of sacrifices consisting of pieces of meat in copper relic-boxes were found in a sanctuary on the River Gnilka. Among the sacrificed animals elk, reindeer, bear, vixen, beaver and water-fowl have been identified. In the lower part of the same cultural layer, fairly well-preserved logs were found, which most probably had originally been part of a construction forming part of the sacral complex.

A later level of archaeological material from those sanctuaries (from the eleventh to thirteenth centuries) provides reliable evidence of close and regular contact between the ancient population of the mainland tundra and the seasonal population of Russian traders/hunters and tributaries (Khlobystin & Ovsyannikov 1973, pp. 248–57) (Figs 4.5, 4.6). It is significant that the Russian influence, which can be discerned in all these sites, and which accounted for the 'Chudski' features found in the material culture of the local inhabitants of the tundra, disappears in the late thirteenth to early fourteenth centuries. At the same time, the local tribes themselves – the bearers of that culture – begin to disappear as well. Most researchers link these phenomena with the radical change in the population in the belt of the northeastern tundra in the first half of the eleventh millennium AD, and with the changes in cultural-economic patterns that followed (Lashuk 1958, p. 55).

One of the problems of studying sacred sites in the Russian Arctic is the inadequacy of inventories for sites of this type. The main reason for this is that in the context of an atheistic state, although traditional beliefs were not victimized by the official church, they were condemned by society at large and by the state. The result was that the sacred sites of the Nenets people were fairly well concealed from the sight of outsiders, although some information can be gleaned from descriptions of sites, most of them dating from the beginning of the twentieth century.

At this stage it is only possible to draw up a provisional and far from complete list of the sacred sites of the Nenets people in the tundra. These sites (shown in Fig. 4.1) are Vaygach Island, Kozmin Copse, Kanin Nos (Figs 4.7, 4.8), Yugorsky Shar, Mikulkin Nos, Lake Kharveye, Bolvanskaya Hill on the Timan River, Gubistaya River, Kiiskaya Hill – on which there once stood idols of the Kanin Samoyed (the Russian name for Nenets), Peschanka River, 'Pytkov Stone' – a stone mountain between the Bolvansky Ridge and Lake Varandei. There are also tribal sanctuaries in the Varandei tundra: Savdy Seda ('sharp-peaked hill'), Labakhei-to ('lake with steep shores'), Khaktsyarka ('hill like a man's ears'), Khurtvoi-seda ('steep hill'), Sivngevak ('seven-headed hill') and Siyara (or Sivera) Hill (Figs 4.9, 4.10).

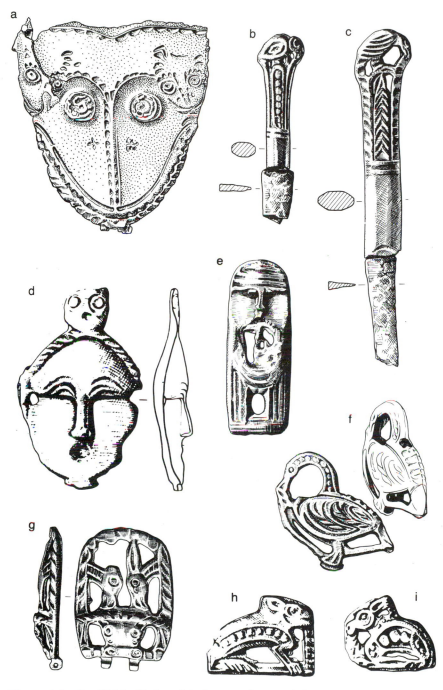

Figure 4.2 Sacrificial offerings (ninth to tenth centuries).
a, d, f, h, i – Vaygach Island
b, c, e, g – Gorodets Sanctuary

Figure 4.3   Bone articles (sixth to tenth centuries) from the Gorodets Sanctuary.
a, c – 'little hammers' fashioned from bone for playing the tambourine; b – a bone
stamp

Ethnographic considerations

Ethnographers have now collected a considerable amount of empirical material, shedding light on the traditional culture of the Nenets people. This
material makes it possible to progress from the study of this culture at an
external, superficial level to the identification of deeper religio-mythological
ideas, concepts and categories, and to construct a model of the spatio-
temporal, causal, ethnic, quantitative and semantic dimensions of the Nenets'
world (e.g. Khomich 1966, 1977; Lashuk 1958).

One of the Nenets' most fundamental cultural categories was the spatial
category, which embraced a range of ideas related to the ordering of the
universe and the ways in which it might be settled. The Nenets' ancient model
of the world was determined by the specific features of their nomadic way of
life, which gave rise to their linear (dynamic) perception of space (as opposed
to the static or radial perception of space found in cultures of settled peoples).

The dynamic conception of the ordering of space was embodied in the structure of the Nenets dwelling – the *choom* (Islavin 1847). The concept of the *choom*, its organization and symbolic divisions, has many parallels in the mountain Saami *kåhte* (tent) (Yates 1989). In traditional Nenets culture the *choom* not only performed the utilitarian function of protecting humans against their environment but also provided a most important means through which they were able to reflect the ordering of the world, by creating a tangible model of it.

The *choom* embodied both the dynamic and static aspects of the universe. The very idea of the Nenets dwelling, its ability to be dismantled and transported, reflected the dynamic aspects of the Nenets' way of life, whereas its construction reflected its static aspects. All operations connected with the erection or dismantling of the *choom* had religious significance, while cosmological features could be attributed to its constructional elements. The erection of the *choom* constituted a re-enactment of the creation of the world, being an 'assembly' of the basic elements of nature and human culture (fire, wood and deerskins). It is no coincidence that the assembly operation was carried out by women since, according to the cosmological myths of the Nenets, a woman figured as the primogenitrix of the world.

Figure 4.4 Sacrificial offerings (sixth to tenth centuries) from the Gorodets Sanctuary.
a – a 'piece' of meat in a little bronze box; b – a bone comb decorated with a polar bear

Figure 4.5   Sacrificial offerings (eleventh to thirteenth centuries).
a, f, h, j – Vaygach Island; b, e, g, i – sanctuary at Gorodets

While the assembly of the *choom* embodied the process of the positive ordering of the world, its dismantling provided a model for the destruction of the cosmos, reflecting critical, transitional situations linked with the onslaught of the destructive forces of chaos. These situations stemmed from important events of a cosmological character such as birth, disease, death and disruptions in ecological or seasonal processes.

The birth of a child was considered to disrupt the established pattern of nature and that of the social unit. It thrust the world into the abyss of the primal (chthonic) female element, the primeval chaos from which the cosmos had been born. The tangible model for this engendering element was the special *choom* provided for women in childbirth. This was referred to as the 'unclean *choom*', since women, as well as the actual act of giving birth, were perceived as impure.

If a birth took place in an ordinary *choom*, it was considered to be defiled and

Figure 4.6 Sacrificial offerings (twelfth to thirteenth centuries), Vaygach Island.
a–g – warriors, saints; h – small votive axe

became impure, or unclean. To cleanse a *choom* after a birth the midwife would pour water into a cauldron, drop a birth sponge into it, boil up the water over a fire and then sprinkle this water over the objects and people inside the *choom* (Islavin 1847, p. 121). For the eight weeks following childbirth, a woman was regarded as so unclean that she would not even dare to share food with her husband. After that period she was purified with heather or deer-fat and the *choom* transferred to another spot (Islavin 1847). The destruction of the world, resulting from the birth of a new human being, was depicted through the destruction ('rolling up') of the *choom* and its transference to a different place. This then acquired the significance of a sacred centre and served as the starting-point for the 'unrolling' of a new dwelling, a 'new world'.

Figure 4.7 Kanin Nos Peninsula: the holy stone.

Figure 4.8 Bronze ornaments (a, e, f, g) and iron rivets (b, c, d) found by the holy stone on Kanin Nos Peninsula.

Similar sacred significance was ascribed to the operations involved in the dismantling and transfer of a *choom* made necessary by epidemics of disease, or by disruptions of ecological or social equilibrium.

It is, however, in the burial rites of the Nenets people that the parallels between the collapse of the world and the collapse of the *choom* are the clearest and most obvious. Within the traditional social unit, focused on the identity of the tribe, or group, the death of an individual member was experienced as a group death, bringing in its wake the dismantling of all ties within the social unit, within the tribal world.

The *choom* was a model of the world itself and for that reason all dynamic processes operating within the universe were depicted through one or other of its transformations. Death, for example, that ushered in the onset of the end of the world, led to a partial deformation or complete collapse of the *choom* and its transfer to another more favourable (more sacred) place:

> If a Samoyed dies inside a choom, then at the spot opposite which
> the deceased lies the outer covering of the choom is torn open, the
> poles supporting that covering are broken, and it is through that
> same gap that the deceased is carried out.
>
> (Islavin 1847, p. 137)

This ritual process for carrying the deceased out through a specially prepared opening, instead of through the ordinary entrance, is one of the ethnographic phenomena which reflect the upside-down (inverted) world of the dead in relation to the world of the living. Similar concepts and corresponding procedures have been noted in the ritual and mythological traditions of the Nenets people. Objects buried alongside the deceased, for example, must be deformed in some way: 'All these objects have to be broken to signify that in the next world they are used in a different form from that found on earth' (Islavin 1847, p. 137). The sledge on which the deceased was transported was left at the cemetery and 'it was always turned over with runners uppermost, since it was believed that in the world beyond the grave everything was "upside down"' (Khomich 1977, p. 24). Sometimes sledges would not only be turned upside-down, but the right runner would also be broken, and the front ends of the runners were always turned towards the north (Yevsyugin 1979, p. 87). This was done because, in the symbolic classification of space used by the Nenets people, the right was associated with the 'female' principle and with the 'north', with tribal territory and with ancestors. Thus, breaking only the *right*

Figure 4.9 Siyara Holy Hill among sand dunes.

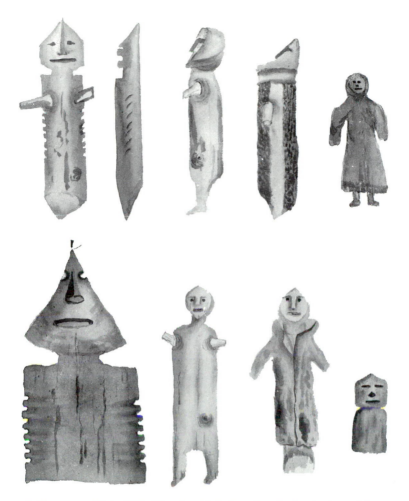

Figure 4.10 Siyara Holy Hill. Wooden idols found at the beginning of the twentieth century.

runner of the burial sledge, and positioning it to face northwards, reflected the concept of the realm of the dead, a realm built in accordance with the principles of inversion.

The ritual of sacrifice made after burial of the dead was also organized in accordance with these principles: 'A deer was sacrificed over the grave, as during all traditional ceremonies. It was then subjected to an agonizing death having a sharpened wooden pole plunged into its anus' (Islavin 1847, p. 137). The unusual nature of this sacrifice (the agonizing death of the victim, the role of the rear part of the sacrificial deer's body) points to the inverted nature of the burial ritual, orientated towards a link with the world of the dead.

A somewhat different description of the funeral sacrifice also exists:

After covering the grave with boards and scattering earth upon it, the deer, on which the dead body was borne forth, is positioned with its hindquarters pointing to the head of the buried man. Four Samoyeds, armed with staves, suddenly begin to strike the beast from all sides, until it be wounded in so terrible a fashion as to be incapable of the slightest movement, when all the Samoyeds are satisfied with the success of this slaughter. Yet if it were to raise its head or make any other movement, then they run and cry out with a desperate cry: 'Vayenza, vayenza . . . woe, woe' convinced that once again one of their kind shall die.

(Atlas of the Archangel Province 1797, p. 37)

Two factors stand out in this description of a burial sacrifice: the turning round of the sacrificial deer so that its hindquarters point towards the deceased and the painful killing of the offering, during which all participating in the ritual believe they discern their own fate and the fate of their kinsmen in the behaviour of the animal. These elements in the sacrificial rite dovetail into the overall pattern of the burial ritual, which re-enacts the critical and marginal situation in which the old world is destroyed ('turned upside-down'), while the new is merely reconstituted from its fragments. Hence the high degree of uncertainty which gives rise to divinations and prophecies regarding the future.

Such inversion of spatial relations was also characteristic of the final stage of the burial ritual – the return of the funeral procession from the cemetery: 'At the end of the funeral ritual all move away from the grave stepping backwards, climb on to their sledges and ride back to the "choom", which they only enter through fire' (Islavin 1847, p. 137). This walking backwards from the grave, and also the return from the cemetery by a different route, not only served to reproduce the inverted nature of the other world but were also designed to deceive the deceased, so that he or she should not find the way home and alarm living people. This strategy reflects the Nenets' attitude to the cemetery as an impure place, fraught with danger. A similar perception of death space is to be found in the beliefs of many peoples, but the special feature of Nenets tradition lay in the fact that virtually all links between the deceased and their kinspeople ceased immediately after the burial. According to Nenets beliefs the cemetery did not possess special religious status, but was endowed with properties that made it impure and dangerous for humans; as a result, there was a system of clearly defined taboos and restrictions relating to behaviour in a cemetery:

For the Nenets, reburying the dead was inadmissible, even changing anything or modifying the coffin or place of burial. Parents would not rectify an accidentally destroyed child's grave, since it was held that then someone else from the family would die. If a Nenets woman were to erect a fence around a grave she would be censured for the same reason.

When visiting a grave (a year after the death or during

Khalmerkh Khanuront) all that was permissible to touch was the little bell on the cross-piece at the head of the deceased.

(Khomich 1977, p. 24)

The existence of clearly defined taboos and restrictions, in relation to contact between living people and the world of the dead, sheds light on essential features of traditional Nenets beliefs. In the dynamic, nomadic conception of the world the frontiers of the world beyond the grave acquired a flexible, mobile character. For this reason Nenets cemeteries, in their capacity as static phenomena, lose their link with ancestor worship and merely serve as 'sign-posts' indicating the presence of the other, chthonic world within the sacred space of the tundra.

Ancestor worship is transferred from the cemetery into the *choom*. An image (*pytarma*) is made of the soul of the deceased, which comes to embody the ancestor; this image is made after his/her death and through it the deceased allegedly continues to live among the living. The *choom*, representing the static as well as the dynamic aspect of the world, is divided into two parts (*va'av* and *si*), providing a model for the dualistic organization of the cosmos, the singling out of a world for the living and a world for the dead. The *pytarma* is placed on the *va'av* (bed), and not on the *si* (the holy spot opposite the entrance) (Khomich 1977, p. 27).

The division of the *choom* into two parts was one of the fundamental principles on which Nenets etiquette was based. Woman, as the primogenitrix of the world and humankind, was associated with ancestor-space. Therefore she was strictly banned from crossing the dividing-line demarcating the holy part of the *choom* (*si* or *sinikui*).

The Christianization of the Nenets people did away with the sacred space of the *choom* and the domestic etiquette based on it. The abolition of the system of values relating to the space within the *choom* reflected the overall strategy of the first Christian missionaries, to neutralize and 'reconsecrate' the whole of the religious topography of the Nenets tundra. This process first and foremost affected the most significant sacred objects – the sanctuaries or sites of sacrifice.

The Nenets' sanctuaries were organized hierarchically, thus reflecting the universal laws underlying the organization of sacred space. The centre of this sacred hierarchy was the shrine on Vaygach Island, whose positioning on such a remote island was bound up with mythological conceptions of the centre of the world as the starting-point for the space within which the process of creation had begun. This island, surrounded by the waters of the ocean, provided an ideal model through which to depict the creation of the world (its growth, development and rising up out of the chaos of the watery element). According to one of the Nenets' myths regarding the origin of Vaygach Island, a stone cliff appeared out of the middle of the sea, and grew and grew until it assumed the shape of a man (Islavin 1847, p. 118). Vaygach Island was perceived as the 'first earth' on which there appeared the 'first man' (an anthropomorphic stone idol). In the course of time it became the 'Mecca' of the whole Nenets people, and pilgrims took holy relics (fragments from the body of the stone deity) home from the island. According to Islavin (1847, p. 114): 'All the stone idols in Nenets dwellings have their origins in the stone idol on Vaygach.' The hierarchy of Nenets sanctuaries branched out from this ancestral centre on Vaygach Island, and incorporated a whole system of cult places of lesser religious importance than Vaygach.

Nenets sacred sites can be roughly divided into two groups: the permanent and the occasional. Permanent sacred places originated in the process of settling space in the tundra. They constituted a special category of topographical signs to regulate economic activity and behavioural stereotypes in time and space. For example, when people were crossing the Ob or the Tazovsky inlet, on the way from summer to winter pastures and back again, a deer would be killed on the shore and its antlers hung on the branches of a larch tree, believed by the Nenets to be the 'tree of light' (*yalya pya*). Similar sacrifices would be performed when they were crossing the strait between the mainland and Vaygach Island – the traditional waters for hunting walruses and polar bears.

Holy places were also established on the shores of rivers and lakes, near large stones and on mountain summits and passes. Sacrifices performed at these permanent sites were calendrical in character and revealed the stable, durable and secure methods by which the Nenets settled their world and incorporated it into the eternal cycle of time.

While the permanent sites underlined the durable nature of the Nenets' world and its essentially clan-based structure, the emergence of their occasional holy places was linked with threshold, or marginal, situations in the life of the individual. For example, a place where someone had taken fright, fallen through ice and drowned, or where someone had seen a vision, might then, on the instruction of the shaman, become a holy place; if so, he would say that it should be venerated and that some object should be placed there, to be regarded as the *khekhe* – the master of the given holy place. Alternatively, the object concerned might simply be an unusual stone in the middle of the tundra, a larch tree 'on seven trunks', or something else slightly out of the ordinary that fired the Nenets' imagination, and made them single out the place as a *khekhe ya*. These occasional holy places provided a special kind of danger signal, or disaster sign, and as such they were incorporated into the symbolic classification of space.

Independently of their geographical location and functional purpose, the Nenets' cult places (both permanent and occasional) were constructed according to a common pattern: 'Resembling each other in character and their main components, the holy places of the Nenets varied only with regard to detail' (Khomich 1977, p. 17).

The construction of sacrificial sites incorporated two elements – stone and wood. The use of these construction materials for the institution of holy places was linked by early Soviet ethnographers with the worship of stone and wood. Advocates of the 'cult' approach to religious activity declare that the whole of the world inhabited by the Nenets, and its most important elements (earth, water, fire, stone, wood, etc.), are objects of veneration, i.e. cult objects. This approach stems from the erroneous idea that ancient humans worshipped the very substance of nature, lending it 'spirit' and 'soul'. In this cult-based conception of the origin of the holy places, the human being thus assumes the functions of creator, who alone possesses the exclusive capacity to attribute soul to the world thus created.

However, stone and wood as such were not venerated by the Nenets, but were merely material representations of a higher reality. The construction of the Nenets' religious edifices from stone and/or wood reproduced the image of the 'world tree' as the universal conception of the ordering of the universe. The cosmological functions of Nenets sanctuaries can be traced in the appearance of the anthropomorphic wooden idols which had *three* sides and *seven* faces, these numbers being considered sacred by the Nenets. The construction of the sacrificial site discovered by Verbov in the northern part of the Yamal Peninsula consisted of a pile of stones with a larch branch driven into it. The branch had *seven* notches (Khomich 1977). On the same peninsula, Zhitkov discovered a shrine consisting of *seven* groups of wooden idols, each group having a dry larch branch standing in the centre (Khomich 1977).

Thus the construction of Nenets sacrificial sites, based on the sacred numbers three and seven, reveals the link between such sites and cosmological diagrams, or a mathematical model of the world. In his description of the seven-part construction of the shrine in the Yamal Peninsula, Zhitkov calls attention to the clan-based character of the organization of ritual activity. Each of the seven groups of idols, lending shape to the sacred space, 'is regarded as a place of worship for specific tribes of Samoyed' (Khomich 1977). Thus the construction of this sanctuary and the special features of its ritual significance suggest parallels between cosmological diagrams depicting the ordering of the universe (seven worlds) and social structures (seven clans). The parallel between Nenets cosmology and sociology, that can be deduced from the organization of sacred space, bears witness to the important role which sanctuaries and holy places played in the ritual and everyday life of the Nenets people.

Holy places, and the ritual activity tied to them, performed a variety of functions. Nenets sacrificial sites constituted the 'holy book' of the tundra, preserving memories of the people's history and individual destinies. The culture of the Nenets, who had no written language, had other means by which they could record and transmit information over the course of time. One such means was provided by sacred objects that performed specific functions, and thus served as reminders. Given these important mnemonic functions, it is clear that the destruction of sanctuaries (and the annihilation of the shamans, the professional bearers of sacred knowledge), which began during the era of Christianization and assumed catastrophic proportions in the period of collectivization, to a great extent destroyed the historical memory embodied in them, and the culture based on that memory.

Mass-scale Christianization of the Nenets people began in the first third of the nineteenth century, bringing destruction of their traditional culture and the dissemination of new cults and rites. However, in spite of this, and notwith-standing the barbaric invasion of modern 'civilization', at a time when the ecological situation was steadily deteriorating, the Nenets people survived, mainly because traditional values and structures re-emerged, and because of the preservation of those cultural monuments which by some miracle had survived, and still retain their sacred importance.

Kozmin Copse

In the course of Christianization, crucially important ancient centres of the Nenets' religion were destroyed, namely the sanctuaries on Vaygach Island and in the Kanin tundra. The Kozmin Copse sanctuary in the Kanin tundra (Figs 4.11–4.17) is among the most significant cultural monuments and sacred places of the Nenets people, and was investigated in 1986 by the Archangel Arctic Expedition. The monument had been destroyed in March 1837 by Christian missionaries led by Archimandrite Veniamin (State Archives of the Archangel Region n.d.). The name 'Kozmin Copse' is now used to refer to a cutting made in the narrowest strip of forest, which is the dividing-line between patches of tundra in the basin of the River Pyya (25 km from the town of Mezen) and the edge of a wood. The path through the cutting is only used when the deer-breeders are making their way to the Kanin Peninsula in early spring, and when they return to the mainland at the beginning of winter. The site of the ancient sanctuary was venerated by the Nenets until quite recently, and remains of sacrifices were found in the trees on both sides of the cutting, from the lowest part of the trunk up as far as the height of a man when standing on a sledge. All the trees lining the cutting were examined carefully, the nature of the 'offerings' found on them was recorded, and the species of the trees on which they were hung. At the same time, the path itself and the soil around the trees were examined with the help of metal-detectors. The finds indicated that the sanctuary had begun to be used again as a sanctuary in the mid–nineteenth century.

The fieldwork carried out so far has revealed that the ancient sanctuary of Kozmin Copse, even in its present form (the expedition did not succeed in finding traces of the monument destroyed in 1837), is not only of significant interest to ethnographers studying the Nenets people today, but is also, first and foremost, a monument of the traditional culture of that people. Investigation of this sanctuary provides a starting-point for a reconstruction of the ancient concepts of the Nenets regarding the ordering of the cosmos and society, and the relationship between humans and nature.

The sanctuary at Kozmin Copse occupied an important place in the hier-archy of Nenets centres of worship. According to legend, it was founded by one of four brothers – the sons of Vesako and Khadako ('old man' and 'old woman'), two stone idols standing in the very centre of the Nenets' sacred world, Vaygach Island. The brothers had scattered north, south, east and west

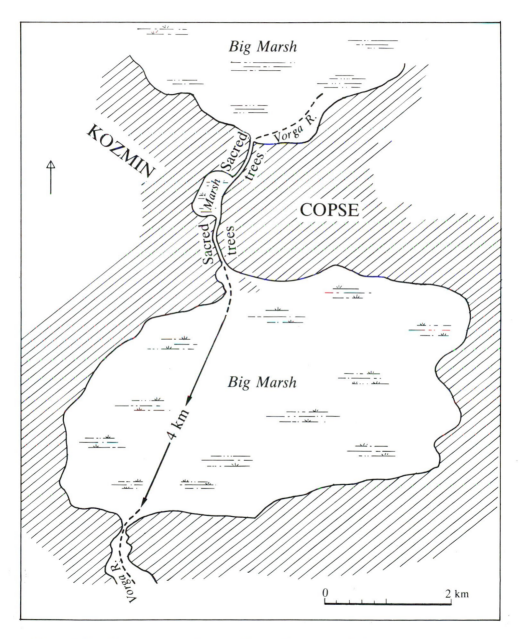

Figure 4.11 The sanctuary at Kozmin Copse. Diagram of the location.

Figure 4.12 Kozmin Copse. Part of the cutting with sacrificial offerings.

Figure 4.13   Part of Kozmin Copse.

and founded new sanctuaries, which provided symbols marking the frontiers of Nenets territory. The holy place on the western border in the Kanin tundra had two names: a Nenets name (Kharv Pod meaning 'larch grove', or the path within it) and a Russian name, Kozmin Copse. The Nenets associated a toponymic legend with the Russian name:

> Some Russian fishermen (*vataga*) led by a man named Kozma were travelling to the lakes through this place of sacrifice. They made fun of the idols and the decorations hanging in the trees. Suddenly, their horses refused to move and stood still, until the fishermen made a vow that they would respect the Nenets places of sacrifice. Kozma was the first to hang his coloured sash on a birch-tree as a sign of conciliation.

> (Khomich 1966, p. 199)

Figure 4.14 Part of Kozmin Copse.

Figure 4.15 Kozmin Copse. Part of the cutting.

This legend reveals the function the holy grove played in marking frontiers, through which strangers could not pass without first offering a sacrifice for purification.

The trees in this grove were considered to be sacred, and this sacredness was reflected in the ritual practice of the Nenets. During the field-study of the sanctuary, sacrificial remains were found on 242 trees. Over half these traces of ritual activity were found on birch-trees, a quarter on fir-trees and the rest on aspen and rowan-trees. The distribution of the ritual trees over the area of the sanctuary is also of interest. In the southern part of the holy grove the sacrificial offerings were most frequently found on fir-trees and in the northern part the majority were on birch-trees. The special importance of the birch and

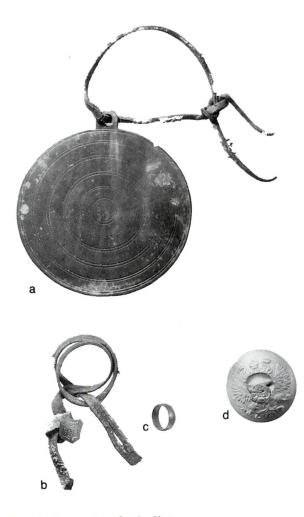

Figure 4.16 Kozmin Copse. Sacrificial offerings.
a – mirror; b – ring with a stone; c – ring; d – button

Figure 4.17 Kozmin Copse.
a, e, f – little bells; b, c, d – bronze brackets

fir in the religious beliefs of the Nenets people is revealed by the writings of Veniamin, who stated that the sacrificial 'trimmings' were hung on birch-trees, while fir-trees specially hewn in the sanctuary were transported, together with idols, on holy sledges (State Archives of the Archangel Region n.d.).

At the sacrificial site under investigation the main category of sacrificial offerings found consisted of various belts, ribbons, straps, cords and scraps of cloth (these accounted for 200 of the 242 finds). The second largest group of traditional objects consisted of objects made from copper and bronze (a mirror, little bells, rings, including one with a stone, and decorative copper discs). The third major category of finds consisted of reindeer skulls and antlers hung on trees. Other articles found in the sanctuary were mainly of modern origin (dolls, teapots, a thermos flask, an alarm-clock and the steering-wheel of a tractor, etc.). Although it is possible that certain objects from modern households turned up in the holy grove by chance, it may well be that within Nenets culture modern industrial products have associations of which we are unaware, for their appearance within the range of sacrificial offerings does not seem to be coincidental. The characteristic ways in which objects are used by a particular people, and the rules according to which certain objects are used in conjunction one with another, are far more durable than objects themselves.

The long-standing continuity of the traditional elements of sacrificial sites is borne out by missionaries' descriptions of rites performed in the sanctuary at Kozmin Copse:

> On the first day of March in the grove that is known as Kozmin Copse, 20 versts from the town of Mezen, one of the most splendid of the idol shrines of all generations of Samoyed in the whole of Archangel City province was destroyed. This grove lies beyond the Piya River and its whole length stretches over ten versts, while its breadth is half a verst. It was venerated as a holy place by the Samoyeds, commanding respect almost equal to that enjoyed by the idols themselves.
>
> The *tadibeis* (shamans) from all the Samoyed tundra forests were duty bound to hew a tree for their *penzer* or drum from this grove alone. Many of the simple Samoyeds upheld the custom of cutting down a small fir-tree from the grove and then transporting it on their sledge together with their idols till the very end of their days. In this grove a hundred wooden idols of diverse size and aspect were committed to the flames: the idols were hung with all manner of trappings, almost two thousand in number. Of particular note among the idols were: (a) twenty large fat idols with round heads similar to those of men; (b) ten thin ones with a height of one sazhen [2.13 m] which were hewn with four sides, on each of which were seven faces positioned one above the other. The first variety were arranged in rows standing on their smoothly trimmed bases: those of the second variety had a tapered end which was driven into the ear so that they were arranged round a large birch-tree close both to the birch-tree and to each other; (c) others were made out of tree-stumps still rooted in the earth. No less than two thousand trappings from the grove were burnt together with the idols. They had been hanging on birch-trees and consisted of pieces of cloth of diverse colours and animal skins, also of buttons and other copper baubles. Samoyed women used to hang them there every time when they made their way to the town of Mezen through this same grove. A large number of deer-antlers were also burnt in the grove, antlers from deer that had been brought as sacrifices to the idols that had once stood there. After they had been burnt the grove was consecrated with holy water and on the very

spot where the large idols had once been the life-giving Cross of Christ was erected.

(State Archives of the Archangel Region n.d.)

The use of a strictly specified range of sacrificial offerings (ribbons, straps, cords, bronze objects, deer) over such a long period testifies to the important role they played in the ritual-mythological concepts of the Nenets people. In order to shed light on the meaning of these objects, it is essential to determine the functions of the actual rite of sacrifice. It is suggested by Novik (1984), a researcher working on Siberian shamans, that we should 'regard the offering of sacrifices as a means for establishing communication between the holy and the secular worlds via sacrifice' (pp. 136–7). Thus holy trees and sacrificial offerings placed on them can be interpreted only as devices providing a link between men and spirits (Startsev 1930, p. 39; Yevsyugin 1979, p. 17). It follows that the various objects found in the sanctuary at Kozmin Copse played a subsidiary role in the rites of sacrifice and served as a means of ensuring a link between those performing the ritual and those in whose honour it was performed. To be more precise, the offerings were the material embodiment of that link, and their function was similar to that of the shaman's tree, which provided a model for the structure of the universe.

This function of the objects involved is also revealed by their characteristic colour range, red, white and green (and see Mutoro 1994). This reflects the nature of the Nenets' world as depicted through colours. In Nenets cosmology white signifies the Upper World, red the Middle World and black and green the Lower or Subterranean World. A cluster of red, white and green ribbons tied to a tree constitutes a highly original colour model of the Nenets' world, and ensures the link between people and the world of spirits in the course of the sacrificial ritual. Colour symbolism is also apparent in the clothes worn by the Nenets. It is clear from the writings of Veniamin (*Archangel Provincial Gazette* 1849) that it was women who tied ribbons and pieces of material to the trees of the holy grove, and that these were scraps of material torn from their clothes. It follows that the colour symbolism in the costumes of Nenets women also reflects the cosmological ideas concerning the three-layered construction of the world. Also linked to these concepts is the three-coloured wedding flag, prepared by relatives of the bride and taken by the wedding procession to the *choom* of the bridegroom's parents as a symbol of the marriage ties between the two clan-groups (Yevsyugin 1979, p. 73).

It is suggested that not only the colour symbolism, but also the actual way Nenets women's clothes (coats from beaver and squirrel skins) were made has certain cosmological implications. According to Khomich, clothes of this type were made in three parts. The upper part was made from pieces of squirrel, beaver and fox fur, the middle part from reindeer skins and the lower part from strips of dog fur (Khomich 1966, p. 134). This vertical division of the costume reflects the Nenets' cosmological ideas about the threefold ordering of the world, expressed through zoomorphic forces (the Upper World is that of the beaver, squirrel and fox; the Middle World that of the reindeer; the Lower World that of the dog). The link between the beaver and the Upper World can be traced in the purification rites of a sacrificial site, which would be fumigated with the smoke from smouldering beaver's hair (Yevsyugin 1979, p. 19). The reindeer is the zoomorphic symbol for the Middle World, and in this way becomes like humans, who also occupy a middle position in Nenets cosmography. The dog is a creature from the Lower (impure) World, which is why dogs were used in sacrifices 'to the evil spirits and their chief master Noa living deep down beneath the Earth, beneath the eternal frost' (Yevsyugin, p. 18). Dog fur was held to be unclean (Startsev 1930, p. 106); it is thus clear why dog fur was used specifically for the lower part of Nenets women's clothes.

Among the ribbons, straps and cords found on the trees of the holy grove at Kozmin Copse there were also small bells, a mirror, rings, ornamental discs and other objects made of bronze. In his description of the sacrificial rite, Veniamin (*Archangel Provincial Gazette* 1849) commented upon the use of buttons and other small objects made of copper. Both bronze and copper were considered holy and to have supernatural qualities and properties. Copper was believed to possess cleansing properties and was therefore widely used in traditional medicine. For example, when someone broke a limb: 'the patient would be given boiling water containing copper dust and deer-fat to help his bones grow together again more quickly. The copper dust was obtained by scraping kettles or cauldrons with a knife' (Yevsyugin 1979, p. 82). The power of copper was thought to be active even through mere proximity:

> A sick woman would make a vow that she would sew a sash in honour of the idol-figure kept in her home and would wear it. Yet before donning this belt she had to pass it three times under the handle of a kettle or another copper object, since copper, according to Nenets beliefs, was held to be a noble metal.
>
> (Yevsyugin 1979, p. 83)

The cleansing properties of copper were also exploited in sacrificial rites. Because women were regarded by the Nenets as impure, they had to go through a special purification rite when visiting a sanctuary, which among other things involved ritual ornaments made from copper (or bronze): 'Women were allowed to be at a sacrificial site to satisfy their curiosity, only if they placed some copper object (an ornamental disc, ring, kopeck, etc.) into their reindeer–skin boots' (Yevsyugin 1979, p. 19).

The cleansing properties of copper stemmed from its functions as a sacred metal, mediating between men and gods. In Nenets burial rites, the shaman would turn to the spirits, using a copper ring taken from an ornamental harness. Among the objects found in the sanctuary at Kozmin Copse were bronze rings, one of which was inset with enamel, and a bronze mirror. Since all these objects had an obvious mediating function, it is far from coincidental that they were also used to decorate a shaman's costume, which 'symbolized first and foremost the social role played by the shaman as an intermediary or mediator between different worlds' (Novik 1984, p. 68). Among the objects worn by the shaman for decoration on his costume, small bells and other 'noisy trappings' were particularly important, since they were the source of the special acoustic code of shaman culture. The Nenets' fondness for bells and bell chimes was remarked upon by Christian missionaries, who sought to make use of these elements of traditional culture in the propaganda of the new faith.

The traditional culture and way of life of the Nenets were to a considerable extent determined by the natural, biological cycle. Since men are almost totally absorbed into nature's wilderness, women, in their capacity as pre-servers and transmitters of social and cultural experience, had important functions to perform and thus played a vital role. One of the mechanisms that enabled them to perform this role was the system of taboos circumscribing their behaviour, and the very existence of such a system of taboos, and their strict enforcement, were constant reminders of the fact that there were funda-mental rules underlying the organization of society and the cosmos. Violation of the rules could lead to universal catastrophe, and women in particular were responsible for maintaining the existing order of things since, according to mythological and poetic stereotypes, they were endowed with enormous capacities for both destruction and creation. The specific features of this traditional perception of women enable us to shed light on the significance of ritual acts carried out in the holy grove at Kozmin Copse. Women, being impure, were not allowed to walk over holy objects. Therefore, when travel-ling through Kozmin Copse, they had to purify themselves by bringing sacrificial gifts. Among these, ribbons, small belts and scraps of red cloth were particularly important (State Archives of the Archangel Region n.d.). In Nenets colour symbolism, the colour red was associated with women; it was the colour used to deck the earth on which the mythological primogenitrix of the Nenets lived, and was also the colour of the cords used for tying loads on to purified women's sledges, and for bridal wedding flags.

The holy grove at Kozmin Copse was a 'pathway' sanctuary, situated at the southern end of the path along which the seasonal migration of the reindeer herds passed. In Nenets spatial symbolism, the north was linked with the female sphere and the south with the male sphere. In his description of the sacral topography of Vaygach Island, Veniamin noted that 'on that island since time immemorial two main idols had been venerated, one idol of the male sex at the southern tip of the island and the other of the female sex at the northern tip' (*Archangel Provincial Gazette* 1849, p. 79). The link between the north and the female (mother-ancestor) or clan-based sacred principle can also be traced in Nenets burial rituals. Khomich, quoting Verbov's description of the vestiges of clan patterns to be found among the Nenets, wrote:

> If, in the winter when the tundra Nenets are migrating to the South, to the zone of the tundra forest . . . hundreds of kilometres

from their clan territory, and someone dies, he will often not be buried but wrapped in skins or a 'straight jacket' of birch and loaded on to a sledge. At the end of the spring migration to the North, when the Nenets have reached their clan territory, the deceased will then be buried in one of the clan cemeteries.

(Khomich 1966, p. 218)

The reindeer-breeders' spring migration to the south meant that women had to abandon 'their' sphere (the north and the tundra) and live in alien (male) space (the south and forests). It was precisely at the dividing-line between the 'male' and 'female', the forests and the tundra, that the Kozmin Copse sanctuary was sited. The border provided a special kind of initiation zone where the transition from one condition or status to another took place. When performing the sacrificial rite in the holy grove, a woman was not only cleansing herself from all that was impure in her clan, but was at the same time associating herself with the values of the alien (male) sphere. This action corresponds to the rite of the bride's passage to the house of the bridegroom, during which she associated herself with the sacred relics of an alien clan. Correspondingly, during the spring migration to the north, it was the men who had to carry out a sacrificial rite in the holy grove, thus preparing themselves for re-entering the clan (female) territory. During the field study carried out at the sanctuary, remains of 'male' sacrifices (deer-skulls and antlers) were found, and all such finds were concentrated at the northern end of the holy grove.

The Kozmin Copse sanctuary can therefore be considered to have had considerable ritual significance. On the one hand, it marked off the clan (ethnic) territory of the Nenets people, and on the other it was a place at which calendrical (spring/summer and autumn/winter) rites were enacted, pinpointing the most significant transitional periods of the reindeer-breeders' seasonal migrations. The sacrificial rites performed in the holy grove at Kozmin Copse not only marked the transition from one of the main types of economic activity to another (reindeer husbandry to hunting), but also provided tangible expression of the most important categories in Nenets traditional culture: male/female, wild/domestic, raw/cooked, pure/impure, nature/culture.

Crosses

In the course of the Christianization of the Samoyed clans in the Arctic tundra, one set of sacred symbols, which was linked with a pagan religio–mythological system of beliefs, was replaced by a Christian one. Christian topography incorporated sacred places such as cathedrals, parish churches, chapels that belonged to lay communities, private chapels (belonging to individuals or families) and monasteries with their attendant church-owned estates. Wooden crosses played a tremendously important part in the propagation of

Christianity through the Arctic: crosses in cemeteries and those on graves outside cemeteries, crosses to mark the taking of vows, crosses that were objects of veneration and crosses used during funeral ceremonies (Figs 4.18–4.24).

Between 1982 and 1987 the expedition from the (then) Leningrad section of the Institute of Archaeology carried out work aimed at charting the sites at which ancient crosses had been erected by the inhabitants of the shores of the

Figure 4.18 Old cemetery on the southern shore of Kolsky Peninsula. Kuzomen village.

northern seas: on the shores of the neck of the White Sea and the Kolsky
Peninsula; on the winter shore of the White Sea; on Morzhovets Island and on
the lower reaches of the Mezen River (where there were nearly 100 crosses).
The northern coast-dwellers erected crosses on the shores where they fished, as
a symbol of their faith, but also to signify a territorial claim to a specific
fishing-ground. Peasants erected similar crosses on their land, mainly on the
fields where they grew crops. Thus crosses that are found nowadays next to

Figure 4.19 Old Saami cemetery on Kolsky Peninsula in the estuary of the River
Ponoi.

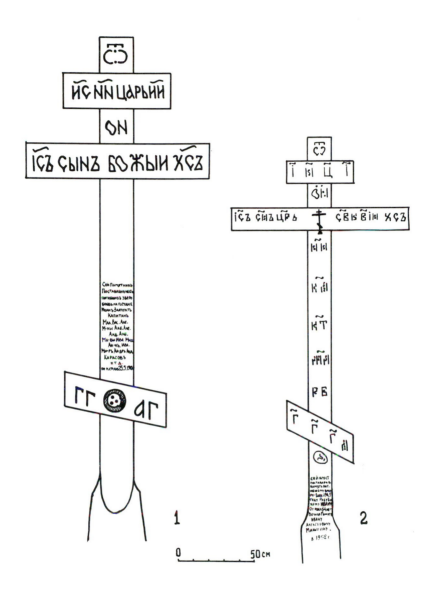

Figure 4.20 Cenotaph crosses in the home of drowned coastal dwellers. Koida village.

peasant houses can be interpreted as property markers. After the collectivization of the northern villages they were taken out of the fields by their owners
and re-erected by their dwelling-houses.

   The right of family ownership of crosses, which were perceived as sacred
clan relics, has survived until the present day, and extends to a fairly wide
range of relatives. In other cases, crosses formerly used as field-markers were
brought to secret sites in the forest, where they were transformed into chapel-
substitutes. Near one such cross was found a large chest containing icons.

Figure 4.21   Cross transferred from the fields to a house. Lower reaches of the River
Mezen.

Mention should also be made of funeral crosses, which represent symbols of burial, i.e. cenotaphs. In the case of fatal accidents, such crosses were generally erected either near the spot where the death had occurred or, if this was unknown, at the home of the dead person.

Peasants' crosses in the fields, and coast-dwellers' crosses near Arctic hunting-grounds, were phenomena of the same type – they served as thanksgiving for life, for harvests, for successful hunting and as a request for protection from all manner of evil, disaster and accidents. Funeral crosses, votive crosses, crosses that were objects of worship and protective crosses are

Figure 4.22   Cross for worship. Lower reaches of the River Mezen.

therefore also part of the special triangle of sacred space that moulded the patterns of people's everyday life and the norms of their ritual and day-to-day behaviour. This space included space for worship (churches); space for the clan or family (houses, crosses, the family iconostasis, chapels) and space for the individual (crosses worn on the person, small wooden incense-burners worn round the neck and pouches containing relics).

It is possible, from archaeological, historic and ethnographic material, to identify three main stages in the medieval history of the organization of sacred

Figure 4.23 Cross in a field with an abbreviated version of a prayer for protection on its side. Lower reaches of the River Mezen.

space in the Arctic tundra. These stages correlate fairly clearly with the special features of the ethnohistory of the region in question.

The first stage (sixth to thirteenth centuries) is characterized by a fairly precise pattern of sacred sites: clan sacrificial sites (on the River Gnilka, Kheibidya–Pedar, in the Adakskaya Cave on the River Usa and on Vaygach Island), and sites that belonged to tribes prior to the Samoyeds (the Pechora or Siirtya). Links between the Russians and the Pechora, which were firmly established between the eleventh and thirteenth centuries, did not at that time influence the ordering or organization of sacred space. 'Russian' influence can

Figure 4.24   Cross in a forest 'chapel'. Lower reaches of the River Mezen.

be traced only in the range of objects used for sacrifices. It can safely be assumed that, by the end of that period, local tribes were beginning to be subjected to powerful pressure from the Samoyeds from beyond the Urals.

The second stage begins in the fourteenth century, when the contacts between Russians and the Pechora were abruptly broken off. It extends to the end of the eighteenth century, when the official church began to make its mark on the sacred patterns of life in the tundra. In the first quarter of the nineteenth century this influence took the form of all-out Christianization, including the physical destruction of everything associated with the sacred traditions of the Samoyeds. This Christianization in its turn resulted in partial use being made of the sacred sites of the preceding period. From the end of that period, and particularly in the first half of the nineteenth century, elements of religious dualism can be discerned in the traditions of the Nenets. Side by side with adherence to the official Christian religion, pagan religio-mythological patterns continued to function.

References

Archangel Provincial Gazette 1849.

Atlas of Archangel Province complete with topographical, historical, economic and administrative descriptions 1797. C(entral) S(tate) A(ll-Union) I(nstitute) of A(rchaeology), 1. VUA, archive item 18588, Part III, quire 614.

Chernov, A. G. 1951. The sacrificial site Khibidya – Pedar. *Short Bulletins from the Archaeology Institute Affiliated to the USSR Academy of Sciences* 39, 84–8.

Islavin, V. A. 1847. *The Domestic and Social Life of the Samoyeds.* St Petersburg: Printing House of the Ministry of State Property.

Khlobytsin, L. P. 1986. Work on Vaygach Island and Yugorsky Peninsula. *Archaeological Discoveries of 1984*, 32–3. Moscow.

Khlobytsin, L. P. & O. V. Ovsyannikov 1973. The craft of the ancient jeweller in the polar regions of western Siberia. *Questions of Archaeology in the Urals and Siberia.* Moscow.

Khomich, L. V. 1966. *The Nenets: historical-ethnographic studies.* Moscow & Leningrad: Nauka.

Khomich, L. V. 1977. Religious cults of the Nenets. *Bulletin of the Museum of Anthropology and Ethnography* 33, 5–28.

Lashuk, L. P. 1958. *Outline of Ethnic History in the Pechorsky Krai: an attempt at a historical-ethnographical study.* Syktyvkar: Komi.

Lotman, Y. M. 1973. Canonical art as an information paradox. In *Questions of Canon in the Ancient and Mediaeval Art of Asia and Africa*, 16–22. Moscow: Nauka.

Murygin, A. N. 1984. Kheibidya-Pedar – place of sacrifice. Syktyvkar: Komi.

Mutoro, H. W. 1994. The Mijikenda *kaya* as a sacred site. In *Sacred Sites, Sacred Places*, D. L. Carmichael, J. Hubert, B. Reeves & A. Schanche (eds), 132–8. London: Routledge.

Novik, E. S. 1984. *Rites and Folklore in Siberian Shamanism.* Moscow: Nauka.

Oborin, B. 1976. *Ancient Art of the Peoples in the Kama Valley. Perm animal-style.* Perm: Perm Book Publishers.

Ovsyannikov, O. V. 1985. The sanctuary at Gorodets. Unpublished paper delivered at the Soviet–Finnish Symposium, Helsinki.

Ryabtseva, E. N. & V. A. Semyonov 1990. *The Adak Cave Sanctuary on the River Usa and Problems Encountered during the Settlement of the Polar Urals*. Short Bulletins from the Archaeology Institute affiliated to the USSR Academy of Sciences, 66–72.

Startsev, G. A. 1930. *The Samoyeds. A historical-ethnographic study*. Moscow & Leningrad: Printing House of the First Workshop of Soviet Printers.

State Archives of the Archangel Region. n.d. f. 6. op. 12, archive item 2, quires 1–2.

Yates, T. 1989. Habitus and social space: some suggestions about meaning in the Saami (Lapp) tent ca. 1700–1900. In *The Meanings of Things: material culture and symbolic expression*, I. Hodder (ed.), 249–61. London: Unwin Hyman.

Yevsyugin, A. D. 1979. *The Nenets of the Archangel Tundra*. Archangel: North-Western.

5   Sacred sites in Madagascar

CHANTAL RADIMILAHY

Madagascar, like everywhere else in the world, contains 'sacred sites', places which have special importance in terms of their impact on both the spiritual and daily life of the population (Molet 1979). Their multiplicity, and also their diversity of forms, demonstrate the importance of their place in the Malagash mentality.

In Madagascar the meaning 'sacred' is represented by the term *masina*, whose primary meaning is 'salted'. In addition, *masina* also incorporates a notion of power and efficacy, and of sanctity. In fact, *masina* is derived from the term *hasina* which, among other meanings, expresses the virtue and strength which accompany certain beings, certain things and certain places (Molet 1977, pp. 185–94). The latter are characterized by the capacity to produce extraordinary and miraculous events. For example, the earth and what derives from it, such as soil, trees and water, are endowed, as people are, with a supernatural power, to which are attached these powers and these *hasina* qualities; to be more precise, they are called *manan-kasina*, that is to say, full of *hasina*.

A site is considered as sacred, *masina* or *manan-kasina*, when it is inhabited by *zavatra* (literally 'things'), by *angatra* ('spirit') or by the spirits of ancestors who focus these qualities and these powers. These various spirits animate everything which is found on the earth and in the earth, and they must always be taken into account.

The multiplicity of 'sites' and of 'sacred places' can take different forms, and it is possible to construct a typology with regard to certain of their characteristics. The best known sacred sites are those which were occupied in ancient times by chiefs or kings, and are found where their actual tombs are located. These are the most appropriate places to go to to be in touch with the ancestors, in order to receive their blessing. Ancient palaces are also sacred because they were the everyday living places of these chiefs or kings, who are considered to be the representatives on earth of the supreme power, coming after God and the ancestors. This characteristic holds good for the whole island, although it is expressed in different ways and in different dialects. For

Figure 5.1 Sakalava cemetery, near Morondava. Photo: P. Vérin.

example, in the central highlands, as on the coast, one finds cult centres called *doany*. The primary meaning of *doany*, which originates from West Sakalava, signifies the village where nobles and, above all, the reigning monarch have their permanent residences. Whereas the *zomba*, in the west, are the places where the royal reliquaries are kept, their equivalent in the central highlands are the *trano manara* (literally 'the frozen houses'). These are small houses, on top of the tombs of nobles, which are believed to be where the ancestors live when they visit the earth (Fig. 5.1).

Among other places that have spiritual importance are springs, lakes, caves, upright stones and the roots of trees such as tamarinds and other *ficus*, trees that are considered sacred, and which were planted by the ancestors' tombs – thus they are signs that this area was inhabited in ancient times. In addition, the altars where the people come to pray, to sacrifice or to give offerings (as they do also in cemeteries) form an integral part of these 'sacred places' (Figs 5.2 and 5.3).

I now present some examples to illustrate the proposed typology. In Madagascar, particularly in the central highlands, use of the term 'sacred sites' is connected with the *vazimba* and the ancestors. In traditional belief, the *vazimba* are the first known inhabitants of the earth, memory of whom is retained in tradition and in popular culture. In general, the exact places where they lived are not remembered, nor the areas they moved about in. Tradition attributes a certain amount of positive power to them, but more often it is

Figure 5.2　A Merina tomb at Kaloy. Photo: P. Vérin.

Figure 5.3　An Islamic tomb at Antsoheribory. Photo P. Vérin.

negative power. Thus calamities, as well as illnesses, are due to the discontent of the *vazimba*, and, in fact, the *vazimba* are more feared than venerated, and many people worship at their 'tombs', at stones or at springs which they haunt, because they must be respected and appeased by various sacrifices and offerings. Elsewhere, their sites are 'sacred' and are the places for prayers. When the latter are answered, the sites become sites of sacrifice and acquire a specialist reputation for dealing with everyday preoccupations: healing, for example, fertility, or success in life. The ancestors, for their part, are the sources of the life which is transmitted to their descendants.

How can one know of the existence of 'sacred sites'? Sometimes place-names include a term that indicates the sacred nature of an area. For example, referring to hills: Ambohitrimasina or *Ambohimasina* ('sacred hills'); or to rocks: *Ambatosikidiana* (literally 'to the rock where one carries out divination'); or trees: *Ankazomasina* (literally 'to the sacred tree'); or in connection with springs: *Andranonandriana* (literally 'to the water of prince') and *Tsiandrorana* ('there where one is not allowed to spit'); or lakes: *Ampijoroa* ('there where one carries out *joro* sacrifices'). In Madagascar, the facility that the people have in recognizing sacred places or sites which have a special importance – and are thus the objects of respect (Molet 1979) – appears to astonish foreigners.

From infancy onwards, education is focused to a great extent on respect for parents, then respect for ancestors, and then respect for spirits which are unattached and live in different places. Thus, in the house, when one wishes to address the ancestors, one turns to the northeast (*zoro fifarazana*) – the most powerful Malagasy astrological direction (Vérin & Rajaonarimanana 1991) – the corner traditionally reserved for the ancestors. People who are on the point of leaving for somewhere very far away, or intending to carry out actions of great importance, will go to the tombs of their ancestors to request a blessing, or to take away a piece of *tany masina*, literally 'sacred earth', a pledge to success.

In addition to toponymy, oral traditions play an equally important role and each region has its own sacred places, which may be the focus of worship by the local people. These sites have several traits in common; one is that there are prohibitions, most often against pork or garlic, or against saying certain words, such as 'salt'. From time to time strangers in the region are forbidden to go in the neighbourhood of such sites in the fear that such prohibitions will not be adhered to and the sites not be respected, in which case they would lose their 'sacred' nature.

A second characteristic common to such sacred places is related to the occurrence of 'miracles', which are nearly always the work of ancient princes or sovereigns. The examples are numerous, both in the stories and in the traditional knowledge of the site. One example of this is the case of a special spring, Kingory, in the highlands, whose existence is due to the work of a prince called Andrianjakakiry. According to these traditions the prince's wife was complaining to him because the spring from which she had to fetch water every day was too far away. Andrianjakakiry, in order to remedy this, invoked his ancestors, asking them to make a spring appear at the place where he spat. The invocation he used was as follows: 'Raha masin-dray aho ka masin-dreny, dia aoka mba hisy loharano mipoitra eto', that is to say, 'If my father and my mother are sacred may a spring arise in this place'. As soon as the words were said a spring of water appeared, called Tsiandrorana, 'there where one must not spit', a taboo which, if not respected, would 'turn the face of the votive to the back', according to the predictions of Andrianjakakiry. In effect the invocation made by Andrianjakakiry resembles those attributed to fabulous persons in legends, when they had recourse to 'incredible and miraculous' facts. Do they not always say 'Raha andrian-dray aho ka andrian-dreny dia aoka hisy . . .', that is to say, 'If my father and my mother are princes, make it happen that . . . ', and the requested events are always realized?

This excursion into the realm of stories and legends allows me to elaborate on the question of origin myths of 'sacred sites'. It is worth going into some detail about the site and the celebrated myth of Ranoromasina. Literally, this name means the person who is sacred or a saint. Ranoromasina is connected with a sacred site, the location of various rituals, near Antananarivo, the Malagash capital. It is quite obvious that a part of the name is *masina* (salt), a term which has already been referred to above. Indeed, according to the legend, Ranoromasina was a very beautiful undine, who was captured through a ruse by a *vasimba* prince called Andriambodilova, who married her. Ranoromasina apparently agreed to marry him on condition that his wife would never say 'salt' (*masina*); much later, Andriambodilova dishonoured this agreement and Ranoromasina returned to her milieu of origin, water. Since then, and until today, the places habituated by these people are 'sacred'.

In addition it must be recorded that in the highlands such princely ancient sites still remain within the belt of characteristic trees which, according to tradition, cannot flourish except on sites which have sheltered nobles: the trees concerned are the *Ficus* (*amontana*), *aviavy* and *hasina*.

Elsewhere, all over Madagascar, there are 'sacred areas' which are encircled by wooden hedges, or distinguished by memorial poles (Fig. 5.4), or marked by characteristic signs, for example the remains of offerings (sweets, honey, bananas or coins), the remains of sacrifices (blood, or the heads of birds), white or red ribbons or cut-out squares of tissues, or pictures made with chalk or white clay (*tany ravo*, literally, 'happy earth'). The use of these two specific colours, red and white, still needs to be researched in detail in order to discover their symbolic value: white reflects 'joy, light or hope', and red, the royal colour, is associated with might or power, and also with health.

The symbolism reflected by the element water occupies a most important place amongst the 'sacred sites' categories recognized in Madagascar. It is important to remember the springs which are reputed to be haunted by the *vazimba*, the significance given to 'sacred' lakes, where the piragua canoes which contained the remains of ancient monarchs were immersed. Also important is the role played by water in the context of religious royal bathing in a river (an ancestral tradition within the Sakalava Menabe of the west of Madagascar), or even in the context of the enchanted bathing in the sea (*sampi*) in certain other regions of the island, such as on the northwest coast. In fact, it is necessary to trace the migratory movements of the people of the island, for these river mouths are the places of 'penetration' of new arrivals to the island. Eventually there was a confrontation between the first 'owners of the earth' (such as the *vazimba*, among others) and the new owners of the waters, owners of the mouths of rivers (Ottino 1986). The latter are the origin of the different kingdoms known in Madagascar. Thus, in the study of the history of kingdoms, the pre-eminence of these new arrivals is usually recognized, and their origin myth and the recognition of their power refer to beings who originated from water or originated in the ocean (cf. undine). Furthermore, in the highlands, for example in the southerly areas, both the birth and the disappearance of these royal individuals are associated with water. In numerous examples both the power and the sanctity of sovereigns are seen to reside in their association with the waters both of the interior and of the sea. In other

Figure 5.4 Memorial pole at Ambatofinandrahana in Betsileo. Photo: Gueunier.

cases, this concept is widened to refer to all peoples; one such group is the Kajemby of the northwest coast in the Bay of Boina who, according to tradition, came from beyond the seas. The Kajemby bury their dead on the beach, very close to the sea, so that, as the sea ebbs and flows, the burials are taken away by the water. Indeed, the 'spirits' of their ancestors give their benediction to their descendants who live by fishing. In the southwest region, among the Vezo fisher-people, altars or sacred sites called *jiny* are frequently to be found on the beach. The meaning of *jiny* can be linked to that of *hasina* – *mana-kasina* or *manan-jiny* have the same meaning and the same symbolism.

In view of these few examples, and bearing in mind the multiplicity of sacred sites that are to be found in Madagascar, it would be possible to work out a hierarchy of degrees of sanctity of sites. Indeed, I have already drawn attention to the fact that some places are more feared than venerated. One can conclude that the well-known sites were, or are, inhabited by ancestors, and that these would be at the top of any hierarchy: sites such as the sacred hills, the *doany* and the *zomba*. After them come those sites that have acquired a certain reputation, especially those places that have demonstrated their capacity to facilitate miraculous events, extraordinary and beneficial for living people. Lastly come those places that are potentially dangerous, even though they are considered 'sacred'.

The administration has begun to classify the sites in their records (Ministère de l'Art et de la Culture Révolutionnaires). Indeed, the list of classified sites of Madagascar contains natural sites, historic sites and some 'sacred' sites. But the belief in the spirit of ancestors is so strong among the Malagasy that in many cases there is no need to establish any administrative regime in order to secure the conservation of sacred sites.

References

Ministère de l'Art et de la Culture Révolutionnaires, n.d. Les sites et monuments classés de Madagascar. Unpublished document. Antananarivo, Madagascar.

Molet, L. 1977. *La Foi malgache*, vol. 1. Thesis, Strasbourg. Paris: Orstom.

Molet, L. 1979. *La Conception malgache du monde, du surnaturel et de l'homme en Imerina.* Paris: Edition L'Harmattan.

Ottino, P. 1986. *L'Etrangère intime. Essai d'anthropologie de la civilisation de l'ancien Madagascar.* Ed. des Archives Contemporaines, publié avec le concours du Centre National de la Recherche Scientifique.

Vérin, P. & N. Rajaonarimanana 1991. Divination in Madagascar. In *African Divination Systems*, P. Peek (ed.), 53–68. Bloomington: Indiana University Press.

6 Places of power: Mescalero Apache sacred sites and sensitive areas[1]

DAVID L. CARMICHAEL

Introduction

The historical homeland of the Mescalero Apache is centred in what is now southeastern New Mexico and west Texas, in the southwestern United States (Fig. 6.1). Before their confinement on the reservation in 1873, the Mescalero were highly mobile, following a seasonal round of hunting, gathering and raiding that extended into what are now the neighbouring states of Texas, and Chihuahua and Coahuila, Mexico (Opler 1983). Within this region, the core area of Mescalero territory can be defined by reference to a number of sacred sites and named traditional resource procurement areas (Basehart 1974).

A fundamental aspect of traditional Mescalero thought is the belief in the sacred character of specific geographical places. Some are important because of the roles they played in the mythic time of Mescalero tribal history. Others are sources of natural resources required in traditional ceremonies. Most appear to be important because they are places of power, points of intersection between the material world and spiritual world. The specific characteristics of these localities are quite variable and many would not be identifiable as archaeological sites.

Historically, most Mescalero sites were temporary, seasonal camps which have very low archaeological visibility (Carmichael 1990). The archaeological evidence of Mescalero presence is rather subtle overall, and sacred sites, as a group, are among the least visible site types. Although the topographic settings of such sites can be distinctive, the associated spiritual events or activities often leave few or no physical remains. For this reason, protection of sacred sites in the context of historic preservation planning presents a challenge. Because many sensitive sites would not be identified as such during an archaeological survey, both archaeological and ethnographic investigations have been carried out.

This chapter provides an overview of some of the kinds of sites considered sacred or sensitive in traditional Mescalero thought. Despite the diversity of site types involved, all are places of power.

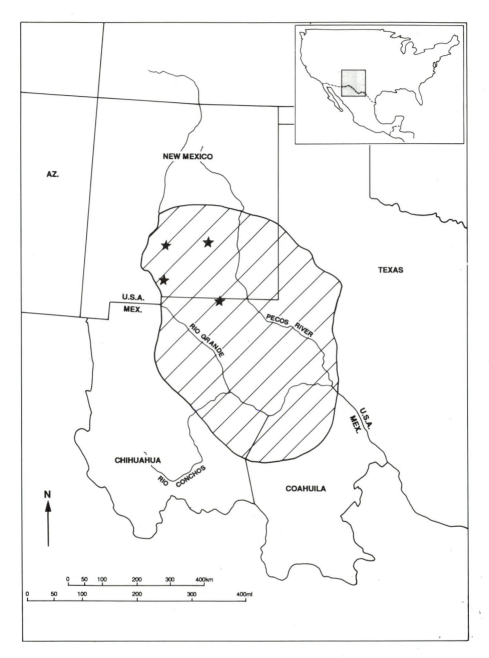

Figure 6.1 Mescalero Apache territory, about 1830 (Opler 1983). Stars indicate the four principal sacred peaks.

Powerful places

The concept of power is a difficult one to express simply in English. Power is a spiritual energy or life force that enables an individual to interact with the forces of the natural and supernatural worlds. Supernatural power derives from a variety of plants, animals and meteorological phenomena. Once obtained, power gives one the ability to influence certain aspects of nature by virtue of a special relationship with the spirits responsible for them (Ball 1980, pp. 61–4; Basso 1971a, p. 270; Opler 1935, pp. 66–7). For the Mescalero, supernatural power is inherently dual in nature: it can be either beneficial or harmful, depending on how it is used. Beneficial power, sometimes glossed as holiness, is called *diyi'* (Opler 1935, p. 69; Basso 1969; Basso 1971b). This connotation of power seems to be analogous to the *wakan* of the Sioux and the *maxpe* of the Crow (Deaver 1986; Hultkrantz 1979, pp. 11–14; Walker 1980).

Power is offered to deserving individuals by the spirits, usually through dreams and visions. People may either accept or decline the offer, depending on whether or not they want to accept what might be significant responsibilities associated with the power. However, not everyone receives power: there is a distinction between people who believe in and seek power and those who actually attain it. Moreover, different kinds or degrees of power may be bestowed on different individuals, depending on which spirits are involved (Opler 1946, p. 275). Powers accepted and used on behalf of the entire tribe are more potent than those, such as healing ceremonies, used by an individual for the benefit of his or her family.

Powerful places are areas where power is received or where power is needed for protection from spiritual danger. Both kinds of places occur at points of intersection between the physical and spiritual worlds. The physical places associated with the receipt and use of power can be more or less *diyi'* depending on the relative potency of the powers involved.

In traditional Mescalero cosmology, the physical and spiritual worlds are identified as two parallel dimensions of existence. The interface between the two can be conceived of as a mirror; the physical, material world is merely a reflection or shadow of the real world, the spiritual dimension behind the mirror (Farrer 1986, pp. 71–2). People in the material world come in contact with the real world mainly under two kinds of conditions: by visiting places where the two dimensions intersect, or by undergoing a transformation. Intersections occur where the structure of the cosmos and physical geography coincide, or where features such as caves provide a portal into the earth, to the spirit dimension. Transformations occur when people make spiritual journeys from one side of the mirror to the other.

Travelling to the spiritual dimension is potentially dangerous for individuals without the appropriate power. In the past, such journeys were made each time men went hunting or went on the warpath. Today most people make the journey only twice: at birth and at death (Farrer 1986). Singers possess the power to make the transition at will, and such journeys take place in the context of curing, divination and other ceremonial rituals.

Sensitive site types

Like other Native American religions, traditional Mescalero practices serve to maintain the knowledge, power and rituals obtained through religious revelation (United States Department of Interior 1979b, p. 10). Places associated with the revelation (i.e. receipt of power) are sacred, but many other places related to the proper performance of the rituals are also sensitive, albeit to a lesser degree. Ceremonies often require the use of particular plant, animal or earth materials. The materials themselves, the locations at which they are obtained, and the places where they are used can all be *diyi'*. A much greater proportion of the landscape is therefore considered sacred or sensitive by traditional Mescaleros than by most Euroamericans. Many powerful places are outside the reservation, and maintaining continued access to them, regardless of present ownership, is very important to the Mescalero people.

The quality of sacredness applies, in varying degrees, to all types of powerful places. The following pages provide an overview of the different kinds of places considered *diyi'* by the Mescalero. For the purposes of discussion, they are organized into three categories: places of intersection, places of transformation and resource areas.

Natural areas of intersection

The physical and spirit worlds intersect at several types of sites. Some of the most important of these are sacred mountains. There are four primary sacred peaks in Mescalero territory (Fig. 6.1): Guadalupe, Salinas, Capitan, and San Augustin. Geographically they define the core of traditional Mescalero lands (Basehart 1974), but their importance relates mainly to their place in cosmology.

The universe is conceived of as a tipi, a hide-covered lodge built on a conical framework of evergreen poles. The lodgepoles support the male sky elements which surround and enclose the female earth elements. A visual metaphor of this cosmology is contained in the Holy Lodge built for one of the most important Mescalero rituals, the Girls' Puberty Ceremony (Farrer 1980, p. 131). The Holy Lodge is a 12-pole tipi supported by four foundation poles, the Four Grandfathers that hold up the universe. In nature, the four principal sacred peaks are the Four Grandfathers. They support the universe (i.e. the sky) and encircle that part of the earth that is the centre place, or homeland, of the Mescalero Apache. The mountains are, therefore, not only physical geographical landmarks, but also part of the very structure of the spirit world. As such, they have been the sources of power for a number of singers.

Caves represent another type of intersection, where it is possible to access the spirit world by going into or under the earth. Caves are considered extremely powerful because they are among the kinds of places where individuals can communicate directly with the mountain spirits (Sonnichsen 1958). Caves are important sources of power, and ceremonial paraphernalia are ritually 'retired' in them.

Springs are also sources of power: they provide contact with the spiritual dimension inasmuch as the water has just emerged from within the earth. Power from the spirit world is carried into the physical world by the flowing water. The significance of *diyi'* in this context is reflected in the distinction between springs and streams, which are classified as 'living' water, and lakes and ponds which are 'dead'. A day after water ceases to flow, it is said to be spiritually (but not biologically) dead.

Places of transformation

The other major category of Mescalero sacred sites consists of places of transformation, where journeys to the spirit world are undertaken. Such sites are perhaps the only kinds of sacred sites that can reasonably be expected to yield archaeological remains. The most sacred, and the most dangerous, of these are burials. At death, individuals are transformed and their spirits begin a four-day journey back to the spirit world. The traditional funeral rites are intended to expedite this journey and to prevent the spirits of the deceased from returning for the spirits of friends and relatives, without whom it is lonely. Until the graves are covered, burials are very dangerous, and any burial remains are handled only under the direct supervision of powerful singers. After attending a funeral, people need to undergo a cleansing ritual so the power of the spirit world is not carried back to everyday life.

The sweatlodge is another type of sacred site where transformations occur. A sweatlodge is a small, domed structure made on a framework of bent branches and heavily covered with hides or fabric. Heated rocks are placed in a pit dug into the floor of the structure and splashed with water, filling the interior with intense steam heat. Sweatlodges have secular uses such as bathing and socializing, but the importance of the site type appears to be related to its role as a place of spiritual transformation. Although sweatlodges are no longer in general use at Mescalero, men were traditionally required to sweat whenever embarking on or returning from a hunt or raid.[2] The hunter was transformed into a predatory animal for the duration of the hunt; his speed, stealth and visual acuity were like those of the animals. The hunter thereby entered the spirit world, a transformation signified by the use of a ritual language (Opler 1940). This warpath language consisted of a male dialect in which everyday items had different names, reflecting their existence in the spiritual dimension. During a hunt or raid, the warrior was powerful and dangerous; it was necessary to sweat again on returning, so that he could safely resume contact with those who had not been transformed. The site of the sweatlodge remained sensitive thereafter because of the power involved in making the spiritual journey.

The ceremony for which the Mescalero are best known is the Girls' Puberty

Ceremony. The Holy Lodge used in this ritual is another type of sacred site that would be visible archaeologically. The lodge is a large tipi in which the participants dance and receive instructions on proper Mescalero behaviour. During the four-day public ceremony, the girls are transformed into the mythic culture heroine, White Painted Woman, and infused with her healing power (Farrer 1978, p. 10; Farrer 1980, p. 154). While in this transformed state, the girls are so powerful that they cannot be touched by anyone other than a singer or their female sponsors. They use scratching-sticks rather than touch themselves, and they use drinking-tubes rather than touch utensils. When it is occupied by the girls, the Holy Lodge is very powerful and sacred; the entrance is bounded by an invisible but distinct line between sacred and secular space, beyond which spectators are not permitted to pass.

Resource areas

One additional kind of place warrants mention here: the source areas for the materials used in traditional ceremonies. Although not sacred in the same sense as the site types mentioned above, resource areas certainly can be culturally sensitive. That is, they are *diyi'* but not to the same degree as sacred sites. Certain types of native plants, soil, etc. are required to perform, properly, ceremonies associated with the use of sacred sites. The improper performance of ceremonies (without the prescribed materials) would be ineffective at best, and could actually be harmful. The importance of resource areas is indicated by Mescalero testimony at hearings for the American Indian Religious Freedom Act of 1978 (AIRFA).

AIRFA is designed to prevent federal agencies from pursuing policies that interfere unnecessarily with Native American peoples' abilities to practise their religions freely. In 1979, following passage of the Act, a series of hearings was held by a federal task force to identify those agency regulations and procedures that interfered with Native American religious practices. The most common complaint voiced by the Mescalero was the lack of access to public lands for the purposes of collecting materials needed for ceremonies (United States Department of Interior 1979a, 1979b). The materials mentioned include mescal (*Agave parryi*), mesquite (*Prosopis glandulosa*), yucca (*Yucca* sp.), sotol (*Dasylerion wheelerii*), sumac (*Rhus trilobata*), sage (*Artemisia filifolia*), and various types of soil and rocks.

All of these materials have more mundane secular uses, but many of them also figure prominently in the Girls' Puberty Ceremony, which is considered by many Mescaleros to be their most important ceremony. It is viewed as the basis of their tribal identity and critical to their survival as a people (Farrer 1980, p. 126). If the ceremony is to be conducted properly, the materials need to be gathered at the appropriate time and in the appropriate manner. Therefore, the source areas are culturally sensitive, and maintaining at least periodic access to them is important to the Mescaleros.

Discussion

One of the most significant points to be made for archaeologists is that many, perhaps most, Mescalero sacred sites contain few if any physical remains. Mescalero Apache campsites in general are archaeologically inconspicuous, and sacred sites are likely to be even less visible. The archaeological invisibility of many sacred sites and sensitive areas may be part of a more general pattern common to many Native American groups (Winter 1980, p. 123). Nevertheless, it is often archaeologists who, in the context of historic preservation planning, are given primary responsibility for identifying sensitive sites to be avoided. An increased awareness of Native American sensibilities is critical to the effective accomplishment of this task.

In the preceding section, seven different types of sacred sites and sensitive areas were identified. The list is not intended to be exhaustive; at least three other site types are known to be sacred or sensitive: vision quest/ pilgrimage sites, places where specialized knowledge (such as how to make hunting bows) was obtained, and prehistoric observatory sites. A great deal of diversity is represented by these sites, ranging from sacred mountains to stands of native plants. Some are archaeological in nature, but many are not. They are not all equally important or sensitive, but they are all *diyi'* to some degree.

All powers are important and necessary; they serve different, complementary roles, each contributing to the vitality of the traditional belief or system. The power associated with different kinds of sites will vary. Human burials are the most sacred and dangerous, perhaps reflecting the immediacy of the danger presented by the potential for being drawn into the spiritual dimension by a deceased loved one. Burials aside, the relative sensitivity of sites appears to reflect the generality and time depth, in mythic time, of the power related to the site.

At one level, individuals may receive power for personal protection, or healing rituals used at the family level. These types of power, the materials used in the rituals and the places where they are performed may be the least potent and sensitive. The singers who paint and direct the Mountain God dancers who perform in the Girls' Puberty Ceremony represent another kind of power. Their power derives from the time period when the Mescaleros arrived in southern New Mexico, and a number of the singers obtained their power at sites on the principal sacred peaks. The power is also more general in its application, as the dance groups perform for the benefit of families, lineages and the tribe.

Still another kind of power is represented by the singers who perform in the Holy Lodge. The rituals date back to the period before the Apaches came to New Mexico, and they have the responsibility of maintaining the knowledge of how the Mescaleros came to be a people. Their powers are derived from the sky elements, identified by Opler (1946, p. 275) as the most potent sources of power. Their powers are not personal; they are essentially held in trust for the tribe and used at the lineage and tribal levels. The most sensitive sites are those relating to the most general types of spiritual power.

Resource areas would seem to be among the least sensitive of powerful places. However, because they can cover extensive portions of the landscape, they may present greater potential for land-use conflicts than other, more sensitive, sites. Those resource zones containing materials used in the Mescalero Apache Girls' Puberty Ceremony provide a case in point. Not only are specific natural materials required for the proper enactment of the ceremony but it is also necessary to gather them at particular times in their seasonal growth cycle. Unfortunately, these needs have not always been accommodated by government land managers. In the past, the Mescaleros have been prevented from gathering sage on federal lands and from collecting mesquite fruits along state highway easements. They have been charged fees to obtain mescal from public lands. They have even been prevented from picking the flowers and stalks of the Spanish bayonet (*Yucca elata*) because it is the state flower of New Mexico (United States Department of Interior 1979a, pp. 7–12). Even since the passage of AIRFA, the author has been asked to collect sotol stalks and mesquite fruits for ceremonial use because it was believed that a non-Indian would experience less agency interference than would a Mescalero.

Mescalero testimony on the religious importance of native plant and mineral resources has tremendous implications for cultural resource preservation and land-use planning. Not only are specific sites sacred, but potentially large outcrops and habitat areas are also sensitive. Specific stands of native plants are not productive every year, and extensive areas of a given ecological zone may need to be visited to obtain the necessary materials. The protection of large areas of the natural landscape could be viewed, in this context, as a religious freedom issue.

It can only be hoped that damage to sacred sites and infringements on their use will decrease as land managers become more aware of Native American concerns. However, it is unrealistic to expect that all sacred sites and sensitive areas can be individually protected from damage or inappropriate use; we must rely on an educational process to promote a respect for the importance of sites and landscapes to native peoples.

Belief in the sacred character of specific features of the landscape is an essential component of Mescalero self-identity; it has been so from mythic time, and is thus vital to the present and future of the Mescalero people.

Notes

1 Much of the data in this chapter was obtained over a six-year period of ethnoarchaeological research with a Mescalero singer or holy man, the late Bernard Second. Some of the sacred sites were previously reported in the context of tribal land claims litigation (Basehart 1974) and impact assessments for military projects (USAF 1986).

2 Available data on traditional Mescalero use of the features corroborates Luckert's (1975, pp. 142–5) analysis of the religious function of the Navajo sweatlodge.

References

Ball, E. 1980. *An Apache Odyssey: Indeh*. Provo, Utah: Brigham Young University Press.

Basehart, H. W. 1974. Mescalero Apache subsistence patterns and socio-political organization. In *Apache Indians XII*, D. Agee Horr (ed.), 8–178. New York: Garland Publishing, Inc.

Basso, K. H. 1969. *Western Apache Witchcraft*. Tucson: University of Arizona Press.

Basso, K. H. (ed.) 1971a. *Western Apache Raiding and Warfare. From the notes of Grenville Goodwin*. Tucson: University of Arizona Press.

Basso, K. H. 1971b. 'To give up on words': silence in Western Apache culture. In *Apachean Culture History and Ethnology*, K. H. Basso & M. E. Opler (eds), 151–62. Tucson: University of Arizona Press.

Carmichael, D. L. 1990. Traditional patterns of Mescalero settlement behavior and their potential for expression in the archaeological record. Paper presented at the Chiricahua and Mescalero Apache Conference: Cultural Resources and Cultural Heritage, November 9–10, Truth-or-Consequences, New Mexico.

Deaver, S. 1986. American Indian Religious Freedom Act (AIRFA) background data. Report prepared by Ethnoscience for the Bureau of Land Management. Billings: Montana State Office.

Farrer, C. R. 1978. Mescalero ritual dance: a four-part fugue. *Discovery 1978* 1–13.

Farrer, C. R. 1980. Singing for life: the Mescalero Apache Girls' Puberty Ceremony. In *Southwestern Indian Ritual Drama*, C. J. Frisbie (ed.), 125–59. Albuquerque: University of New Mexico Press.

Farrer, C. R. 1981. Living the sky: aspects of Mescalero Apache ethnoastronomy. In *Archaeoastronomy in the Americas*, R. A. Williamson (ed.), 137–50. Los Altos, Calif.: Ballena Press and College Park.

Farrer, C. R. 1986. Looking through the mirror of life. *Parabola* II, 70–3.

Hultkrantz, A. 1979. *The Religions of the American Indians*. Berkeley: University of California Press.

Luckert, K. W. 1975. *The Navajo Hunter Tradition*. Tuscon: University of Arizona Press.

Opler, M. E. 1935. The concept of supernatural power among the Chiricahua and Mescalero Apaches. *American Anthropologist* 37, 65–70.

Opler, M. E. 1940. The raid and war-path language of the Chiricahua Apache. *American Anthropologist* 42, 617–34.

Opler, M. E. 1946. The creative role of shamanism in Mescalero Apache mythology. *Journal of American Folklore* 59, 268–81.

Opler, M. E. 1983. Mescalero Apache. In *Handbook of North American Indians*, vol. 10, Alfonso Ortiz (ed.), 419–39. Washington, D.C.: Smithsonian Institution.

Sonnichsen, C. L. 1958. *The Mescalero Apaches*. Norman: University of Oklahoma Press.

United States Air Force 1986. *Legislative Environmental Impact Statement. Small Intercontinental Ballistic Missile Program*. Prepared for the US Air Force, AFRCE-BMS, Norton Air Force Base, California by Tetra Tech. Inc., San Bernardino, California.

United States Department of Interior 1979a. Consultation meeting before the Task Force to implement the American Indian Religious Freedom Act. Transcript of Proceedings, 22 June, Zuni, New Mexico. Washington, D.C.: Department of the Interior, Office of the Secretary.

United States Department of Interior 1979b. American Indian Religious Freedom Act
    Report. P.L. 95–341. Washington, D.C.: Federal Agencies Task Force, Office of
    the Secretary.
Walker, J. R. 1980. *Lakota Belief and Ritual*, R. J. DeMallie & E. A. Jahner (eds).
    Lincoln: University of Nebraska Press.
Winter, J. 1980. Indian heritage preservation and archaeologists. *American Antiquity* 45,
    121–31.

7   *Sacred sites in the Bamenda Grassfields of Cameroon: a study of sacred sites in the Nso' Fondom*

MARY MAIMO MUMAH

Introduction

It is difficult for a Nso' to discuss an aspect of the culture of the people of the grassfields about which papers in learned journals have already been written, because of the lack of public reference libraries which store such material. Also, for a woman to attempt to study a topic like 'sacred sites' in this hierarchical society is a very intriguing problem, because there are many institutions of Nso' traditional society which are open only to men.

This chapter focuses on the Nso' *Fon*dom (Kingdom), the author's birthplace, which is the largest kingdom in the Northwest Province of Cameroon and one of the most elaborately organized. It neighbours the Kingdom of Bamum on the east and is bordered on the west by Bum and Kom; it occupies most of the Bui Division of the province, which has a population of around 200,000. The chapter investigates the sacred sites around Kumbo, the capital of Nso', where the *Fon* has his residence (*nto'*), and comments on their significance in the traditional setting.

Before the colonization of Cameroon in 1884 (and still today) Nso' traditional society was ruled by the *Fon* or king. The Nso' people believed, as many still do, that their *Fon* was at the centre of the 'world', which revolved around him, and from which he gave directives for almost all activities in Nso', mediated by men of title and secret societies which met at the palace. The *Fon* controlled all the land and people and also 'fed the whole nation'. He had the power of life and death, and was seen by ordinary people as everything but God. With these powers he mediated as the high priest between God and the living people through his ancestors.

Types of sacred sites

The people of the Western Grassfields believe very strongly in life after death. They believe that their failures or successes depend on or come from their ancestors. In order to please the ancestors, who are seen as intermediaries between them and God, the people have special objects and places where prayers are said in honour of the ancestors. These special places are regarded as sacred places belonging not only to the lineage heads but also to the entire lineage, and may also be attended by affinal relatives. Others are associated with sub-chiefdoms. Some sacred places also belong to individuals with extraordinary gifts (healer-diviners, twins and mothers of twins). However, the arrival of Christian missionaries in December 1912, as well as the fifty-nine years of changing colonial presence in Nso' (1902–61), and subsequent 'modernization', has discredited not only these places of traditional worship, but also the significance of the ancestral shrines and sacred sites.

In the west, sacred sites are built places of worship such as churches, mosques, synagogues or temples, which are treated with great respect and reverence. In the Western Grassfields, however, a sacred site is not necessarily a building, but is a powerful place or spot, an area or feature believed to be a residence of God. Such sites are places of worship, homes of the ancestors who live or are summonable there, awaiting consultation by their living subjects or children. Failure to offer sacrifices or prayers to God and the ancestors is believed to bring misfortune on the living for this neglect. Actual burials were respected and their disturbance invited accusations of sorcery, a practice associated with the use of bodily remains. Therefore it is taboo to indulge in trade involving any part of the human body, as this is a serious crime attracting serious punishment. Discussing the trade in human skulls in Nkambe District, Mbunwe-Samba (1988, n.p.) says simply that 'the fatal punishment for such disrespect was and is immediate and total'.

Sacred sites may be classified as follows.

The first are those sites in homes or under the care of traditional rulers and lineage heads such as the *Fon*, *Taawong* (a prince and deputy high priest who assists the *Fon* in his religious office (pl. *ataawong*), *Yeewong* (a princess and deputy high priestess), *Shufaay* (the most senior lord of the land) and others. The most important sites include:

> *Kitay ke nshwi*, which means tribute store; once a year, foodstuffs from lineage heads and other subjects are stored here in the palace. The food was stored primarily for the residents of the palace but any lineage head who was seriously in need was served from here. Visitors to the palace were also fed from the same source, hence the claim that 'the *Fon* feeds the whole nation'.

> *Kitav ke shishwaa*, the store of the cult of the earth or 'store of hunger', because it is here that sacrifices and prayers to fight hunger are made. Although it is situated in the palace, in the *Fon*'s residential sector, it does not belong to the *Fon* and the palace residents but to the entire 'nation'. Its members form a 'religious' cult whose chief duty is to sacrifice to the earth in times of calamity, to ward it off. For instance, when climatic conditions are unfavourable, sacrifices are offered to appease the earth. These un-

favourable conditions include floods, drought and epidemics of diseases such as smallpox or cholera. The ritual and ceremonial paraphernalia (the objects of the cult) were kept in the *kitav ke shishwaa*. Members also kept their personal, family or national effects of worth here, perhaps because no one dared to steal from this sacred site, since it was believed that anyone who stole from this store would bring calamity on himself and his lineage. As stated earlier, those with access to the store may now lack the original strong belief and may attempt to steal from this store if they have the opportunity. The young generation is daring indeed!

Lav wong (state house, or house of the country). This is the first place where sacrifices to the nation, and to the earth, are offered. Ritual objects kept in the *kitav ke shishwaa* are used only in *lav wong* and when these objects are taken out the door remains open until they have been used and brought back. Once *lav wong* is opened, no one can farm or use a hoe or cutlass in any way without incurring the wrath of the land and thus inviting a curse on the land. Around April or May every year the cult prepares its medicines, which are put on farms and at crossroads to turn away the evil that may befall the land, and prevent a poor harvest, which may visit the farms as the result of someone making the earth angry.

Other sacred places where the gods live and where sacrifices are offered for the 'nation' are:

Kerësii ke bam nto, the *Fon*'s resting place behind the palace, where the *Fon* officiates alone after his enthronement.

Fëm, the *Fon*'s cemetery or graveyard.

Ntsëndzëv, a special sacred place near a compound called *Ntsëndzëv*.

Bui, the largest river in Kumbo Town used as a sacred site (other such sites are found in different parts of Nso', and all are visited during national sacrifices).

Kidzev, a deep circular pool in the river, believed to be deadly if one dares to go near it. To identify such a place, raffia fibres are tied across the spot where the 'high priest' stands to offer sacrifices to the ancestors.

Ntamir, a junction leading into a home or compound of traditional rulers and lineage heads; also entrances from lineage heads' compounds into farm lands under their control. This is where they make sacrifices when the farming season begins or when new crops, such as corn, are ready. Until these sacrifices are made no one is allowed to farm or harvest. Some symbolic features at *ntamir* are bunches of feathers, or powder scraped from special wood (camwood) and sprinkled on stones on either side of the entrances or junctions (Fig. 7.1).

Maandzë se nggay (sing. *maandzë nggay*), the central courtyards of traditional rulers and lineage heads. A large tree and/or *vikeng* (green peace plants, or

Figure 7.1 Some distinguishing features at sacred sites. A lineage head sacrificing at *ntamir* (junction leading to his compound or leading to his farmland). Drawing: Wilfred Loyu (Bamenda, Cameroon).

Dracaena species are grown here). Features similar to those at a *ntamir* are sometimes found here.

Verësii (sing. *kirësii*), the private sitting places of lineage heads, usually close to the graves of the former lineage heads.

Nggaisii (sing. *nggay*), the sacred assembly halls in which all members of the lineage assemble. It is in this hall that serious disputes are discussed, and both joyous and sad occasions are organized. When the need arises for sacrificial offering, a leader of the *nggay* (*taala'*) tears the beak of a chicken or slaughters a goat and allows the blood to run over the threshold of the door, as every member has to cross this blood when entering or going out of the *nggay* (Fig. 7.2). The whole of the sacrificial animal is eaten by all members of the lineage as a sign of oneness or communion.

Kongsii – some waterfalls are regarded as the abodes of gods and are therefore used as sacrificial sites.

Another class of sacred sites is formed by those belonging to members of cults or secret societies such as *ngwerong*, *nggiri*, *rum*, *mfu'*, and *ncong*. Although they do not offer sacrifices, the cult houses are reserved houses, hence they are considered here as sacred places. These cult houses are organized so that even initiated members have to undergo further initiation and pay fees in kind before they are allowed to move to certain parts of the house or eat certain parts of an animal. The initiation is followed by the provision of the where-withal for feasting, and failure to keep to the rules of the cult house can involve heavy fines or have fatal consequences. For instance, it is believed that, if a young member eats a gizzard of a chicken, a reserved portion, he is likely to develop an incurable disease which results in death, unless the victim or his parents pay heavy penalties immediately. Members of some cult houses use *visusung*, elephant grass stems, and *kilun* (wild garden egg, *Solanum* sp.) is also used during their ceremonies. *Kilun* is also used in divination, and by a masked *juju* (*kighevshu*) empowered to unveil any hidden evil (Fig. 7.3). Further details concerning some of these secret societies can be found in Mzeka (1978) and Chem-Langhëë (1985). Sacred objects include musical instruments, pots, masks and bags of medicine, and their appearance is heralded by so-called 'running *jujus*' warning non-members not to approach.

Figure 7.2 A *shufaay* or *taala'* killing a beast to allow the blood to run over the threshold of the *nggay* door (family assembly hall). Drawing: Wilfred Loyu.

Figure 7.3 A masked *juju kighevshu* with special spears ready to remove any hidden evil. The spear ends have wild garden eggs (*kilun*) to enable him to spot the hidden area faster. Drawing: Wilfred Loyu.

Another group of sacred sites consists of those belonging to individuals with special healing powers (native doctors) and those with special privileges (twins and their mothers). The sites belonging to this class include special termite mounds (*kikfëkfë*) where some diseases like infertility, madness and bed-wetting by adults are said to be cured, and domestic shrines for twins.

Lav se shiiv (sing. *lav shiiv*) – the consulting-rooms of native doctors, where the traditional doctors call on the ancestors to assist them in the art of curing the various diseases (Fig. 7.4).

Objects considered to be sacred are *mebvëm* (sing. *shibvëm*), the medicated statues or figurines (anthropomorphic statues) and objects like twins' property or *vifave won nyuy*, which means 'property of God's children' (referring to the twins). Their property consists of a native raffia bag, a calabash and a basket of foofoo meal, served with a suitable accompanying soup, which must contain a lot of egusi mounds. These items are honoured and must always contain food, water and *vikeng* (*Dracaena* sp.) because it is believed that God feeds with the twins, and therefore starving the twins would mean attempting to starve God.

This could cause the sudden death of one or both of the twins, thus causing lamentation in the family.

The rulers and people empowered to offer sacrifices have various rites to perform in order to reinforce the power and authority of the ancestors and gods. They sprinkle the area or object with camwood, *kiwooy* (a slimy concocted liquid for removing pollution and for blessing by asperging with a whisk). Palm-wine is also poured on the object or put in special gourds (*ngiv*) for the ancestors and gods to drink. As a mark of their high office, these diviners wear wreaths of *ror*, a special creeping green plant (*Basella alba*) which is wrapped round their necks during offerings.

Most of these sacrifices, usually involving incantation, fall basically into four major groups:

Kinka – prayer, incantation or calling on the ancestors to protect or to shower blessings on the living.

Figure 7.4 Some features found in traditional doctors' consulting-rooms. The doctor stirs a pot of medicine and calls on the ancestors to assist him to cure diseases. Drawing: Wilfred Loyu.

Ntangri – offering of animals and other objects in sacrifice to the ancestors or gods when something goes wrong or in thanksgiving for the blessings received. The term *chu* is used for libations.

Shikan or *menkan* – anointing an afflicted person with powder scraped from a special hardwood in order to drive away evil spirits.

Kidiv – a reconciliatory offering using concocted palm-wine to settle an outstanding grudge between the dead and the living. The palm-wine mixture in a calabash is placed over a three-stone fireplace containing very little fire. As the prayers are said, the wine bubbles, indicating that the ancestors are awake and providing adequate heat. It is believed that if the wine boils over, the prayers are not heard, which means that the dead person is still angry about the evil done to him while on earth. The wine should rise to the brim three times, then settle to the bottom to indicate reconciliation.

Because of the importance attached to these sacrifices and prayers, special days are set aside for them. These days are known as gods' days (*vi shiiy ve anguy*) and are called *kilovëy* and *nggoilum*, and are automatically regarded as traditional rest days. No farm work involving disturbance of the earth is allowed on these days. Any woman who violates this rule risks losing her farm, as the lineage heads punish such disrespectful acts by seizing the farms, or heavy penalties are paid to the lineage heads who further offer sacrifices to appease the earth.

Nso' palace sacred sites

The palace is the name reserved only for the residence of a traditional ruler of the entire 'nation'. This overall ruler in Nso' is the *Fon*. According to Mzeka (1978, p. 28):

> The *Fon* is looked upon as the link between the living and their ancestors and the gods. It is he who sacrifices and communicates with the gods by the intermediary of the late *afon* and by which fertility and concord are brought to the land. His person is sacrosanct.

This description of the *Fon* shows that the Fonship in Nso' is sacred. The *Fëm*, which is the most important sacred site, is the graveyard where *Fons* of Nso' are buried. It is also, in so far as the graveyard in Kumbo is concerned, the hut built over the grave. The link between the *Fëm* and the palace is the grave, which must have the same features as those of the palace. For instance, the palace, the *Fon*'s compound, is made up of open courts (*maandzë nggay*) where the *Fon* receives the populace, *taa kibuu*, where the *Fon* receives his councillors and important visitors (*faay kishiiy*), the *Fon*'s bedchamber, and the royal mortuary (*faay kibvë*).

According to the Nso' people, the *Fon* never dies. He is immortal, being a Nso' god (*nyuy Nso'*). The people see him only as 'missing', and his burial a matter of being 'stored'. This calls for sacrifices to cleanse the land polluted by his death. When the *Fon* is missing (dies), the corpse is taken from the *faay kishiiy* to the *faay kibvë*, where it is washed, smeared with camwood, wrapped in royal cloth (*kilanglang*) and capped with the cap of rank and dignity (*tanmbam* or *ngwerong* cap) with which the *Fon* is installed. Two rams are slaughtered, one at the grave before digging begins and the other sacrificed at the *nggay* (the family assembly hall of the palace).

While the corpse is in the royal mortuary, the deputy high priest (*Taawong*) continuously plays the state gong (*nggem wong*) round the corpse, at intervals, to announce that the 'Nso' sun has set' and also to awaken the ancestral *afon* and gods in the *Fëm* (Fig. 7.5). The grave is usually larger and deeper than a normal grave. For instance, the *Fëm* has a double terrace on one of the walls, symbolizing some apartments of the palace, described above as *maandzë nggay*, *taakibuu* and *faay kishiiy*. At the opposite wall to the terrace of the grave a cavity, about 1 m square, is dug deep enough to represent the *faay kishiiy* where the corpse will be seated before burial rites begin. This cavity, which is now called *faay kishiiy*, is decorated and furnished with bamboo boards, overlaid with *kilanglang* (royal cloth) and decorated with special wall mats (*mban*). The bamboo throne (*kavaa*) is then put in position in the *faay kishiiy* of the grave, on a dais covered with leopard skin, the symbol of royalty, power and authority. The *Fon* is the only person in Nso' who may sleep on a leopard skin or put his feet on it.

When the grave is ready, the corpse, still wrapped in *kilanglang*, is carried, head first, in procession by *vibay ve duy* (burial priests descended from former *ataawong*), led by the *Faay Ndzeëndzëv* (senior lord and leader of the *Fon*'s councillors, and installer of *Fons* of Nso'). *Taawong* follows, playing the *nggem wong* at intervals, and then *Yeewong*, who cleanses the path with aspergings of a slimy liquid, consisting of palm-wine or water and herbal infusion, which is necessary for removing pollution and for blessing. Before the corpse is carried to the *Fëm*, led by the great lord of sacrifice, the palace is cleared of everyone who is not authorized to see the corpse. At the *Fëm*, the corpse is blessed by *Yeewong*, and then a burial invocation (*kinka*) is said both by *Taawong* and *Yeewong*.

The *Faay Ndzeëndzëv* removes the cap (*tanmbam*) from the head of the corpse, calling him by his birth name in order to remind him of the name by which he will be addressed as an ancestral *Fon* during future sacrifices and libations. The *tanmbam* is preserved for the installation of the new *Fon* in order to ensure continuity, and this transfer of the *tanmbam* and attributes of the *Fon* commits the new *Fon* to carry out his duties strictly as Nso' tradition dictates.

The burial rites consist of the corpse being taken to the *faay kishiiy* (Fig. 7.6) and seated on a bamboo *kavaa* (royal stool) with its feet resting on the leopard skin (*juv baa*) to underscore the royalty, power and authority which he has as the ancestral *Fon* of Nso', which are transferred to his successor. The corpse is secured in position with pieces of camwood and *kirun*, which are very durable trees, said to be resistant to ants or bacterial destruction. The hind legs of the

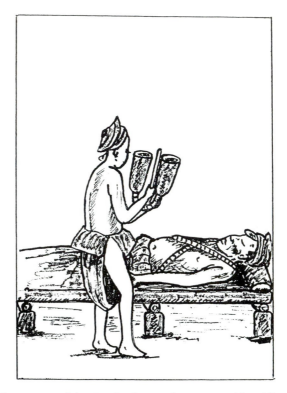

Figure 7.5 The corpse of the *Fon* in the royal mortuary (*faay kibvë*). *Taawong* goes round playing on the *nggem wong* at intervals to announce that the 'Nso' sun has set' and also to awaken the late *afon* in the *Fëm* to receive him. Drawing: Wilfred Loyu.

ram slaughtered earlier are flavoured and preserved with salt, then placed in front of the corpse as his own share of the sacrifice. A beast is sometimes left there. A new container of salt, which is one of the 'things of the earth', is also placed in front of the corpse. The entrails of the sacrificial beast are also placed there on a special leaf (*kiman*) in order to appease the earth.

A royal drinking-cup is forced into the left hand of the corpse to emphasize his power and authority as an ancestral *Fon*, since only the *Fon* drinks from the left hand in Nso'. A long Indian bamboo with one end reaching out of the grave is inserted into the gourd (*ngiv*) containing wine which had been placed before the corpse (Fig. 7.6). Because of the *Fon*'s supremacy, his wine or its container is known as *bom*. The future libation wine for the ancestral *Fon* will be sent through the inserted Indian bamboo. Lastly, a special creeping plant (*koonte*) is tied on the left wrist of the corpse, as a symbol of the deceased *Fon*'s bravery and heroism. It is led out of the grave to grow, in order to connect the dead hero with the living heroes. The filling of the grave with earth is done slowly with special music (*nsii*) used for burials of *Fons* and Nso' heroes, and also of the aged. A grass thatched bamboo hut (*Fëm*) is built over the grave, as a special honour to protect him from rain. No other person in Nso', irrespective of his economic or political weight or wealth, can have a hut or any other form of covering over his grave. After the first sacrifice to the most recent ancestral *Fon*, offered by *Taawong*, and the final invocation by *Taawong* and *Yeewong* to end the burial rites, preparation begins for the mourning and final selection of the new *Fon* (Fanso & Chem-Langhëë 1989, pp. 50–66).

From the care and diligence taken in burying a *Fon*, it is evident that the Nso' people strongly believe in life after death. For instance, the sitting position in the grave and the number of symbolic objects given to him clearly suggest he is still alive. The *Fon*'s grave is therefore considered sacred because he is not dead, and waits there for consultation. Because of the lower regard for women in Nso', they are never allowed to see either the corpse of the *Fon* or the *Fëm*. They are not even allowed to go anywhere near it or talk about the corpse or *Fëm* because of its sacredness. *Yeewong*, the high priestess, is the only exception (Fig. 7.7).

Figure 7.6 The corpse seated in the *faay kishiiy* of the grave. Note the real and symbolic things done to the corpse (his share of the sacrificial beast and wine (*bom*), his feet resting on a leopard skin, a drinking-cup forced into his left hand, a *koonte* plant tied on his left wrist is let out to grow and a passage through which his wine will be sent during future libation is provided by the long Indian bamboo inserted into the *ngiv* at his right). Drawing: Wilfred Loyu.

Figure 7.7 *Yeewong* is the only female who enters the *Fëm* and she plays an important role during sacrificial offerings. Drawing: Wilfred Loyu.

Other important sacred sites are the *say se ayeefon*, token graves of *Fons'* mothers. They are tokens because in actuality their mothers are never buried in the palace. No one except the *Fon* dies in the palace. If any palace inmates (the *Fon*'s wife, a princess or prince) is very ill, he or she is taken out of the palace, and if this results in death, the *Fon*, because of his sacredness, does not see their corpses but he sends things for burial. *Fons'* mothers' graves are considered sacred sites because it is believed that any woman, so blessed that she can give birth to a 'god', must also possess divine powers.

Another sacred site is the *kilan ke nyuy* – a massive, flat stone in the palace which has unique features, believed to be the goddess who cares for the *Fon* and the palace inmates. It is at this site, therefore, that the ruling *Fon* and his diviners start prayers each time they call on the ancestral gods.

The yearly offering in the *Fëm*

This takes place once a year or when an unusual event dictates it. The *Fon* and his diviners, carrying sacrificial paraphernalia, move silently in single file with heads bowed, because they are in communion with the ancestors (Fig. 7.8). The *Fon* is always in the middle for protection. The items used for the offering consist of camwood, wine in a *ngiv* (carried in a state bag), palm-oil, salt, herbs and a beast. The sacrifice starts at the *kilan ke nyuy*. On arrival at the *Fëm*, the *Fon* utters some words of prayer to the ancestors (Fig. 7.9). He calls the names of the late *afon* and pours libation saying:

> This is your wine to appease you and to inform you that . . . [the message].
> Grant favours to the land.
> Let all evil disappear.
> Let a lot of good come to the land.
> Give fertility to the land and the people.
>
> (Mzeka 1978, p. 48)[1]

Requests for fertility to both the land and the people are included in all sacrificial prayers. After the libation ceremonies, the wine, camwood, salt, herbs and palm-oil are mixed together and applied to the doors of the huts

Figure 7.8 The procession of diviners going to the *Fëm* for the yearly sacrifice. Note *Taawong* leading, playing on the state gong (*nggem wong*) while *Yeewong* blesses with the *kiwooy* using a piece of a *Dracaena* plant. Drawing: Wilfred Loyu.

Figure 7.9 The *Fon*, *Taawong* and *Yeewong* in sacrifice at the *Fëm*. Note that everyone offering sacrifices wears *ror* round the neck. They also wear limited clothes and go without shoes to underscore the supremacy of the ancestors. Drawing: Wilfred Loyu.

(*femsii*) built over the graves. Everyone taking part in such ceremonies wears *ror* round their necks to drive away evil spirits and also to bring peace to the 'nation'. In earlier times, the diviners wore no clothes but today they may wear limited clothes and shoes (Fig. 7.9). Still in a solemn manner, they return to the *kitav ke shishwaa* to restore the sacrificial items and, finally, they cleanse themselves in order to communicate with non-members, by burning incense (*kilaay*), and blessing with palm-wine. It must be emphasized that the ceremonies carried out at sacred sites are efficacious because it is believed that the 'people' there are alive with full authority and power to mediate for the living when the need arises.

Because weeds are likely to grow in the *Fëm*, and huts may need repair, a special group of people known as *won jemeer Fon* are authorized to care for it, weeding any grass, repairing the thatch and noting unusual signs which, according to the Nso' tradition, calls for sacrificial prayers to the ancestors. No other people are allowed to enter the *Fëm*, except the burial priests. Even the *Fon* only goes there for ceremonies. *Won jemeer Fon* have been described as follows:

The fourth to the fifth generation of a prince or princess is known as *duy*. If a *duy* daughter marries a commoner lord (*mtaar*) and when the lord dies, the son of the *duy*'s daughter succeeds him. Such a successor is styled *won jemeer Fon*.

(Interview with *Yeewong*)

The lineage formerly of the commoner clan is now assimilated to that of the extended royal clan, but its members can have nothing to do with the things of *nggiri* or *ngwerong*, the major cult houses of the palace, but have their own house called *taamban*, and are eligible to care for the *Fëm*.

Conclusion

Although this subject–matter looks simple, my experience with the people I have interviewed has shown that there is much difficulty in obtaining information from the cultures we are supposed to know.

Being a woman, I encountered real hardship in trying to get information. Some of the people I questioned were so shocked and embarrassed that they either just frowned, saying nothing, refusing to give answers to my questions, or left me, shaking their heads as if to say 'Oh gods of Nso'! There is evil on the land. A woman daring to talk about the *Fëm*, the sacred home of the ancestral *Fons*, is calling evil on the land. Help us!' I remained patient, however, as I know that the traditional Nso' man has little or no regard for a woman, especially where such a delicate topic is concerned. It was necessary to work through a relative who herself is a traditional title–holder (*yaa*) and who, from time to time, takes part in some of the sacrifices. She went with me to the different traditional title–holders, as she knew that I could not get any help on my own. With each one, she introduced both my lineage and the objective of my visit. Still they hesitated, but finally gave spontaneous and positive responses to my questions. These were some of the diviners responsible for directing sacrifices on the sacred sites discussed in this chapter.

From what I have gained doing this short enquiry, I strongly recommend that historians, ethnologists and archaeologists should devise appropriate syllabuses, which would include traditional history that can be taught in our schools, for much is still unknown about the very culture we think we know well enough, together with the cheap publication of books suitable as teachers' guides.

On a different note, I would like to emphasize here that Christianity has brought nothing new in terms of 'prayers and worship to God' to the Bamenda Grassfields of Cameroon.

Note

1 Information about this ceremony was also given in a personal interview with the *Yeewong* who had taken part in the last two deaths and burials of late *afons* of Nso'.

Acknowledgement

Special thanks are due to Professor Sally Chilver, for her invaluable comments and corrections to this chapter.

References

Chem-Langhëë, B. 1985. Palaces and chiefly households in the Cameroon Grassfields. *Paideuma* 31, 151–81.
Fanso, V. G. & B. Chem-Langhëë 1989. The transfer of power and authority in *nto* Nso'. *Paideuma* 35, 49–66.
Mbunwe-Samba, P. 1988. Towards a national policy for museum and tourism development in Cameroon. Unpublished paper.
Mzeka, N. P. 1978. *The Core Culture of Nso'*. Agawam, Montana: Jerome Radin Co.

8   Bukusu sacred sites

SIMIYU WANDIBBA

Introduction

The Babukusu constitute the largest of the ethnic groups which inhabit the Bungoma District of Western Province, Kenya (Wandibba 1972). They are to be found mainly on the southern slopes and plains of Mt Elgon, an extinct volcanic mountain which is the most conspicuous single topographical feature in the 3074-km area of the Bungoma District.

Linguistically, the Babukusu belong to the main Bantu-speaking community in western Kenya known as the Abaluyia. This community is made up of sixteen or so ethnic groups who speak mutually intelligible languages and also share many other cultural features. The community practises both patrilineality and patrilocality. In this chapter the main shrines or sacred sites of the Babukusu are presented and discussed.

Indigenous religious beliefs

The indigenous religious beliefs of the Babukusu revolved around a supernatural power and the spirits of the dead. The supernatural power was manifested in deities, jointly referred to as *wele*, which could be translated as 'god'. The supreme deity was known as Wele Khakaba (god the giver), who was the creator of the world and all living creatures, including human beings. The Babukusu believed that God did not simply create the world and the creatures that are seen, but also created an order which enables humans to live in the world. Thus, 'God provided man with a woman so that he might multiply, with air to breathe, a sun to shine for him in daytime and a moon to light up at night, with water to drink, plants and animals to eat, and so on' (Wagner 1954, p. 43). Wele Khakaba was, therefore, responsible for all the good things that people enjoyed – fertility, health, wealth and good luck.

Wele Khakaba and his two assistants were benevolent towards people and were therefore referred to as good gods, as opposed to the two bad gods, Wele

Ebimbi (god of the wild) and Wele kwe Luchi (god of the river). Wele Ebimbi was responsible for all evil things in life – suffering, death, pain, bad luck, infertility and natural calamities, whereas Wele kwe Luchi was responsible for abortions and child mortality. These bad gods were not used as tools of evil by the supreme deity – they were independent, though weaker, forces than the creator god.

The spirits of the deceased were regarded as being possessed by mystical power that could affect human welfare. The Babukusu distinguished between two types of spirits, the good and the evil. The good spirits were referred to as *basambwa* (sing. *omusambwa*) or *bakuka* (sing. *omukuka*), and the bad spirits were known as *bimakombe* (sing. *simakombe*). Both types of spirits had a permanent abode called *emakombe*, which was believed to be underneath the earth. From this subterranean abode, the spirits visited their living kinsmen and appeared to them in a variety of ways, the commonest manifestation being in the form of dreams. The good spirits played a central role in the everyday lives of the people, and it was to them that the living turned in cases of need. Thus, whereas prayers were offered to the supreme deity, sacrifices were generally made to the *basambwa* of immediate relatives, especially the male ones. Eurocentric scholars have referred to this phenomenon as 'ancestor worship'. This is totally wrong because ancestors are never worshipped. They merely act as intercessors between the supernatural deity and the people, in the same way that saints do in the Christian religion. Whereas sacrifices were made to the good spirits, the evil spirits were expiated. This was done by killing a black sheep, which was believed to have the power of sealing off any contact between the evil spirit and its victim.

Sacred sites

The sacred sites of the Babukusu were based on Babukusu belief in the existence of a supernatural power as well as in what could be termed life after death. These beliefs meant that people had to respect both the supernatural power and also their departed relatives. The respect was not just in the form of awe, for these beings also had to be appeased, not only in times of trouble but also as a means to good health, prosperity and the general well-being of the family, clan or community. The appeasement was expressed in the form of sacrifices and/or prayers offered to the deceased. Such sacrifices and prayers were usually offered at specific places, which were recognized as sacred places or shrines.

There were family as well as communal sacrifices, and these family sacrifices were of three different types. The first type consisted of daily food and libations offered by a widow during the first few months after the death of her husband. These food offerings were placed on the loft or beside the centre-post of the house as food for the spirit of the deceased. Food offerings were also made by some diviners to their 'guardian spirits'. The second type of sacrifice was performed on all important occasions and turning-points in the life of an individual and the family, such as birth, naming, circumcision, marriage and death. In this case, the sacrifice would be addressed to the ancestral spirits believed to be in charge of the well-being of the family or individual on whose behalf the sacrifice was being offered. Finally, there were sacrifices which were normally offered when illness or other misfortune had overcome the family. Such sacrifices were offered after consulting a diviner, a person believed to have power from god to identify a definite ancestral spirit responsible for the misfortune. In this instance, the sacrifice would be addressed to that particular ancestor. These ancestral sacrifices involved the blessing of the ancestral spirits and, through them, of god. If the sacrifice involved the killing of an animal, meat was offered to the ancestral spirits, by placing it either inside or on top of the sacrificial shrine.

Communal sacrifices were performed by either clans or the community as a whole. Clan sacrifices were offered to clan founders, and could be held either at the main shrine or by the graveside. On the other hand, sacrifices that involved the whole community were usually made in response to calamities such as severe droughts or epidemic diseases. The community was also involved in sacrifices offered before a war was waged, or in those sacrifices associated with agricultural activities, such as planting and harvesting.

The Babukusu traditionally recognized three main sacred sites: *namwima*, *wetili* and *silindwa*. *Namwima* was a sacrificial shrine which consisted of a sometimes minute (between 6 cm and 2.13 m high), hut-like structure erected either in front of the entrance to the living house or at a nearby ant-hill. It was built of pliant twigs of the *kumulaa* tree (*Combretum collinam*), and thatched with a specific type of grass known as *ebonga*. The trees and grass used are known to be effective in increasing fertility, and this could be the reason why they were used. As a rule, *namwima* had a centre-post and walls like a house for living in. However, unlike in the case of a real house, the walls of *namwima* were not covered with daub. Wagner has observed that a stone called *libale lia Wafula* (Wafula's stone), because the first such shrine is said to have been built for a particular Wafula, was always placed on the left side of the entrance (Wagner 1970, p. 283). To the right of the entrance to *namwima*, a leafy branch of the *kumunyubuti* tree (*Clausena anisata*) was placed to provide shade for the ancestral spirits who were believed to be sitting in front of the sacrificial hut. This was done whenever a sacrifice was to be offered.

Namwima constituted the universal shrine of the Babukusu. 'The sacrifices made at this shrine were mainly addressed to the spirits of one's father and grandfather as well as to remote ancestors in the paternal line' (Wagner 1970, p. 283). This is not surprising in view of the fact that, as already pointed out, the ancestral spirits were believed to have the ability to intercede between god and his people. Thus, if any calamity befell a family, a sacrifice was made not directly to god but to the spirit of an immediate ancestor. The sacrifice made at the *namwima* involved killing cattle, goat, sheep or chicken. Beer was also occasionally poured into a small pot and then placed in the *namwima* as a form of sacrifice. In addition to sacrifices made in response to a misfortune, sacrifices were also made to ask for favours from the ancestral spirits.

The second sacrificial shrine was known as *wetili*, which was a 'tunnel-shaped, vault-like structure' (Wagner 1970, p. 283). Unlike *namwima*, this shrine was not universal; it was built by only some of the Babukusu clans. In contrast to *namwima*, which was constructed in front of the house, *wetili* was built behind the house, under the eaves. It was also built of pliable twigs of the *kumulaa* tree, and the structure was then covered with cow dung and fruits of the *sirarandura* shrub (*Solanum incanum*) were placed on its top (Wandibba 1972). According to one scholar, the sacrifices offered in this shrine consisted of a small gourd of milk or a spleen and a portion of the sacrificial animal's neck called *enjasi* (trachea). 'Such sacrifices were in the first place addressed to Malaba, a younger son of the eponymous founder of the Babukusu known as Mubukusu. Sacrifices were also made here to the less important spirits of old women' (Wagner 1970, p. 283).

These two sacrificial shrines were owned on a family basis; thus in each homestead there would be a *namwima* and/or *wetili*. In most cases they were constructed for use at a particular point in time, and once the sacrifice had been made they could be left to decay, and then, when the need arose again, a new shrine would be put up. Specialists in various ritual fields, however, always had a *namwima*, which would be of an unusually large size and regularly maintained. Once a shrine was abandoned, practically all the physical evidence of its existence was destroyed, and the site then no longer commanded the respect and awe that it had done previously. The only way in which future visitors to the site would recognize it as having been sacred was by the stone which, as already stated, was always placed to the left of the entrance to the *namwima*.

Silindwa (pl. *bilindwa*), the grave, was the third type of sacred site. The grave was, and still is, in the form of a raised oblong mound. In general, any grave was treated with respect; thus livestock were usually kept away from burial-grounds, and cultivation was not undertaken on such sites. However, the graves that commanded the greatest respect and awe were those of elderly people, especially men. At least one year after the burial of a mature or elderly person, a special ceremony was performed at the grave, which involved clearing the grave and then smearing it with black mud from a river bank. Beer was brewed and an animal killed for the occasion. In the case of a woman's grave that was the last of the burial ceremonies, unless the woman buried there was identified, by a diviner, as being responsible for misfortunes which had befallen her living relatives, in which case further sacrifices would be performed at the grave. For a man, however, another ceremony was performed two or more years later, which consisted of pulling down the deceased person's house. For this ceremony, beer was brewed and a bull or ox slaughtered by the graveside. In the case of an elderly man, the central post, and some of the daub from the house, were piled on the grave. A white stone was also placed at the head end of the grave, and this stone, together with the pillar, served as the marker point for the grave. A further ceremony was performed much later at which the pillar was split and the stone moved to the home of the eldest surviving son of the deceased. Although this ceremony marked the end of sacrifices by the graveside, respect for the site continued. For a family, the grave of an ancestor served as a place where sacrifices could be made to appease the deceased and also to ask for favours. Such a grave was highly respected and would never be cultivated.

There are two reasons why graves of clan or family heads were venerated. One was that sacrifices had to be performed there, for example when boys were to be circumcised. This was based on the Babukusu's belief that the dead looked after the interests of the living. The other reason had to do with the changing patterns in the ownership of land. Traditionally, land was jointly owned by the community as a whole, but with the coming of colonial rule individual ownership became the norm. Thus, a person whose forefathers had been buried in a particular place could claim the land in question and, on that basis, would get ownership of it.

Conclusion

In this chapter, the main sacred places of the Babukusu have been described. It should be borne in mind, however, that there are many other sacred sites which have not been dealt with here. Such sites are generally restricted to particular clans and, within those clans, to particular individuals. Among these are the smithy and the sacred places of certain specialists such as rain-makers.

The main point which emerges is that the sacred sites of the Babukusu were intricately tied into the everyday activities of the people. These activities were believed to be governed by the spirits of the dead as well as by the gods. Thus, prayers were said and ceremonies performed before important activities such as planting and harvesting. Prayers were also offered in the morning when people woke up, and before they set out on a journey, or to hunt. The spirits of the dead were seen as intercessors between god and the people, and because of this, prayers and offerings were, in the first instance, generally addressed to the spirits rather than to god directly. Although the spirits and god were believed to be everywhere, the Babukusu felt that sacrifices offered at specific places carried more weight than those performed just anywhere. This was probably the main reason why the two types of shrine described here were constructed, and also why sacrifices were made at the gravesides.

It has also been shown that the Bukusu concept of god was dualistic: it was believed that one side of the supernatural power represented the good god while the other side represented the bad god. The same concept of good and bad was extended to the spirits of the dead.

Acknowledgements

I would like to express my sincere thanks to Dr V. G. Simiyu and Dr Wembah-Rashid, and Stevie Nangendo, for reading through and commenting on earlier drafts of this chapter. I found their comments both stimulating and challenging.

References

Wagner, G. 1954. The Abaluyia of Kavirondo. In *African Worlds*, D. Forde (ed.), 27–54. London: Oxford University Press.
Wagner, G. 1970. *The Bantu of Western Kenya*, vol. 1. London: Oxford University Press. [Published in 1949 as *The Bantu of North Kavirondo*, vol. 1. London: Oxford University Press.]
Wandibba, S. 1972. The Bukusu forts. Unpublished B.A. dissertation, Department of History, University of Nairobi.

9 Sacrificial places and their meaning in Saami society

INGA-MARIA MULK

Introduction AUDHILD SCHANCHE

The Saami people are the indigenous people of the northern parts of Norway, Sweden and Finland, and of the northwestern part of Russia. The earliest written sources about the Saami date from around the beginning of our chronology, but archaeological indications of Saami ethnicity go back to a much earlier date.

Saami territory became divided by the borders of the national states from the sixteenth century until the end of the nineteenth century. Prior to that, the Saami had been taxed by, and engaged in trade with, Norwegians, Swedes and Russians – sometimes by all three of them at the same time – for hundreds of years. In the Viking and early medieval ages, when furs were highly prized in Europe, Saami people probably engaged in the trade on more equal terms than in later history, when Scandinavians and Russians colonized the north (Hansen 1990).

Originally, the Saami lived mainly by hunting and fishing. Between the eleventh and thirteenth centuries, small-scale stock-holding seems to have been included in the economy in some areas along the coast. Domesticated animals included a few sheep and cows, and also reindeer (Odner 1992). The tradition of seasonal movement between hunting and fishing grounds within family districts continued, possibly in a somewhat altered form. Specialized reindeer herding, today the most typical Saami occupation, was fully developed around AD 1600 (Vorren & Manker 1976). Its earliest appearance among the Saami is still being debated (Storli 1991; Storli, Arronson, Carpelan, Odner, Mulk & Hansen 1993).

Today, the Saami constitute the majority population in a few fjord and inland communities in northern Norway, but generally Saamis are totally outnumbered by Norwegians, Swedes, Finns and Russians. The total number of Saamis does not exceed 100,000, most of them living in the Norwegian parts of their old territory (Solbakk 1990).

Saami history has many similarities with the history of other indigenous peoples. It is a history of colonization, deprivation of land and suppression of language and religion. However, because Saami territory is part of Europe, *Sápmi* (the Saami term for their nation) was not 'discovered' in historic times, even though cultural contacts between Saami and non-Saami actually predate the time when the Germanic peoples of northern Europe became Christianized.

The pre-Christian Scandinavian religion, replaced by Christianity around AD 1000, had no missionary goals. Although land suitable for farming and crop-growing was slowly taken over by pre-Christian Scandinavians, Saami religion and religious practices were not persecuted in this early contact period. Persistent and intense Christian missionary activity started in the seventeenth century (Solbakk 1990). Part of its fulfilment was the destruction of items connected with the Saami religion, such as burning of the shamans' drums. Today's remnants of the old Saami religion are the knowledge of and respect towards some of the sacred places and burial sites, some of the myths and legends (kept alive by their connection to the landscape), the tradition of healing and the existence of the sacred and sacrificial places themselves, burial sites included. Some of them are known because early missionaries and others recorded them, some because oral tradition has managed to survive, and some because archaeological and ethnographic investigations have revealed them.

Saami pre-Christian religion was deeply rooted in Saami territories. The divine powers and the natural powers of the earth were not divided; they were one and the same. Between the people and the land which they lived on and moved in there existed a spiritual unity. Both religion and religious practices were deeply rooted in space, not, as with Christianity, in linear time. 'Natural' features, such as special rock-formations, cliffs, boulders, mountains, forests, lakes, springs and the ocean, and also wind, sun, stars and heaven, manifested gods and goddesses (Vorren 1987; Fjellström 1987).

The powers of nature were not considered evil, but could be dangerous if one did not maintain a good relationship with them. This was achieved through a set of sacrificial practices and also through general rules of behaviour in relation to the natural world. The rules were maintained and passed on by tales and oral tradition. For instance, one tale told people never to yell or boast in nature, in order not to disturb or challenge the spirits. Another told of the beauty of the fat-smeared sacred stone, glistening in the sun, of the danger that would come upon those who mistreated it, and of the deep sorrow and feeling of loss when a sacred stone was destoyed by fire (Qvigstad 1927).

Certain religious activities demanded human-built structures of stone or wood (Vorren 1985). But these were not of monumental character, and thus did not express the idea that humans were in any way above nature. The gifts that they were to offer, while passing by sacred places or during ceremonies, were also usually the products of nature, such as animals, blood, fat, horns and bones, milk, cheese and sometimes porridge (Fjellström 1985). In addition, certain metals that were believed to hold special powers were left as offerings (Zachrisson 1985).

Offering natural products to the powers of nature may be seen as a symbolic act of giving back nature's gifts. This might be done in order to secure further gifts, to please the gods or to achieve good luck for certain activities. On an ideological level, such acts will enforce the idea of humans being part of nature, contrary to the idea that their task on earth is to conquer and subordinate nature. Offering special objects to sacred natural formations can be interpreted as serving the same purpose.

On a general level, the old Saami religion bears resemblances to many other indigenous peoples' religions. Christian missionaries regarded these religions as sinful, savage and primitive. The alternative they offered was a religious practice that served to separate earth and heaven, body and soul, humans and nature, the secular and the sacred.

Saami sacred sites   INGA-MARIA MULK

Traces of Saami trapping and reindeer-herding cultures are strikingly unlike the traces of agrarian and urbanized societies, since the traditional lifestyle and culture of the Saami make use of natural resources, the remains of which are integrated parts of the environment. The most frequent types of Saami remains are hunting-pits, hearths, hut foundations, graves and sacrificial places. Saami sacrificial places were important components of Saami society. They were part of the pre-Christian conception of the world, with a strong belief in the presence of ancestors and other spiritual beings at certain locations. These holy places, sometimes consisting of entire mountains, were objects of different kinds of ceremonies. They are to be found everywhere in the Saami landscape – along the migratory routes, at the dwelling-sites, in the hunting-grounds and by the fishing-waters.

Distribution, location and function (Fig. 9.1)

Archaeologists, ethnologists and historians of religion have paid particular attention to the remains of sacrificial places. Most of our knowledge about Saami pre-Christian religion and Saami sacrificial ceremonies originates from records written by clergymen during the seventeenth and eighteenth centuries. In addition to these sources, a great number of sacrificial places have been investigated, many of them in northern Sweden. Among the fundamental archaeological works in this domain are the investigations of Hallström during the years 1909–43 (Fig. 9.2; Hallström 1932), and the listing and analysis of remains from eleven of Hallström's sites by Serning (1956). The character of Saami sacrificial places has been well described by Manker (1957), who documents over 500 sacrificial sites. In her thesis on Saami metal deposits, Zachrisson has analysed the sacrificial places in the light of a recently discovered sacrificial site in southern Lapland (Zachrisson 1984). Layers of bones, antlers and other sacrificial gifts have been found on several of these sites. Among the artefacts found there are buckles, rings, chains, spirals, pendants,

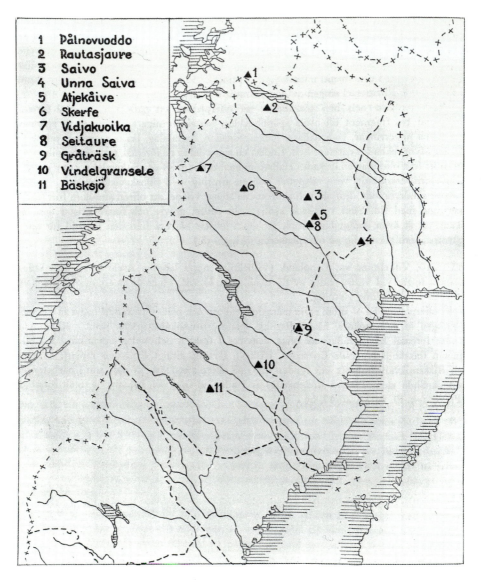

1 Pålnovuoddo
2 Rautasjaure
3 Saivo
4 Unna Saiva
5 Atjekåive
6 Skerfe
7 Vidjakuoika
8 Seitaure
9 Gråträsk
10 Vindelgransele
11 Bäsksjö

Figure 9.1 Saami places of sacrifice, with finds from the Iron Age and Middle Ages in northern Sweden. From Serning 1956.

beads, mountings and clasps of different metal materials, simple sheet-metal pendants, arrow-points made of iron and about 600 silver coins (Serning 1956; Zachrisson 1984). Most of the artefacts found at the sacrificial places originate from either western or eastern Europe, but there are also objects of native Saami manufacture. Those objects can be dated to late iron age or early Nordic medieval time. According to Zachrisson (1984, pp. 68ff.) they can be dated to the period between the eighth and the middle of the fourteenth century AD.

One of the characteristic features of such sacrificial places is their location on outstanding formations in the landscape, implying that the choice of location was primarily governed by topographical conditions. As a rule, sacrificial places are naturally demarcated from the surrounding landscape. Of all the holy places known today, the majority are found on or close to hills or mountains, on islets or places in lakes (so-called Saivo-lakes), close to rapids or waterfalls or on meadows or heaths (Manker 1957, p. 23). In some cases a whole mountain could be regarded as holy, but most of the sacrificial cere-monies were practised at places where there were either existing sacrificial stones or transported stones or wooden idols. Many of these sacrificial places are naturally shaped stones, rocks or caves, but there are also constructed sacrificial places in the shape of rings (Vorren 1985, pp. 69ff.). Historical documents also mention sacrificial ledges, built up from organic material.

In the Saami pre-Christian conception of the world every significant moun-tain, lake or stream would have holy places and sacrificial places. These places were considered to be animated by spiritual beings or divine forces. Natural forces such as sun, thunder and wind were personified as divine images; disease and death were spiritual beings, and livelihoods such as hunting, fishing and reindeer-herding had their own protective gods or spirits (Manker 1957, p. 11).

Information on the spatial distribution of sacrificial places can be recon-structed from investigations and historical sources, and with the help of place-names and information from the Saami people of today. Common place-names that indicate holy places and sacrificial places are names which include one of the following words: *seite*, *passe*, *ailes*, *vidja*, *vero*, *sjiela*, *tjekku*, *halte*, *saivo*, *akka* or *attje* (Manker 1957, pp. 13ff.).

The sacrificial stones, or *seite*-stones (Fig. 9.3) as the Saami call them, generally consist of amphibolite, and are naturally ground and shaped through erosion by water, ice and wind. At many places there have been found *seite*-stones personifying the god, or the so-called *halte*, of animals, fish and birds, as well as wooden idols with human-like features. At most of the find-sites these objects are found in groups. The majority of them represent animals or birds, but a few resemble human beings. As a rule they are rather small and easily transportable, but there are also larger ones.

The function of sacrificial places in Saami society

In Saami trapping culture, and later in their intensive reindeer nomadism, the main sources of livelihood were land and water. The Saami attitude to the

Figure 9.2 Sacrificial place on a cliff ledge beneath Vidjavare mountain, excavated by Gustaf Hallström in 1909, at Lake Rautasjaure in Kiruna Commune, northern Sweden. Hallström found a rich cultural layer dating to AD 800–1000, including sacrificial animals (mainly reindeer) and more than 500 sacrificial objects (including coins, jewellery and a horn hammer).

Figure 9.3 A *seite*-stone from a sacred site near Lake Stora, Lulejaure, northern Sweden.

environment was reflected in the ideology of the entire Saami society. Everything was regarded as living, as a part of the cosmos. Through tradition handed from generation to generation the people developed a strong bond with their territory.

The relation to the surroundings was a determining factor for the continued existence of Saami society. Each local community, or *siida*, consisted of a limited number of families, together making use of a limited territory for living, hunting and fishing. The *siida*-systems were geographically demarcated units, with naturally defined or otherwise declared borders. Those borders were often the subject of disputes and discussions between representatives of different *siidas*. It was not unusual that two or more *siidas* had at their disposal common land for hunting and fishing. Hunting-pit systems and other trapping constructions may have been utilized by two or more *siidas*. Between groups of fishing Saamis there may have been collective ownership of fishing-waters and fishing-tools such as seine nets.

Economies based on hunting, fishing and reindeer-herding are dependent on prevailing natural conditions, and therefore they must be based on a stable relation between humans and nature. A necessary prerequisite for survival was knowledge about the distribution of the natural resources within the territory, and knowledge about the best way to take care of those resources. From such knowledge strategies were devised for the group to make use of the territory, by the development of appropriate technology and social structures. Holy mountains, and places where different ceremonies were held, constituted important parts of this social structure. These ceremonies varied according to different social groups. Many of the sacrificial places close by the winter-villages were used by the whole community (Tornaeus 1900), and other places were used by hunting and fishing groups, reindeer-herders and by family groups. But there were also ceremonies which were held inside the houses and which were carried out in honour of the female goddesses: Juksakka, Sarakka and Uksakka.

According to Johansen the functions of sacrificial acts can be divided into three (Johansen 1980, pp. 101ff.). In the first, comprising gifts to the gods, there is a relation between giver and receiver wherein the receiver expects the gift, and the giver expects something in return. The second, comprising collective sacrificial ceremonies, includes holy sacrificial repasts, where some animal, identified with the divinity, would be slaughtered and eaten according to fixed rituals. Johansen (1980) claims that such meals rendered strength as well as fellowship. In the third, comprising propitiatory sacrifice, the tribute was paid to conciliate a divinity when some sin had been committed, or in order to facilitate some imminent activity.

It is probable that most sacrificial ceremonies involved more than one of these functions. At those sacrificial places where the remains of slaughtered reindeer have been found it is likely that the sacrificial act has been followed by a ritual sacrificial repast. Some ceremonial repasts, such as that held in connection with bear-grave rituals, do not necessarily involve animal sacrifice (Bäckman 1981).

The Saami habitation pattern and the utilization of resources vary between coast, mountain, tundra and forest, depending on the conditions provided by the surrounding environment. Two main categories are discernible in northern Sweden: the mountain Saami and the forest Saami. The habitation pattern and resource utilization of the mountain Saami extended over *siida* territories including areas from the alpine zone in the west to the woodland in the east. During summer and autumn these people hunted wild reindeer in the mountains and then moved eastwards for the winter to their dwelling-places by the fishing-lakes in the woodland. The forest Saami, on the other hand, made use of a more restricted area along one of the major watercourses in the woodland.

The spatial distribution of sacrificial places can shed light on Saami social structure during prehistoric times within the *siida* territories of the mountain Saami and the forest Saami. The sacrificial places of the woodland are in most cases richer in finds than those in the mountains, and they also contain a greater number of find categories.

An example of a sacrificial place in the mountains, with few find categories, is Vidjakuoika, in the parish of Jokkmokk, Lapland. This sacrificial place is situated in waterlogged terrain near one of the rapids of the river Vuojatätno. The site consists of about forty *seite*-stones, a thick layer of bone and horn, some arrowheads and some bronze sheets (Serning 1956, p. 134). The bones collected during Hallström's investigation in 1909 proved to be bones from reindeer. The fact that all marrowbones were split confirms, according to Hallström, the stories told by his Saami informants about ancient sacrificial repasts in this location. He was told by Saami Nils Kuoljok of the Sirkas *siida* that major sacrificial repasts were held in his grandfather's day (Manker 1957, p. 171). Close to this sacrificial place there are hut foundations as well as hunting-pits, and the sites mainly consist of groups of hut foundations. These have been dated primarily to late iron age/early Nordic medieval times (Mulk 1988, 1991). This location is still an important summer dwelling-site for reindeer-herding Saami within the Sirkas *siida*.

Characteristic features of this sacrificial place are the location close to a rapid, whose name includes the word *vidja* ('holy'), the great number of *seite*-stones, bone and horn, and arrowheads made of iron. At this site, hunters of wild reindeer may have sacrificed them as thanks for the luck of their chase, perhaps with a following ceremonial repast. Sacrifices may also have been made to give thanks for good luck in fishing, but the closeness to hunting sites and hunting-pits, as well as the sacrificed arrowheads, makes it most plausible that the ceremonies were held in connection with wild reindeer-hunting.

The sacrificial place of Saivo, in the parish of Gällivare, Lapland, is situated in woodland on an islet in a small lake of the same name. At this site there was a more differentiated set of finds, as well as a great number of *seite*-stones. Furthermore, bone, reindeer antler, fish and birds were found, and also different kinds of metal objects such as arrowheads, knives, ornaments, chains, beads, etc. It is possible that this location was the main sacrificial place for a mountain-oriented *siida*, being located within their winter land. Another possibility – but less likely – is that the place belonged to a forest-oriented *siida*.

The large sacrificial places at the winter dwelling-sites, *dalvadis*, like the one described above in Saivo, were probably used by the whole population; such sites, and their ceremonies, may have been symbols of cultural affinity, strengthening the ties between the families in the *siida*.

Many such sacrificial places have been in use over a considerable period. The sacrificial places have been dated by the metal finds, which are restricted to a few hundred years, but although these sacrificed metal objects originate from a period limited in time, sacrificial slaughtering may have been executed earlier as well as later in time. It is probable that sacrificial places with *seite*-stones have been used continuously since the early Iron Age, but this is difficult to prove.

In northern Sweden, by Lake Seitaure, there is a sacrificial place where fragments of asbestos, pottery, bronze sheets, a glass bead and a small piece of quartz have been found (Serning 1956, p. 135). A comparison between archaeological investigations concerning Saami bear-graves, and written sources concerning bear-hunting and bear-grave ceremonies, shows that written sources accord well with archaeological findings. It is noteworthy that datings from a bear-grave by Lake Karats, in the parish of Jokkmokk, indicate that this grave was made during the ninth or the tenth century, thus demonstrating that the Saami have buried bears in a similar way from the late Iron Age until historical times (Iregren & Mulk 1988). Consequently, there is reason to assume that the Saami conception of the world has included similar means of expression over a considerable space of time.

The importance of sacrificial places for the Saami of today

The pre-Christian Saami religion survived until the seventeenth century, when the Swedish church intensified the mission among the Saami of northern Sweden. Saami shamans were subjected to severe persecution as their activities were considered to be expressions of total heathenism and barbarism. The shamans were forced to hand over their drums for destruction and burning, and they were urged to cease their activities. Even the slightest transgression led to the death penalty. The oppression and persecution exerted by the Swedish church led to the concealment of old rites and ceremonies, in fear of reprisals. Oppression was clearly displayed; anyone who was caught was punished, and as a consequence the Saami people went 'underground' with their activities. The Christian religion became official and the Saami religion became unofficial, but although a good many Saami officially became Christians this does not imply that all parts of the Saami conception of the world disappeared. It is important to note that even today sacrificial places and *seite*-stones carry a strong emotional significance. Furthermore, the knowledge of old Saami manners and customs have been passed down from generation to generation. Still to this very day there are Saami who have knowledge of old Saami popular beliefs, some of them practising as medicine-men. Many Saami are also familiar with the sacrificial places of their ancestors, that is to say they know who or what family or *siida* was using a certain sacrificial place.

Accordingly, many Saami today experience a strong historical and social anchoring to the cult places of their ancestors. They are taught how to conceal the existence of these places, so that they will remain unknown to the uninitiated and so that the *seite*-stones may stay where they belong. Thus, from a Saami point of view, there are no ambitions to submit the sacrificial places to investigations by archaeologists or any other scientists.

References

Bäckman, L. 1975. *Sájva: föreställningar om hjälp-och skyddsvasen i heliga fjäll bland samerna*. Stockholm Studies in Comparative Religion 13. Stockholm: University of Stockholm.

Bäckman, L. 1981. Commentary on: Fjellström, Pehr, Kort berättelse om lapparnas björnafänge samt deras wid brukade widskeppelser. *Norrländska Skrifter* 5, 43–59.

Fjellström, P. 1985. Sacrifices, burial gifts and buried treasures. In *Saami Pre-Christian Religion*, L. Bäckman & Å. Hultkrantz (eds), 43–60. Stockholm: University of Stockholm.

Fjellström, P. 1987. Cultural and traditional-ecological perspectives in Saami religion. In *Saami Religion*, E. T. Ahlbäck (ed.), 34–45. 'Abo, Finland: Donner Institute for Research in Religious and Cultural History.

Hallström, G. 1932. Lapska offerplatser. In *Arkeologiska Studier Tillägnade H. K. H. Kronprins Gustaf Adolf*, 111–32. Stockholm: Norstedt.

Hansen, L. I. 1990. *Samisk fangstsamfunn og norsk høvdingeøkonomi*. Oslo: Novus Forlag.

Iregren, E. & I.-M. Mulk 1988. Björngraven i Karats: arkeologisk-osteologisk rapport från en undersökning av en björngrav i Karats. Unpublished MS Ajtte svenskt fjäll- och samemuseum. Jokkmokk.

Johansen, Ø. 1980. Forhistorien, religionsforskningens grense. *Viking* 43, 96–106.

Manker, E. 1957. *Lapparnas heliga ställen: kultplatser och offerkult i belysning av Nordiska museets och landsantikvariernas fältundersökningar*. Acta Lapponica 13. Stockholm: Nordiska Museet.

Mulk, I.-M. 1988. Sirkas, ett fjällsamiskt fångstsamhälle i förändring 500–1500 e Kr. *Bebyggelsehistorisk Tidskrift* 14, 61–75.

Mulk, I.-M. 1991. Sirkas – a mountain Saami hunting society in transition, AD 500–1500. In *Readings in Saami History, Culture and Language II*, R. Kvist (ed.), 41–57. Umeå: Center for Arctic Cultural Research, Umeå University.

Odner, K. 1992. *The Varanger Saami. Habitation and economy AD 1200–1900*. Oslo: Scandinavian University Press.

Qvigstad, J. 1927. *Lappiske eventyr og sagn*. Oslo.

Serning, I. 1956. Lapska offerplatsfynd från järnålder ochmedeltid i de svenska lappmarkerna. Acta Lapponica 11. Stockholm: Nordiska Museet.

Solbakk, A. (ed.) 1990. *The Saami People*. Kautokeino: Saami Instituhtta.

Storli, I. 1991. *'Stallo'-boplassene. Et tolkningsforslag basert på undersøkelser i Lønsdalen, Saltfjellet*. Tromso: Institutt for Samfunnsvitenskap, Universitetet i Tromsø.

Storli, I., K.-A. Arronson, C. Carpelan, K. Odner, I.-M. Mulk & L. I. Hansen 1993. Discussions. Sami Viking age pastoralism – or 'The fur trade paradigm' reconsidered. *Norwegian Archaeological Review* 26, 1–48.

Tornaeus, J. 1900. Berättelse om Lapmarckerna och Deras Tilstånd. Utg. av K. B. Wiklund. *Svenska Landsmål* 7, 3.

Vorren, Ø. 1987. Sacrificial sites, types and function. In *Saami Religion*, E. T. Ahlbäck (ed.), 94–109. 'Abo, Finland: Donner Institute for Research in Religious and Cultural History.

Vorren, Ø. & E. Manker 1976. *Samekulturen: en kulturhistorisk oversikt*. Tromso: Universitetsvorlaget.

Zachrisson, I. 1984. *De samiska metalldepåerna år 1000–1350 i ljuset av fyndet från Mörtträsket, Lappland*. Archaeology and Environment 3. Umeå: Department of Archaeology, University of Umeå.

Zachrisson, I. 1985. New archaeological finds from the territories of the southern Saamis. In *Saami Pre-Christian Religion*, L. Bäckman & Å. Hultkrantz (eds), 83–100. Stockholm: University of Stockholm.

10 The Mijikenda kaya as a sacred site

H. W. MUTORO

Introduction

A sacred site is a place which is considered holy, and is partially or wholly reserved for magico-religious or ceremonial functions. Because of this it is venerated and revered and is kept free from contamination by sin and evil. Sacred sites vary in size from very small places covering a few square metres to large areas covering several hectares of land. They are usually characterized by the presence of artefacts, ecofacts and features that are unique to them; they may be in the open air, or in rockshelters, caves and forests. In many cases, sacred sites have frightening tales told about them, in order to scare off those who would want to destroy or defile them. In the archaeological record, sacred sites may initially be identifiable as burial sites, ceremonial sites or butchery sites. It is on the basis of such clues that other attributes that are typical of sacred sites can be identified, isolated and studied. It is against this background that this chapter discusses the Mijikenda kaya (pl. makaya) as a sacred site.

The Mijikenda

The Mijikenda are a Bantu-speaking people who inhabit the immediate Kenya coastal hinterland. They comprise nine closely related ethnic groups, hence the name Mijikenda (miji – 'towns or villages', kenda – 'nine'). The Mijikenda themselves call these nine villages or towns makaya chenda. Each of the nine towns bears the name of its founding ethnic group: Giriama, Rabai, Chonyi, Kauma, Kambe, Jibana, Ribe, Digo and Duruma. The Mijikenda are distributed over a wide territory of approximately 65 km broad stretching about 150 km from slightly north of latitude 3° south in the Jilore region in the north to latitude 4° 30′ south on the Kenya–Tanzania border. To the west, the Mijikenda have the nomadic Oromo, Kwavi pastoralists and Waata elephant-hunters as neighbours. The three latter groups live in the marginal environments of Taru Desert. To the east, the Mijikenda's neighbours are the

Waswahili, who live on the coastal plain and adjacent islands such as Lamu, Pate and Manda (see Abungu 1994).

The sacredness of the Mijikenda *kaya* can best be understood in the light of the Mijikenda traditional system of government. This was gerontocratic in character (Brantley 1978) and emphasized the age-set grades known as *rika* (pl. *marika*). The most senior age-set subgroup (*kambi*) in each of the nine ethnic groups contained the oldest men in their *rika*. The highest rank of the *kambi* was known as *mvaya* and was subdivided into three cults: *nchama*, *mondo* and *fisi*. The *nchama* cult consisted of elders who were still energetic and could perform menial and other tasks for the *mondo*, who were older than the *nchama*. The task of the *mondo* was to advise members of the *fisi* cult on day-to-day matters of the society. The *fisi* cult not only comprised the oldest members in the Mijikenda society but was also the most sacred cult in the society. Initiation to this cult was solemn and was preceded by a special type of dance known as *mung'aro*. The significance of the *fisi* ('hyena') cult to Mijikenda society is highlighted by Charles New (1873, p. 5), a pioneering Christian missionary in the region in the late nineteenth century. He observed that:

> The greatest funeral ceremony held by Wanika (Mijikenda) are those which they get upon the death of a hyena. They regard that animal with the most singular superstition. They look upon it as one of their ancestors or in the same way associated with their origin and destiny. The death of the hyena is the occasion for Universal morning. The *mahtanga* (wake) held over a chief is nothing compared to that of a hyena. One tribe only laments the former, but all tribes unite to give importance to the obsequies of the latter. . . . It is the *ada* (custom).

New apparently interprets the word *fisi* simply to mean the animal 'hyena', whereas *fisi* actually refers to the most sacred cult members of the Mijikenda society, whose death would almost bring the entire society to a standstill.

The *kambi*, as a body, wielded considerable power. They arbitrated in community disputes, punished offenders, instituted laws and ensured that they were obeyed. They were seen by the public as the only people who had the ability to appease and be listened to by the departed spirits (*korma*) of their ancestors. The *kambi* wore a special dress called *kitambi*, which was held to the waist by a red belt, and they walked with a pronged staff, *mtsatsa*, as a symbol of their office. In general all the *kambi* members were allowed to sit at the *moro* where the sacred objects that signified their office were stored. These objects included wonderful relics of the past, such as victory trophies, magic horns, instruments and drums.

The *kaya*

The *kambi* carried out their secular and religious functions inside their sacred settlements, known as *kaya* (Fig. 10.1). The *kaya* is unique to the Mijikenda people, and as such remains a symbol of their identity, defined by the presence of the ritual symbol, the *fingo* (Mutoro 1985), a complete pottery vessel filled with medicines and magic charms to protect the *kaya* and its occupants from evil spirits and enemies. The Mijikenda built their *kaya* in the heart of dense forests. This means that every *kaya* is a forest but not every forest on the Mijikenda ridge on the coastal hinterland is a *kaya*. Dry-stone walling on the *kaya* was restricted to the entrances and gates, where wall enclosures (about 1 metre in thickness and 3 metres in height) were built, each wall supporting a wooden door-frame and shutter. The number of gates on each *kaya* entrance varied from two to four, depending on the degree of its significance. The entrances and exits to the *kaya* were arranged in an east–west or north–south orientation. At each entrance and exit was buried a *fingo*, the size of which similarly varied from *kaya* to *kaya*, depending on its size and significance. The small *kaya* settlements covered 5 to 8 hectares of land while large or principal ones covered 20 to 30 hectares (Mutoro 1987). At the centre of each *kaya* was the *moro*, a large dome-shaped house built between a fig tree (*mugandi*) and a baobab tree (*muyu*), which was the meeting-place for the *kambi*. The *moro* was looked upon with great awe by the people because only the initiated were allowed to come near it. Inside it were kept insignia of office, important relics of former days, trophies of victories won in the past, magic horns, drums and other instruments. The most dreaded of these drums were the *muanzia*, of which there were two, one belonging to the men and the other to the women. The *muanzia* were played only on special occasions, at night, in order to have maximum impact on the people.

The sacredness of the *kaya* can be explained in terms of the various functions that it performed: it was a residential, political, burial and religious centre. The residential part of the *kaya*, known as the *boma*, housed all the clans of the respective Mijikenda ethnic groups, both the ordinary citizens and the *kambi*. It is here too that they were buried after they died, and the graves of the more important members of the society can be identified by their grave-posts, *vikango*, or by the sizes and approximate ages of the trees that mark the original positions of the graves. While the *vikango* for ordinary people consisted of undecorated, termite-resistant posts stuck at the head of the grave, those of the *kambi* or *fisi* were grotesquely carved human-like life-size posts, whose image is said to resemble that of the deceased. Because it is the resting-place of the *korma* (departed spirits), the *boma* within the *kaya* is sacred and prohibited to youths in general, and foreigners or strangers in particular, as their entry would disturb the prevailing peace. The trees within the *kaya* forest are similarly sacred because they represent the grave sites of some of the founding fathers of the society. The sacredness of the *boma* is also confirmed by the presence of whole and fractured animal bone remains. The meat on these

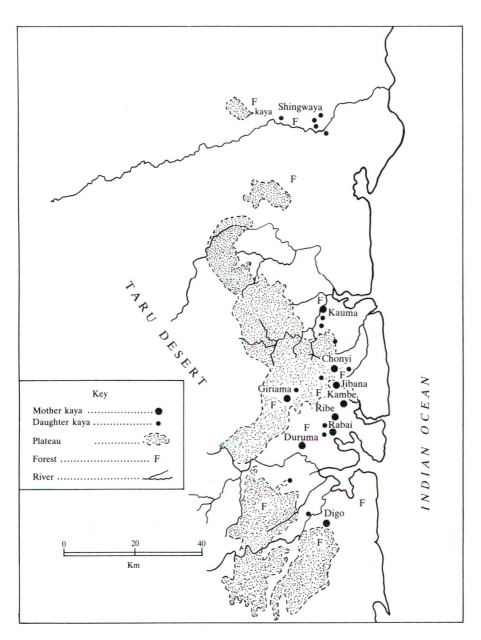

Figure 10.1 Distribution of *kaya* settlements.

bones was eaten as part of the offering to the dead. In addition to animal bone remains, calabashes of coconut shell have been found, placed at the head of the graves or at the base of the tree stems. These are frequently filled with palm-wine during ceremonies to give thanks or appease the dead. The potsherds found in the *boma* are elaborately decorated in various motifs, which is in sharp contrast to the plain pottery that is found outside the *kaya* (Mutoro 1988). Finally, the large tree stems in the settlement are frequently decorated with bands of red, white and green cloth. While the significance of the colours need further investigation, it is evident that the ceremonialism that goes with them supports the sacred character of the site (and see Abungu 1994; Ovsyannikov & Terebikhin 1994).

The most sacred part of the *kaya* is the *moro*, whose sacredness, as pointed out above, lies in the fact that within it are stored all the secrets of the society. It was here that different ceremonies were performed by the *kambi*. New (1873) described an initiation ceremony he witnessed at the *moro*:

> [T]he candidate to be admitted into the order I found . . . behind a screen of plaited palm leaves, stretched at full length upon the ground. He lay stone still, as if dead. Over his head had been spread a covering of soft mud an inch thick, looking like a close fitting cap, and he was lying in a manner I have described till the mud should be baked and hardened in the sun. But this was only a foundation of further ornamentation. By the man's side I observed a basket of red clay, a quantity of grey wool, which had been shorn from some-body's head. These materials I was told would be mixed together in a stiff mortar and then spread over the entire man's head and face. Horns were to be mounted over his eye, one upon the middle of the forehead and two others at the back of the head. The ears were to be filled and nostrils plugged with clay. . . . Everything was to be done to make him look as hideous in appearance as possible. . . . When this 'get up' is finished, the man is turned to the woods and is allowed to do as he pleases. He prowls around like a demon, making frightful noises and is the terror of the country. He is to kill someone before the ceremony is over.
>
> (New 1873, pp. 108–9)

Initiation ceremonies such as this one were always carried out in the *moro*. Associated with this ceremony was the *muanzia* dance, which was performed while beating the *muanzia* drum. According to New, the vibrations of the *muanzia*, which was 'nicely carved and painted', produced the most hideous sounds imaginable: 'sometimes [the vibrations] resemble the roaring of distant thunder, now the roaring of a lion, and now what can be imagined to be the mourning of some demon in agony' (New 1873, p. 113).

The *moro* area was not only used for performing initiation ceremonies but also for religious functions, such as the exorcism of evil spirits from sick people living in the area. In the process of healing the sick and exorcising evil spirits from the possessed, the *kambi* elders used beads to attract the spirits; a staff, painted black, was decorated with white and blue beads and a red feather before being stuck into the ground, in order to attract the evil spirits and thus make them abandon the sick person. One such healing exercise was observed by John Ludwig Krapf (1860, p. 189):

> We came upon a band of Wanika who informed us that they were bent on expelling an evil spirit from a sick person. In the centre of the throng stood a wooden mortar filled with water. Near the mortar stuck into the ground was a staff, which they call *moro*: about three feet long and of the thickness of a man's finger, painted black and ornamented with white and blue glass beads and that his attention becomes gradually drawn to them until he finally forsakes the sick person and fastens on the beads.

In addition to serving as a centre for healing and exorcising evil spirits, the *moro* was also used as a centre for performing fertility rites, and for praying for rain during long droughts, for food during famine and for peace or victory during war.

Conclusion

This chapter has focused on the *kaya* as a sacred site, and demonstrated that it was the centre for political, magico–religious and ceremonial functions. Over time the *kaya* has, in some respects, become less central to the Mijikenda people:

> By the end of the 19th century Mijikenda society had been radically altered through the attrition of some characteristics, the redefini- tion of others, and the introduction of new elements. Kaya and clan were no longer the significant corporate groups, while sub-clan and lineage became more important. . . . Political power was no longer solely a function of age and esoteric knowledge, as younger men gained control over people through economic success.
>
> (Spear 1978, p. 126)

However, although uninhabited today, the *kaya* as a sacred place has not been abandoned altogether, and this area is still looked upon with reverence and fear. It remains the resting-place of the founding fathers of the Mijikenda society, and Mijikenda elders still wish to be buried in the *kaya*. They also continue to retreat there for several weeks at a time, to perform rites and make offerings to their ancestors as they pray for rain, or give thanks for a good harvest. The concept of sacredness persists, and today, as in the past, the *kaya* is administered with very rigid rules. For example, visitors have to leave their shoes at the gate and dress in the Mijikenda traditional robes before they can enter the settlement. Entry into, and movement within, the *kaya* is followed by incantations stressing that none of the visitors has any bad intentions, and by prayers requesting that they should come out of it safely.

As in the past, only the very elderly members can go near the *moro*, the most sacred part of the *kaya*, and even they are unsure about their cleanliness of spirit as they approach, and solemnly pray that they are not struck dead while standing at the *moro*. Because of this fear, an outsider hoping to see a *moro* may well be disappointed, and a visit to the *kaya* may end without the elders going towards it, or even looking in its direction.

Beyond the *moro* is the *boma*, which used to serve both residential and funerary functions. As in the past, the Mijikenda people still bury their dead in the courtyard not far from the doorsteps. What used to be a *boma* is today filled with *vikango* (grave-posts) of the ancestors of the Mijikenda people. This area is similarly venerated and visitors are forbidden to come close, as their movements would disturb the dead. Trees in the *kaya* are similarly still considered to be sacred because they represent the grave sites of the ancestors of Mijikenda society, and may not, as a rule, be cut down.

Finally, today, as in the past, the *kaya* remains not only the symbol of identity for Mijikenda society but also the sacred centre at which magico-religious and ceremonial functions are performed. It remains the focus of Mijikenda culture, and is held in high regard not only by the old but also by the young, who are aware that the *kaya* is the nerve-centre of their culture, now and in the future. It is partly as a result of this continuing role of the *kaya* as the sacred centre of Mijikenda society that the government intends to protect and gazette *makaya* as national monuments.

Acknowledgements

This chapter is based on field research carried out under the auspices of the Urban Origins in Eastern Africa project, sponsored by SAREC. I wish to express my sincere thanks to SAREC for their generous and continued support for the project.

References

Abungu, G. H. O. 1994. Islam on the Kenyan coast: an overview of Kenyan coastal sacred sites. In *Sacred Sites, Sacred Places*, D. L. Carmichael, J. Hubert, B. Reeves & A. Schanche (eds), 152–62. London: Routledge.

Brantley, C. 1978. Gerontocratic government: age-sets in precolonial Giriama. *Africa* 48, 248–64.

Krapf, J. L. 1860. *Travels, Researches and Missionary Labours during an Eighteen Years Residence in Eastern Africa*. London: Trubner & Co.

Mutoro, H. W. 1985. The spatial distribution of the Mijikenda *kaya* settlements on the hinterland Kenya coast. *Transafrican Journal of History* 14, 78–100.

Mutoro, H. W. 1987. An archaeological study of the Mijikenda *kaya* settlements on hinterland Kenya coast. Unpublished Ph.D. thesis. Ann Arbor University, Michigan: Bell & Howel Information Co.

Mutoro, H. W. 1988. A nearest neighbour analysis of the Mijikenda *makaya* on the Kenya coastal hinterland. *Kenya Journal of Sciences* 1, 6–17.

New, C. 1873. *Life, Wanderings and Labours in Eastern Africa.* London: Hodder & Stoughton. (3rd edition: 1971. London: Frank Cass & Co. Ltd.)

Ovsyannikov, O. V. & N. M. Terebikhin 1994. Sacred space in the culture of the Arctic regions. In *Sacred Sites, Sacred Places*, D. L. Carmichael, J. Hubert, B. Reeves & A. Schanche (eds), 44–81. London: Routledge.

Spear, T. T. 1978. *The Kaya Complex: a history of the Mijikenda peoples of the Kenya coast to 1900.* Nairobi: Kenya Literature Bureau.

11 The perception and treatment of prehistoric and contemporary sacred places and sites in Poland

KATARZYNA MARCINIAK

For most people in Poland their tradition and history is based on more than 1,000 years of the Polish state and of Christianity. As far as social consciousness and identification is concerned, Poland's past can be divided into two periods: prehistoric and historic times (Christianity). The way people identify with their national heritage differs according to the period, and each period is responsible for different kinds of tradition and social identification. The prehistoric period left many kinds of objects and places which may be treated or interpreted as sacred. In the historic period, sacred places functioned as centres of great importance, with which a given group could identify its religious, traditional and cultural roots.

Poland lacks any tribal communities. There is no direct cultural identification between modern communities and prehistoric groups, and no ancient ritual places with which any contemporary community can identify itself in terms of cultural links and common ancestors or roots. Cultural identification does exist with historic sacred places, however, and this is expressed in different ways by the Roman Catholics and by the religions of the national minorities in Poland. This tradition of cultural identification created one of the most important, characteristic and unique forms of the Roman Catholic church.

It is suggested that the variations in the perception and treatment of so-called sacred places and sites in Poland, whether prehistoric or historic, depend on the roles that they play and fulfil in contemporary society.

Prehistoric sacred places and sites

As far as Polish prehistory is concerned, from the first traces of human groups until the Slav period, it is extremely difficult to establish distinct criteria which allow classification of a given place as a sacred site. My concern here is not how many sites and places existed in a particular prehistoric period, but the way in which they are treated today. The basis for such a classification is usually the lack of any traces of permanent habitation, or the presence of a special kind of artefact, for example a cluster of hearths, objects of unusual shape, content, etc. Some of the most typical prehistoric cult places are sacred groves and some lakes, streams, marshes and other natural features. On the basis of previous research (Bender 1972) it appears that cult places in central European communities were situated mainly in the open, which is why the objects are difficult to distinguish archaeologically, leading in turn to difficulties in interpretation.

Because of their unusual character, exploration of places regarded as sacred sites attracts relatively greater interest among archaeologists, and such work is more likely to get published in the press or popular scientific journals. Otalazka, near Warsaw, is an example of such a site which raised considerable interest about twenty years ago. It is a typical marsh site dated to the end of the Roman/Iron Age (fourth to sixth century AD), with unique finds consisting of a conical stone circle 6 metres in diameter with animal bones within it, which is interpreted as a kind of altar; and a so-called oval-shaped grill where, over a surface of approximately 10 square metres, pillars and thin vertical and transverse beams were driven into the ground. Within this construction a huge quantity of pottery and animal bones was found, and there were also places in which sacrificial pots had been deposited. Otherwise, this site has the typical characteristics of a marsh site (Bender 1972). The only basis and criterion for classifying this place as a sacred site was the 'unusual' character of its finds. The modern perception of the site's characteristics as 'uncommon' meant that, from the very beginning, it was the subject of numerous articles in newspapers and archaeological journals.

Such spectacular events do not happen very often in Polish archaeology. It may be assumed that cemeteries and certain objects from settlements, some types of pottery, amulets, clay figurines, treasures, etc. would also have had sacred meaning for a given community. However, objects which are likely to have been connected with ritual activities in prehistoric times – unless judged to have exceptional aesthetic value – are not treated by archaeologists any differently from secular objects.

There are also places in Poland which have attained an accepted place in social consciousness today because of their aesthetic and landscape values, as well as their atmosphere of mystery. Complexes of peaks in Lower Silesia are examples of this type of place, their features preventing them from being classed with ordinary settlement areas. Peaks such as Sleza and Lysa Góra, are well known in Poland, and information about them exists in almost every tourist guide; they have become very important tourist centres. It should be stressed in this context that archaeological monuments are not commonly a focus for tourism in Poland.

Stone circles have been found surrounding the four peaks of the Sleza Massif – Sleza, Radunia, Wiezyca and Lysa Góra. Excavations have shown that they are not part of a fortified system, and thus the peaks had no strategic significance. In addition, sources of drinking water are outside these circles, which

Figure 11.1 Stone carving of a she-bear from Sleza.

demonstrates that they were not hill-forts. On Sleza, which is regarded as a major cult centre, there were two circles: one, which surrounded the peak, was constructed with stones of different sizes, joined without any kind of mortar; the other circle, half-way up the mountain, is crescent-shaped, with a circumference of *c.* 400 metres. In addition to these circles there are monumental stone sculptures, including two she-bears (Fig. 11.1), a man with a fish, a 'monk' and a mushroom. All of these, which are very well known in Poland, are marked with an 'X' sign, a feature which has fascinated archaeologists, and which has been taken to be a sign of Celtic significance. The date of these objects is not clear; they were probably used by people of the Lusatian culture or by Celts, and this Sleza area may have been a centre of importance in both of these periods (Cehak-Holubowiczowa 1959; Gediga 1979). The Sleza complex undoubtedly functioned in the Middle Ages, and a German chronicler wrote about Sleza: 'Because of its quality and size, when the accursed pagan cult was kept, Sleza was treated with great adoration by the people' (Gierlach 1980, p. 110). One must remember that this was written at a time when Christianity was a strong influence in Poland. Today, the special treatment given to the stone circles, and their wide reputation as tourist attractions, is not because of their special 'sacred' character, but rather because both circles and stone monuments are spectacular.

Thus it can be seen that, although prehistoric sites may be significant in contemporary social consciousness, this is not because the sites have religious or sacred significance in the present. They are important either because of the nature of the artefacts found on them, which indicate a special significance to the people who placed them there in the distant past, or the sites are, in themselves, so spectacular that their impact is, in a sense, inescapable to living populations, even if their original significance is unknown.

Contemporary sacred places and sites

Within contemporary Poland, therefore, the places that function, both cognitively and empirically, as sacred sites, are those that have been created within the Christian period. This does not mean that all the sites are Christian sites. The current claim that contemporary Poland is a mono-religious country is not true. Inside its borders coexist not only different kinds of Christian religions but also other religions, such as Islam and Buddhism, which have emerged in different cultural contexts. Within each particular tradition there are different places of special importance, not only because of differences in religion but also as a result of history, tradition and culture.

It is not easy to construct a useful classification of sacred places which takes into account all the different religious traditions that exist in Poland today. One of the largest categories of sacred places consists of places with pictures and/or sculptures which are regarded by the church authorities as holy and miraculous. Another group consists of places where religious revelations have taken place, and another consists of places where supernatural phenomena have occurred, e.g. crying pictures in Lublin and Wyszków (in 1949) and bleeding crosses in Slupsk (in 1980), Olecko (in 1981) and Rudnicki (in 1991).

Sacred places in contemporary Poland are normally perceived mainly through their religious, magical, historical-cognitive, and political functions. Generally, at least two such functions coexist at the same place. Among the most frequently cited examples are the sanctuaries of the Holy Virgin, which are very numerous in Poland and are still increasing in number. Religious communities usually gather around their parish churches, which are under the care of priests, Orthodox priests, mullahs, monks, etc. Their main task is to strengthen the faith of their congregation, and one of their very characteristic ways of doing so is to organize pilgrimages to sacred places in different parts of the country.

The religious functions of sites are undoubtedly the most important in contemporary Poland, but the manner in which they influence the congregation is changing over time. Pilgrims are influenced by a series of stimuli of various human senses: eyesight, hearing and smell. The most extreme example comes from the Lichen Sanctuary of the Holy Virgin, a relatively new sanctuary created about 100 years ago, in a period which can be described as a time of glory and magnificence. On the few hectares which belong to the parish of the Marian order (*ksieza Marianie*), which has been taking care of this sanctuary since 1949, many chapels (Fig. 11.2), grottoes (Fig. 11.3), altars, etc. have been built in order to commemorate different episodes from the Old and New

Testament, the history of the Catholic church in Poland, and the history of Poland, including the political events of modern Poland (Makulski 1984). In spite of the fact that these references are so blatant, the sanctuary is socially perceived as an exclusively religious sanctuary, without political or historical significance.

Despite the long history and rich liturgical tradition of the Polish Catholic church, new elements are continually being introduced. For example, in Górka Duchowna, Good Friday mystery plays (Fig. 11.4) began to be enacted two years ago.

The Holy Virgin sanctuaries in Poland, apart from their religious functions, fulfilled, and still fulfil, crucial political functions. The biggest Polish sanctuary, the Jasna Góra Sanctuary of the Holy Virgin in Czestochowa, is also the best known, outside as well as inside Poland. It is not only the most important religious place in Poland but also a centre of Polish culture and tradition. There are many monographs concerning Czestochowa which show the importance and significance of this place for Polish culture. This sanctuary came to special prominence in the last decade, when the Pauline monks, who are responsible for it, protected and helped people who were being persecuted because of their political convictions, and also their families. Masses were celebrated for the country during which people prayed for the liberation of Poland from the rule of communism. All Poles, especially practising Christians, were supposed to make a pilgrimage to Czestochowa in order to demonstrate not only their godliness but also their political attitude. It was a relatively easy task to distinguish ordinary 'religious' pilgrims from 'political' ones. The latter usually had a rheostat attached to their lapels or sweaters, which was the symbol of resistance against communism, the sign of 'Solidarity' or 'Fighting Poland'. Such people also assumed a very characteristic position, kneeling on both knees with their hands crossed on their chests (a sign of deeper religious initiation than the ordinary joining of the palms in prayer), and having their heads bent submissively onto their chests.

Another sacred site which has political significance is the Sanctuary of the Holy Virgin in Stoczek in the Warmia region. This sanctuary is famous not only because of its holy picture (which is a copy of a picture of the Holy Virgin of the Snows from Rome) but because it is the place where the Cardinal Stefan Wyszynski, the Primate of Poland, was imprisoned in the 1950s.

An important place of pilgrimage is the Church of St Stanislaw Kostka in Warsaw, where priest Jerzy Popieluszko preached and where he is now buried. Father Popieluszko was brutally murdered by the Polish intelligence service and is regarded as a symbol of Poland's fight for freedom and independence.

The St Anna Mountain Sanctuary in Silesia is completely different in character. It is the place of pilgrimage for people of German origin, and as such is the place where the German minority manifests its separate character. Official post-war propaganda proclaimed that Poland is a homogeneous country without national minorities; thus the Germans living in Silesia were treated as Silesian citizens (*Slazacy*), and the St Anna Mountain Sanctuary is

Figure 11.2 Chapel of Revelation of the Holy Virgin at Lichen. In the centre of the chapel there is a stone with the footprints of the Holy Virgin.

Figure 11.4 A scene from the Good Friday mystery play at Górka Duchowna, commemorating the death of Jesus Christ.

the central pillar of their religion and culture. Germans from all parts of Poland meet at the sanctuary, and celebrate masses in their own language. This place has a very important impact on the integration of the German minority in Poland.

Other minorities living in Poland – Ukrainians, Byelorussians and Lithuanians – also have their own sacred places. Thus, the Sanctuary of the Holy Virgin from the Holy Mountain of Grabarka near Bialystok is the centre of the Orthodox church in Poland (Fig. 11.5). There has been an Orthodox church there since the seventeenth century (until it was burnt down in the summer of 1990) with a very famous icon of Spas Izbownik from the twelfth century. A dynamic movement has emerged, concentrated around the sanctuary, in order to defend their own, mainly Byelorussian, culture. The core of this movement consists of young people who, through religious practices,

Figure 11.5   Grabarka – expiation crosses in the ground and on a tree.

Figure 11.6   An old Muslim cemetery at Kruszyniany.

want to learn the roots of their own culture and to make Polish opinion aware
that Poland is not a nationally and religiously homogeneous country, and that
the stereotype of the 'Polish Catholic' is false (Madra 1982; Mironowicz 1983).

Even now, many sacred places are categorized as magical, the most famous
being those where one can recover lost health. In order to do this, many ritual
activities have to be performed, e.g. a person has to walk on a pilgrimage from
her/his home to a sacred place of this kind, taking water from the springs and
streams which usually flow near such a site, and which are regarded as having
curative powers. For example, in Grabarka there is the holy well from which a
single gulp of water guarantees good health for the following year. There is
also a small stream near the sanctuary which, it is believed, will cure all
diseases. During this ritual, the hands or face are washed with the water and
then must be wiped very carefully on a towel or rag, which is then left as the
locus of diseases near the stream. That is why, during the annual church fairs,
so many different kinds of towels, rags and scarves are left in the vicinity of the
stream.

Almost all places considered sacred in the sense defined above are also
commonly regarded as tourist attractions, especially for people whose
religions are different from those whose sacred place it is. The most
popular tourist places, because of custom and architecture, are those most
different from Polish culture, e.g. Kruszyniany (near Bialystok), the centre of
Islam in Poland, where there are eighteenth-century mosques and cemeteries

(Fig. 11.6) (Borzyszkowski 1977; Datko 1983), Grabarka and Wojnowo (Fig. 11.7) in the Warmia region (a village settled by members of the old Orthodox Slav church (*starocerkiewnostowianski*)).

The best time to visit Grabarka is on 18–19 August when the traditional annual church fair takes place (Fig. 11.8). At that time, the Heads of the Orthodox church from Poland, Byelorussia and Russia congregate there, wearing very beautiful, rich and unusual canonicals, together with several thousand Orthodox believers of many nationalities, wearing their national costumes. The behaviour of many tourists is the same as elsewhere. Some people discreetly observe the mystery play which takes place all around, mixing imperceptibly with the crowd, while other tourists behave ostenta-

Figure 11.7 The old Orthodox Slav church at Wojnowo.

Figure 11.8   The annual Orthodox church fair at Grabarka.

tiously, loudly and noisily, and take pictures against a background of
Orthodox priests, crosses and coloured wagons.

Generally speaking, conflict between members of different religions does
not exist in Poland. The desecration of sacred sites which sometimes occurs is
typically criminal in origin, and not directed against any particular religious
group, e.g. the theft of a silver sarcophagus of St Wojciech from Gniezno
Cathedral, the theft of an icon from the burnt Orthodox church at Grabarka,
or the theft of icons from Uniate Orthodox churches in the Bieszczady
mountains, in southeast Poland. Only the actions of Nazis and Stalinists in
the past were directed at destroying the heritage of a particular national or
religious group. For example, during the Second World War, the Jewish
synagogue in Poznań was converted into the town's swimming-pool, and
only now is action under way to return this synagogue to its traditional
owners. Also, as a result of the mass displacement in the 1940s of people of
Ukrainian descent, many Orthodox churches in the Bieszczady mountains
were left without any kind of care, falling into disrepair and having objects
stolen from them.

Although they are important to the community, it is clear that, in general,
churches and other sacred places are insufficiently guarded and protected. The
church authorities have direct responsibility for the protection of their
churches, and they are also responsible for all repairs and preservation.
However, all repairs of those buildings which were built before 1939 have to
be carried out under the control of the Vojvodeship Conservator of Art which,

in the last few years, because of the deep economic crisis, has been unable to give religious communities very much help. For this reason the churches are now supposed to become self-supporting.

Conclusion

It has been shown that those places in contemporary Poland that are perceived as sacred, although they may have some historical and political significance, are most important to contemporary believers because of their religious and magical functions. In contrast, prehistoric sites do not have any contemporary function. They may be perceived as having had sacred significance in the past but because people of today have no direct cultural identification with pre-historic groups, these ancient sacred places are perceived almost exclusively as monuments of the past.

References

Bender, W. 1972. Osrodek kultowy na Mogilanka. *Z Otchlani Wieków* 38, 118–33.

Borzyszkowski, M. 1977. Sanktuarium Maryjne w Gietrzwaldzie w okresie mi edzyw-ojennym (1921–1939). *Studia Warminskie* 14, 325–48.

Cehak-Holubowiczowa, H. 1959. Kamienne kregi kultowe na Raduni i Slezy. *Archeologia Polski* 3, 52–100.

Datko, A. 1983. Sanktuaria Maryjne w tradycji polskiej. *Tygodnik Polski* 2, 1–6.

Gediga, B. 1979. Zagadnienie religii. In *Prahistoria Ziem Polskich*, J. Dabrowski & Z. Rajewski (eds), 320–4. Wroclaw: Ossolineum.

Gierlach, B. 1980. *Sanktuaria slowianskie*. Warsaw: Iskry.

Madra, B. 1982. Grabarka. *Projekt* 2/3, 42–8.

Makulski, E. 1984. *Sanktuarium Maryjne w Licheniu*. Lichen: Ksieza Marianie Press.

Mironowicz, A. 1983. Grabarka. *Wiez* 26, 153–6.

Rudnicki, K. 1991. *Cuda i objawienia w Polsce w latach 1949–1986*, Warsaw: Panstwowe Wydawnictwo.

12   Islam on the Kenyan coast: an overview of Kenyan coastal sacred sites

GEORGE H. OKELLO ABUNGU

The Kenyan coast

In Kenya, a sacred site or sacred place is an area reserved for religious and ceremonial functions, it is an area set apart or dedicated (to a god/gods) for the use of the supernatural. It is an area that is seen to be consecrated, devoted and holy, not to be violated; it is above criticism by those who believe in it or its functions, which are religious, and so entitled to veneration (and see Mutoro 1994).

Along the Kenyan coast, with a few exceptions, sacred sites are not 'made' for such purposes, but are 'found'. They are either naturally or artificially created, and their functions and/or uses have changed through time. The sacred sites found along the Kenyan coast vary from small areas covering one or two square metres, to large ones of several hectares (Fig. 12.1). The most common types of sites found on the Kenyan coast are forests, caves, open-air sites, rock shelters, monumental tombs, abandoned and ruined mosques, and large trees (baobab and fig). These sites are mostly characterized by the presence of particular types of objects, such as rose-water bottles, incense-burners, broken pottery, coconut shell, pieces of cloth tied as flags, and other objects. In the case of the Kenyan coast, a combination of red, white and black coloured cloths are invariably used for these 'flags'.

In this area, all the sites seem to be associated with spirit worship and/or spirit possession (Caplan 1979). Their importance as magico-religious centres for those who believe in them is beyond doubt; some of the greatest magicians on the Kenyan coast (e.g. Kajiwe) claim to have received their magical powers from such places. Others have to visit and consult the spirits before they can apply their magical powers in the treatment of others.

As noted above, the sacred places are areas which have changed their function over time, such as abandoned mosques, tombs of great people (founders of lineages and clans) and large trees in desolate ruined settlements. Most of these places are ringed with the red, black and white 'flags'.

The ownership of these sacred places varies: they may belong to individuals,

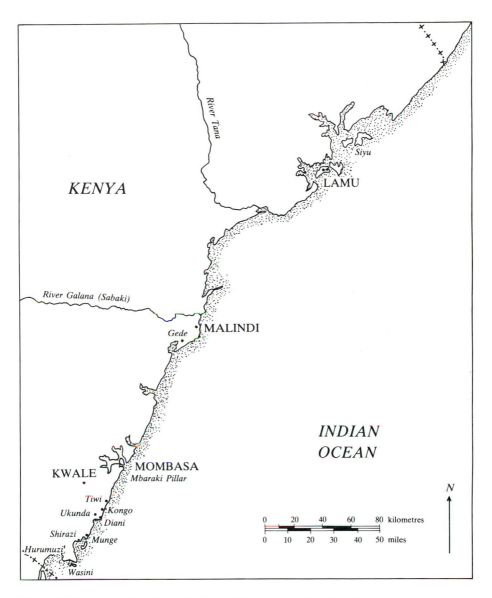

Figure 12.1 Some sites along the East African coast. Drawing: Lorna Abungu.

to families, or to the community. On the Kenyan coast, while the individual ownership of sacred places is limited, both family and communal ownership are prevalent. There are people living today who claim direct descent from the builders of what are considered to be sacred sites (especially in relation to ruined structures).

Different types of sacred places

Non-Muslims (and see Mutoro 1994)

Caves and rock shelters
Within the coast's immediate hinterland are sacred places in the form of caves and rock shelters. These are easily identified by the presence of the above-mentioned 'flags', which are prevalent in nearly all the sacred sites both on the coast and in its hinterland. In most cases, caves are either individual or family-owned, and some have now become important tourist attractions, with individual owners charging fees before allowing people to view them and their associated artefacts. This practice is more prevalent in the Cede area of the northern Kenyan coast, probably because the area is near Malindi and Watamu, two major tourist resorts. The caves and rock shelters seem to be venerated because of their appearance and their unique quality, which means that they are seen as dwelling areas for the spirits and are thus considered sacred.

Muslims
Along the Kenyan coast, the sacred places of the Swahili and the Digo, both of whom are Muslims, are found in abandoned settlements (especially mosques), tombs, and also caves and rock shelters; all of these are most often found near a large baobab tree (Fig. 12.2). These places are either associated with the spirits of the dead ancestors or with jinis (genies). Thus, mosques built by 'famous' departed ancestors, monumental tombs belonging to the patriarchs and/or great ancestors, and large trees associated with jinis are all revered as holy and sacred places. Because of the number of former Swahili settlements abandoned all along the Kenyan coastal strip (Fig. 12.3), there is a very high prevalence of sacred sites.

Mbaraki Pillar and Mosque (Figs 12.4 and 12.5)
One of the most important Swahili sacred places is the Mbaraki Pillar in Mombasa. The pillar and mosque are located southwest of Mombasa town, tucked among baobab trees and what is now rapidly becoming an industrial area. The pillar measures 14.10 metres high and has slits on all four sides, which support the scaffolding used for its construction and subsequent maintenance.

Beside the Pillar, some 5 metres away, was a mosque with a large *musalla* (prayer room), two anterooms at the sides, and stone-built cisterns for storing water on its northeastern and southwestern corners. In view of its small size, the mosque was probably a private one, built by some elderly sheikh. It was constructed between AD 1400 and 1450 and was almost a complete ruin by 1550 (Sassoon 1982, p. 27). The ruins were excavated by Sassoon in 1977 and a new mosque (now hosting a resident imam) was subsequently constructed according to the original foundation plan.

During the excavations at Mbaraki Mosque late seventeenth-century broken pots were found on the east side of the mosque, near the base of the pillar, and in the mihrab of the mosque, the mihrab being the apsidal recess in the wall that faces Mecca (this direction is north in East Africa). The use of pots in mihrabs is not part of Islamic practice, and therefore these findings represent other, non-Islamic, activities. However, such findings and activities are not uncommon along the Kenyan coast; moreover, they are also evident among those who see themselves as Muslims.

Ruined mosques in abandoned Swahili settlements along the coast are used,

Figure 12.2   Tomb of Idarus at Wasini, with large baobab tree behind it. Photo: Lorna Abungu.

Figure 12.3   Kongo Mosque at Diani Beach, on the south coast. Photo: Lorna Abungu.

in one way or another, at the present time. It is a common belief among some groups that ruined mosques are the domain of spirits who can be persuaded to intervene on behalf of needy or troubled people. The same belief applies to some large monumental tombs and large baobab or fig trees, all of which are invariably found in or around abandoned settlements.

Because of the belief in the presence of spirits within these areas, offerings of food, incense and rose-water are often made to please the spirits; also, 'flags' of cloth are hung from the large trees, or from other prominent places in the area. The mihrabs are the most solidly built feature of mosques, much more so than the walls; this makes them the obvious focal point in the ruins and, as such, favoured places for such ritual activities as those mentioned above, including leaving broken pieces of pots. Such evidence, when found in an archaeological context along the Kenyan coast, is an obvious indicator of spirit-worship/possession; these areas are therefore seen as sacred places.

It is important to note that the archaeological evidence in the form of broken pottery suggests that Mbaraki Pillar and Mosque were being used for the propitiation of spirits from around AD 1700. This practice has continued over the years; in relation to the Pillar, up to the present. This points to a long and continuous practice of spirit-worship/possession and the concept of sacred ground and structures.

Mbaraki Pillar is interesting not only because of its monumental nature, but also because of its importance as a religious place. Shown in De Sa's map of 1710 (Sassoon 1982), and thus already in existence in the early 1700s, the Pillar has become a religious landmark in its own right within the region.

Theories about why it was built and about its original function have varied. Some believe it was a lighthouse, others a look-out tower, but its concealment from the harbour entrance and the open sea render both theories unlikely. It is also unlikely to have been a minaret, since it has a very small door, there are no steps within the Pillar, and very narrow openings at the top, which would not suffice for the calls to prayer. Moreover, there is no evidence, along the entire East African coast, for tall minarets (like the ones found in present mosques) before the nineteenth century, except possibly one mentioned by the Portuguese in the early sixteenth century, located at what is probably the Basheikh Mosque.

Unlike the numerous pillar tombs found along the coast, Mbaraki is hollow, very large, and does not appear to have been built as part of a tomb. Unlike the other sacred sites along the Kenyan coast, Mbaraki seems to have been built

Figure 12.4   Mbaraki Pillar, with large baobab tree in the background. Photo: Lorna Abungu.

Figure 12.5 Mbaraki Pillar and Mosque, with *muezzin* calling for prayer. Photo: Lorna Abungu.

('made') to house a spirit or spirits, and thus constructed to be a sacred site; it may well have been built to house the spirit that is still venerated and consulted on this very site.

Members of the community that perform the ceremonies at the Pillar say that it was built by an Omani Arab who had come to Mbaraki and was there released from some evil spell; because of this, he showed his appreciation of the treatment received by building the Pillar. The woman nowadays in charge of performing the rituals at this site also contends that the hollow Pillar was built for the spirit, so that it could live at the very top. This fully corroborates the communal view, and confirms the view that Mbaraki has been an import-ant sacred site ever since it was built. The Omani connection seems plausible, since there is evidence to show that Omanis had settled in this area after expelling the Portuguese in 1698, and the Pillar at Mbaraki was built soon afterwards, between 1700 and 1710.

Today, not only does Mbaraki Pillar remain one of the landmarks of Mombasa, but the community still performs the obligatory ritual functions, and thus maintains the tradition. The ritual activities take place only 10 metres away from the newly rebuilt mosque, whose imam does not approve of what goes on around the Pillar. When asked his views, he said that spirit propitia-tion is un-Islamic and therefore wrong. However, there seems to be a degree of tolerance, and people seem unwilling to talk about it.

Kenyan south coast

Mbaraki Pillar is not the only place along the coast where propitiation of spirits takes place. An archaeological survey of the Kenyan south coast, carried out by the Coastal Archaeology Department of the National Museums of Kenya, revealed that in nearly all abandoned settlements there were areas of such 'un-Islamic' activity. The sites of Hurumuzi, Shirazi, Wasini, Diani, Munge, Ukunda, Tiwi, Kongo and many others produced evidence that unequivocally points towards this conclusion. At Wasini Island (Walsh in press), the grave of an old healer and priest, Idarus, is now a sacred place where people pray for relief from misfortunes ranging from sickness to drought; the gigantic baobab tree at Ukunda is considered a sacred place, and is frequented mostly by Digo elders who go to pray under it. This is an important tree, since it is the only one gazetted in Kenya by presidential decree (by the late Jomo Kenyatta), and therefore cannot be tampered with. This is one of the few sacred sites, along with the *kaya* (Mutoro 1994), that has attracted political attention.

Kenyan north coast

Along this part of the coast there are many sacred places in the form of tombs. In the old Siyu settlement, on Pate Island, there are three groups of tomb concentrations. The first is a large domed tomb adjoined by smaller tombs (Fig. 12.6). The larger tomb, which bears the Islamic inscription date of

Figure 12.6 Domed tomb at Siyu, Pate Island. Photo: Lorna Abungu.

1260 AH (or AD 1411) had all of its facades decorated with imported Chinese and Islamic wares.

The largest of these domed tombs is reputed (through oral tradition) to be the resting-place of a legendary priestess, Mwana Ndia wa Msingi, from Pate town. She was reportedly invited to Siyu by the townspeople to treat a stomach ailment which had nearly decimated the female population of Siyu in the early fifteenth century. As a sign of respect and appreciation for her good work in arresting the epidemic, the people of Siyu built her an elaborate tomb that was completed before her death. On the left side of the tomb, the townspeople built three other smaller domed tombs for her daughters. To this day, this site is revered and considered to be sacred.

A second group of tombs is located next to the present-day Friday Mosque. The domed tomb here is said to house the remains of a famed Islamic scholar and Shea (descendant of Mohammed) who also came from Pate town. At this site, protective rituals are performed to this day by the people of Siyu; they burn incense and hold prayers, especially those people intending to undertake journeys, since it is reputed that carrying out these rituals before a journey will be a good omen and will ensure that it is blessed.

The last group of tombs at Siyu consists of pillar tombs – often misinterpreted (Kirkman 1964) as being phallic symbols – which are very common along the East African coast. At Siyu there is a pillar tomb which is said to hold the remains of Sheikh wa Haswa, reputed to have been a wealthy man within the community who offered part of his land as a public cemetery. He has since become a sort of 'saint' to the local population, and the tomb is thus treated as a holy place. During a recent visit to Siyu in 1990 I witnessed a local imam, accompanied by a group of young women, offering prayers at the tomb.

It would therefore appear that men and women who contributed to the welfare of the community were revered as 'saints', and that after their deaths, their burial-grounds are revered as holy and sacred. Prayers are often offered and the protective powers of the holy places are sought. Thus in death, as in life, their good deeds are believed to continue.

General observations

The situation on the Kenyan coast, especially among the Swahili and other Muslim communities, is of great interest: African customs and religions have become intertwined with Islamic non-African religion to produce a hybrid. Spirit, in an African society, is real and living, and caves and old mosques are areas through which these spirits can be reached, and which are also often inhabited by them. Like Islamic beliefs, Africans also believe that a mosque, even when in ruins, is still a holy place and can be used for worship.

Tombs, on the other hand, are places in which spirits dwell, or rest; these are also holy places where specific spirits (such as those of the ancestors) can be appealed to for assistance. Thus, in most African societies, people do not 'die' as such, but pass on to become higher beings in death. The spirits are in contact with the living, and can either bring good omens when appeased, or bad omens when annoyed.

Along the Kenyan coast, these sacred areas are readily identified by the colours associated with spirits: red, white and black. Colour is an important factor in understanding the idea of spirit propitiation. Other colours, apart from the three commonly used, do not appear to have been in regular use until recent times; the names for these other colours seem to have been lacking in the Swahili vocabulary. While *nyeusi* (black), *nyekundu* (red) and *nyeupe* (white) are nouns, and fall into the class system in KiSwahili grammar, other colours are treated as adjectives, and are preceded by *rangi ya* ('the colour of'). On the other hand, the colour blue does not seem to have a name in any African languages on the Kenyan coast. This seems to point to the fact that the three colours prevalent in sacred places are ingrained in African custom and tradition and, as such, have been absorbed into their spirit propitiation. Giles (1982) has pointed out that dwellings of certain spirits are demarcated by certain colours of 'flags': white is used for Muslim spirits, while red and black, or a combination of all three colours, represent the presence of animist spirits.

Regarding the spirit mediums, there seem to be no predetermined characteristics; anyone can be chosen as the medium for sacred sites, whether young or old, man or woman. However, the role seems to be handed down through lineages. The spirits are said to possess such people and demand that they (the caretakers) look after them (the spirits). The spirit then reveals its dwelling-place, where the chosen person will become caretaker and carry out the various required rituals.

Many of the people involved in spirit propitiation see themselves as Muslims. However, those who see themselves as 'good' Muslims view this as a non-Islamic, unacceptable practice. To a 'good' Muslim, Allah should be approached directly, and not through any other medium. Muslim education has therefore been denouncing spirit propitiation, which is also frowned upon as mere ignorance on the part of those who believe in it. To discourage the practice, the 'good' Muslims in some cases clear the ruined mosques and build new ones on top. This has more or less driven the practitioners underground, and in some areas it is rare to find anyone willing to talk about such practices, or even admit to their existence. This, however, is not the case at Mbaraki.

Conclusion

It can be seen from this account that there exists an intricate system of beliefs and practices which have created a new notion of sacredness based on various locations within the inhabited and uninhabited coastal environment. All this seems to have emerged from a mixture of different customs and religions over several centuries. There are, of course, contradictions within the various beliefs, which are expressed in terms of both condemnation and tolerance.

Thus the sacred sites found along the Kenyan coast appear to be varied and unique.

The National Museums of Kenya, the custodian of these settlements, has made it possible for these sacred sites to be preserved and studied. It is therefore impossible, in most cases, to destroy or interfere with them. Restricted sites, like the *kaya* (see Mutoro 1994), are protected both by their own people, and also by a government Act. It is to be hoped that all the important sacred sites on the Kenya coast will not only be duly protected, but will also be studied and understood in their proper contexts.

Acknowledgements

This present work is based on research being carried out in the SAREC-sponsored Urban Origins in Eastern Africa project. I am deeply indebted to its organizers; not only in making the research possible, but in enabling me to attend WAC 2 in Venezuela. I would also like to thank the National Museums of Kenya for its support and confidence in the work of the Coastal Archaeology Department.

References

Caplan, P. 1979. Spirit possession – a means of curing on Mafia Island, Tanzania. *Kenya Past and Present* 10, 41–4.
Giles, L. 1982. Mbaraki Pillar and its spirits. *Kenya Past and Present* 19, 44–9.
Kirkman, J. 1964. *Men and Monuments on the East African Coast*. London: Butterworth Press.
Mutoro, H. W. 1994. The Mijikenda *kaya* as a sacred site. In *Sacred Sites, Sacred Places*, D. L. Carmichael, J. Hubert, B. Reeves & A. Schanche (eds), 132–9. London: Routledge.
Sassoon, H. 1982. Mbaraki Pillar and related ruins of Mombasa Island. *Kenya Past and Present* 14, 26–34.
Walsh, M. In press. Mwaozi Tumbe and the rain-making rites of Wasini Island: a text in the Chifundi dialect of Swahili. *Études Océan Indien*.

13 A ceremony in the 'cave of idolatry': an eighteenth-century document from the Diocesan Historic Archive, Chiapas, Mexico

INÉS SANMIGUEL

Translated by Ben Alberti[1]

Caves play an important role in the religious and mythic system of the indigenous peoples of Los Altos de Chiapas. They are used for ceremonial practices, both curative and magical, and, being the dwelling place of *el dueño de la tierra* (the master of the earth), clouds, thunder and rain also come from them. In the modern Maya region of Tzotizl, several anthropologists (Bricker 1973; Gossen 1974; Guiteras-Holmes 1961; Holland 1960, 1963; Vogt 1969) have conducted ethnographical studies on the significance of the caves and many of the ceremonies which take place within them. It is well known that, within Mesoamerica, the importance of caves is not a recent development but has its roots in the ancient past. Nonetheless, in the area of Chiapas, the significance of the cave in the historic process is unknown, even though there have been several studies which should help in the understanding of it. Modern works include those by Blom (1954) and Navarrete & Martínez (1977). From the colonial era there are two major sources, the writings of two bishops of Chiapas: Fray Pedro de Feria (1584) and Núñez de la Vega (1702). Because the caves occupy a very special place in the lives of the indigenous peoples, it is essential to make some attempt to understand their historical and ethnographic significance.

This chapter examines one important document, *Sobre ydólatras. Pueblo de Chamula. Año de 1778* held by the Diocesan Historic Archive, San Cristóbal. This document, which relates to a specific cave, consists of twenty-nine records, handwritten on both sides, and is attributed to the town of Chamula, because previously the parish of San Andrés village (now known as Manuel Larráinzar, or more commonly, San Andrés Larráinzar) came under the vicarate of Chamula. There are various aspects of the document that need to be analysed, including the process of legal development. However, only one aspect will be considered here: the comparison between the beliefs and findings of this period (the eighteenth century), and contemporary ethnographic information. Some mention will also be made of funerary practices.

---

[1]Department of Archaeology, University of Southampton SO9 5NH, UK.

The 'cave of idolatry' which appears in this document is known by the name of Sacamch'en ('white cave' in Tzotzil). It is located in Yavteklum, less than 2 km to the southeast of the municipal capital of Larráinzar. Yavteklum consists of an enclave, belonging to the municipality, of approximately 6 hectares in the Stzelejiló region. The Aztecs knew the place as Iztacostoc, which also means 'white cave', in Náhuatl, and for this reason the village appears in the colonial documents as 'San Andrés Iztacostoc'. However, the local people continued to call the cave by the name it had before the arrival of the Aztecs, as is evident in the document: 'This village, in pagan lands, was immediately next to the cave that is called in their language sacumchen, and to this day they call the village San Andres Sacumchen' (*Sobre ydólatras* 1778, f.6v).

According to oral tradition, the apostle San Andrés (patron of the village) originally lived in Sacamch'en, but the cave was too small, so he went to Simojovel in search of a better place to live. He disliked it there, so he went up to Bach'en, but this also being too small he continued to Stzelejiló, which he disliked because it was a high crag. Finally, he found the place where the village church is now, and there the patron saint of San Andrés was definitively established (Ochiai 1985, pp. 55–7).

Following examination of the document, a surface collection was carried out of the artificial agricultural terraces of Yavteklum. Sherds, mostly rims and parts of the body of vessels, as well as stone fragments from hand-mills, were delivered to the Fundación Arqueológica Nuevo Mundo, San Cristóbal, Chiapas, for identification and permanent safekeeping. Part of the ceramic material was identified as late, and the rest as belonging to the Yash phase of the early Post-Classic period, which can be placed chronologically between AD 1000 and 1250 (Douglas Bryant, *pers. comm.* 1981).

During a second survey of the region, several samples of ceramics and human bone were taken from Sacamch'en Cave, all of which had been previously disturbed and were found dispersed over the floor of the cave. The material was examined by specialists in the Mayan period, and some examples of polychrome ceramics, such as the neck and body sherds of an anthropomorphically decorated vessel, were eventually associated, from their form and decoration, with similar material from the late Classic period (between AD 700 and 1000) (Susanna Ekholm, *pers. comm.* 1982). From the archaeological evidence it would appear that this cave has been occupied over a long period of time. Furthermore, it continues to be a very important place for the local people, where secret divination and curing ceremonies still take place.

According to the document, the site was discovered when the priest of San Andrés was told of the existence of a cave, at a place called Sacumchen, by an Indian from the village. The Indian said that while he was preparing the ground for maize planting he had seen three Indians enter the cave carrying fire, candles and an aromatic substance covered with wrapping. The priest of San Andrés went to the cave, explored and ransacked it, and then informed the curate of Chamula of what he had seen:

A type of stone table, over which there was a badly made cross, and at its sides several candle stumps, and the heads of many turkeys which had been consumed there, and some small containers in which they make offerings of incense and liquid . . . around said cross there was an arc made from green leaves, which would take at least eight days to make, and where this arc was attached to the floor, there were some hollows, in which I found bones which appeared to be from the deceased, so I decided to stay there that night in order to finish the next day, which I did, and hardly surprised I found a cadaver, and after which I found many others, large and small, one of which was fresh enough to be able to determine the skin, stuck to the skull, from which I infer that these are graves of idolaters who have sacrificed their lives to the devil.

(*Sobre ydólatras* 1778, f.2, 2v)

The curate of Chamula notified his superior, the bishop of Chiapas, Monseñor Francisco Polanco, who in turn ordered an investigation, and a judgement upon the idolaters. The document makes it clear that the church wanted to find an idol, and needed proof not only of its existence but also of its veneration, as stated by the priest of San Andrés during the interrogation:

I came back to the P. Coadjutor to ask what he felt about the business, and he replied: he was convinced that the idol was in this cave, or an image that was venerated in the pagan world, or another that the Yllustrísimo Señor Nuñes refers to in his Pastoral, and those with the surname, *Poxlon*, *Patxlan*, *Tzihuizin*, or *Hicalahau*. . . . He is convinced of his suspicions, knowing that this village, in the pagan world, was right next to the cave which is called sacumchem in their language.

(*Sobre ydólatras* 1778, f.6v)

An important source on the theory and theology of the Roman Catholic church at that time is the work of Núñez de la Vega (1702), whose writings helped the church to achieve the spiritual conquest of the Indians.

The priest of San Andrés was very familiar with the work of the bishop of Chiapas, and was inspired by it:

Before embarking on a move he warned the P. Coadjutor Dn. Nicolas Morales what he had said before leaving the village, and it is, that when he was in command, that the indians emptied their bellies over the stone slabs, which served as a table where the arc of green leaves was.

(*Sobre ydólatras* 1778, f.9v)

In 1687 Núñez de la Vega had found two idols hanging in the church of Oxchuc, Chiapas: 'It was no small difficulty to take down all of them, and we had it that, reciting the creed in loud voices, all the indians were spitting as they did it' (Núñez de la Vega 1702, p. 133).

From the information in this document it seems that no idol was found in the cave, and even when the idea of an idol (or idols) was pushed hard in the interrogations, there was no reply on the part of the accused that could confirm the existence of such an idol, although the accused were judged and condemned as idolaters. Instead of confirming the existence of idols, the Indians explained their beliefs and ceremonies in the cave, thus leaving some very valuable ethnographic material.

The Indian who had exposed the case was interrogated, and also two young Indian witnesses, two mayors, two festival officials and the previous official of the fiesta of San Andrés (the woman of one of the offenders was accused and gaoled, but not interrogated). The account of the interrogation describes who went to the cave, and for what purpose:

> To the fifth question he replied that, by an ancient custom, he knows that all those who hold offices of fiestas come to make their oration in the cave, and that his companion Nicolas Dias Autumn went with him, carrying liquid, and of the two above-mentioned candles, one was his and the other was his companion's.
>
> (*Sobre ydólatras* 1778, f.15v)

From the account of the Indian who had denounced the fiesta officials, it appears that they went to the cave at various times: 'He had found them, and seen them go at all hours of the day and night, especially festival days, carrying fire, candles, and incense covered with wrapping' (*Sobre ydólatras* 1778, f.8v).

In accordance with ethnographic information collected in San Andrés Larráinzar during the course of several years of investigation, it is known that today the festival officials, when they receive their positions, gather at the Catholic church to deliver their speeches, accompanied by the ritual adviser bearing offerings of candles, incense, flowers and pine branches. They can go any day, although by preference they go on Sunday, since that is the day of the weekly market, a time when the people gather at the municipal capital.

The interrogation also reveals who went to make offerings in the cave:

> To the third question he answered that, four or five years previously, when Alferes de Passion was in the cave asking for prosperity from the sacamchen angel, as it was a custom of the village, and as he was its head and principal flatterer after God, as here in Chamula the same happens at the place called Calvario, where there is a house, and they help him in the growing of his cultivated fields, as to him was conceded prosperity by the sacamchen.
>
> (*Sobre ydólatras* 1778, f.15, 15v)

> . . . though it was a custom of the village that all those that held positions went to ask for prosperity and happiness from the angel

of the cave, and for this they learnt from each other, and they wondered.

> (*Sobre ydólatras* 1778, f.21v, 22)

. . . that it was certain that he had frequented the cave, burning candles and perfumes to the master of the same cave.

> (*Sobre ydólatras* 1778, f.12v, 13)

It can be inferred from this that it was specifically the master of the cave (*yajual balumil*) to whom they went to pray and make offerings, in order to appease him, so that he would not send bad weather during the fiesta. He is not only perceived by the Chiapas Indians as *el dueño de la tierra*, the master of the earth, but also as the creator of the water that runs in the rivers and brooks, and of the rain that waters the maize. If the fiesta officials did not comply with the requisite duties of fasting, sexual abstinence, orations and offerings before the fiesta, they would be punished by rain on the day of the fiesta for which they were responsible.

It is worth extracting further information from this document concerning the master of the earth, since this concept cannot be well understood from existing studies of the Altos de Chiapas:

> He had burnt two candles and liquid with some green twigs, which he placed next to the cross . . . with fluent words he spoke his oration to the sacumchen angel: 'Help me Divine Spirit, Holy Captain, so that it will be fine weather on the days of my fiestas.'
>
> (*Sobre ydólatras* 1778, f.15v)

> . . . he had been taught that the sacumchen is the first-born son of God, which, in his language is: zba znichon Dios, remembering also the village custom, in which they wish to make understood that it is one ceremony only, or sign, which in his language they call hguinagem.
>
> (*Sobre ydólatras* 1778, f.23v)

> . . . that on one occasion, a snake, with eyes like those of a capon, came at them in the cave, and upon seeing it they were afraid.
>
> (*Sobre ydólatras* 1778, f.22v)

Thus it can be seen that the master of the earth is described in a number of ways. For example, he is referred to as the 'first-born son of God', 'divine spirit', or 'holy captain'. He also presents himself in various forms. According to ethnographic information (Holland 1963, pp. 92–4; Sanmiguel 1989, p. 137; Vogt 1969, pp. 302–3), the master of the earth is perceived as a benevolent being who controls the normal passage of life, but at the same time he has the capacity to destroy it. He lives in the subterranean world, dressed in the trappings of a Spaniard, and at times he presents himself in the form of a snake.

Today, the master of the earth is no longer known as 'son of God', but it is very possible that the concept of master of the earth that existed in the sixteenth century, at the beginning of the introduction of Catholicism into Chiapas, had many characteristics in common with the Catholic concept of Jesus Christ, and the two concepts could have merged into one. Over time, the nomenclature of the two became separate, but not their shared essence. That is to say, that even though the place of one is in the temple and the other is in the cave, in the minds of the people both share very similar features and characteristics. The fact that the master of the earth has the physical appearance and dress of a Spaniard could be precisely because of his fusion with the Catholic Christ.

The ceremony mentioned above, known as *hguinagem*, may be a divination practice, since the name could be better read as *vinajel*, from the root *vinaj*, meaning 'to be visible', 'to appear', or 'to be a seer' (Haviland 1981, p. 380). *Vinajel* could thus be interpreted as 'the made visible', 'the appeared'. Given this interpretation of the name given to the ceremony, it may be assumed that the people carried out private divination and curing ceremonies in the cave, as well as having public ones carried out by the festival official. At the present time, even though private ceremonies are still carried out in the caves, the vast majority of curative ceremonies are practised within the Catholic churches, among both the Tzotzil and Tzeltal of Chiapas, despite opposition from the regional Catholic authorities towards such practices.

As already mentioned, there were various prerequisite procedures that festival officials had to follow before carrying out ceremonies in the cave. The document specifies these procedures. For example:

> He proceeded showing him the doctrine of the dead Diego Gansales, whose doctrine is the custom of the ancients, for which the aforementioned Phelipe Dias went with him to the cave to flog himself, and only gave himself thirty lashes.
>
> (*Sobre ydólatras* 1778, f.22)

> . . . but with a view to what the rest had said of him, of the lashes in the caves . . . he confesses to having fasted only two weeks to implore the help of sacamchen.
>
> (*Sobre ydólatras* 1778, f.22v)

> . . . he also says that when they burn the incense, and light the candles, sometimes they take the cross out, other times they take it apart, and other times they put it aside.
>
> (*Sobre ydólatras* 1778, f.22, 22v)

A further example of this self-sacrifice is the meeting, held at the church three Fridays before the celebration of the fiesta, between the officials of the fiestas of San Andrés and Concepción, and the Pasiones de Carnaval, at which they flog themselves on the back, at the same time making speeches and giving offerings of incense.

The document also refers to funerary practices. It reports that bones were found inside the cave, spread over the floor, and there were broken pots and stone slabs over the bodies:

> The excavation continued through very hard earth, covered by some quite small stone slabs put there on purpose . . . until, at some depth, new bodies were discovered, that gave off such putrefaction. . . .
>
> *(Sobre ydólatras* 1778, f.10)

> during the excavation, in between some rocks that resembled snails, a young white boy was uncovered . . . and another hollow was found from where little was completed, and quite a lot of earth fell, small shin-bones and pieces of pots.
>
> *(Sobre ydólatras* 1778, f.10)

Information on early period cave burials from the work of Blom (1954), and Navarrete & Martínez (1977) suggests that this is a type of burial that may go back to the Classic Maya period (i.e. AD 300–900). Unfortunately, the cave has been robbed at least once, and it is not possible to reconstruct what may have been there in terms of the several types of burial from different periods. Consequently, we only have the limited information from the priest of San Andrés.

A burial found by Lee (1975, p. 8), in an open site at Chenalhó, is precisely the same type of burial that is described in the document. The burial at Chenalhó consists of a simple trench in which the body was laid, and later covered by a stone slab. The similarity to the cave burial suggests that this funerary custom may have survived from the prehispanic era up until several centuries after the Spanish conquest, since the bodies found in the cave are said to be recent. The document states that the Indian was asked during his interrogation if he knew whose corpses or bones were buried there, and which had been exhumed:

> He replied that all he knew, and had heard his grandparents say, was that it rained hot water, and that the people took refuge there, and died.
>
> *(Sobre ydólatras* 1778, f.12)

> . . . that he only knew of the aforementioned bones what he had heard, that the ancient village had perished in a hot rain, and that they were buried there.
>
> *(Sobre ydólatras* 1778, f.13v)

In this context it is relevant to add that I was told by an old man from San Andrés that all the ancient inhabitants had perished in a hot rain. He also told me that in the 1950s, upon the opening of a road through to San Andrés, ancient burials had been found in 'stone boxes'. This information is of great interest, if compared with the type of burial found by Culbert (1965, pp. 12, 13), which had walls and floors made from stone, and can be dated by ceramic association to the early Classic, or early Post-Classic period. This suggests an occupation of Los Altos de Chiapas of several centuries.

A second reference to hot rain can be found in a myth collected and published by Holland (1963, pp. 71–2):

> The first world was destroyed and its population killed, so another was created and populated with people. However, these too were imperfect, because they did not remain dead after death; after three days they returned to life and continued living eternally. Neither did this please God, who decided, therefore, to destroy the world with a torrent of hot water. When the water started to fall some people took refuge in the caves, but they all died, and this is why we frequently find human bones in the caves: they are the remains of the inhabitants of the second world.

It is impossible to determine which era this myth refers to, or the stories relating to the 'hot water' mentioned by the Indian from San Andrés, but it is possible to assume that these are allusions to volcanic eruptions, from Chiapas or other regions further afield.

On the basis of the available data, it is suggested that the Catholic church was substituted for the cave. The church had in fact replaced part of the cave, and some of the ceremonies, especially public ones, were moved from the cave to the church approximately 200 years ago. The private ceremonies are still gradually being moved from the cave to the church.

The fact that the officials and Pasiones de Carnaval do not go directly to the caves to ask for 'prosperity' or 'fair weather' from the master of the earth, during and before the fiesta, but go to the church, gives support to the hypothesis that the church has replaced the cave. Gifts of incense, candles, flowers, pines and branches are still made as offerings, as before, but now they are made in the church. To reinforce this hypothesis further, it should be mentioned that, in the carnival fiesta celebrated in San Andrés, there is a scene in which 'black men' (ik'aletik) chase the children, and when they catch them they carry them to the church saying in loud voices: 'chakik'ot batel ta jch'en' ('I'm going to take you to my cave'). Later, in the church, the children are left seated at the foot of the cross at the entrance. It is also relevant to note that caves and churches share certain morphological features: both are large, dark places, they both have crosses, incense, flowers, liquid and pine. One difference would be that within the church there are images of the saints, which the cave does not have. However, the fact that Holland (1960, pp. 127–30) found anthropomorphic figures from the prehispanic period in a cave at Chalchihuitán, not far from San Andrés village, is highly suggestive.

It can be seen that *Sobre ydólatras. Pueblo de Chamula. Año de 1778*, the document on which this chapter has focused, contains a wealth of data, and from this it is possible to suggest that parallels can be drawn between the concept of the cave, and the practices carried out within caves in the eighteenth century, and the concepts and practices that today relate to the church – though there are also observable differences. Furthermore, the study of these similarities and differences, through the analysis of archaeological, historic and ethnographic material, is of great value to the understanding and interpretation of the process, change and continuation of some religious and supernatural concepts of the indigenous peoples of Los Altos de Chiapas.

References

Blom, F. 1954. Ossuaries, cremation and secondary burials among the Maya of Chiapas, Mexico. *Journal de la Société des Américanistes* 43, 121–35.

Bricker, V. R. 1973. *Ritual Humor in Highland Chiapas*. Austin: University of Texas Press.

Culbert, T. P. 1965. *The Ceramic History of the Central Highlands of Chiapas, Mexico*. Papers of the New World Archaeological Foundation, 19.

De Feria, P. 1899. Relación que hace el Obispo de Chiapas (Fray Pedro de Feria) sobre (1584) la reincidencia en sus idolatrías de los indios de aquel país después de treinta años de cristianos. *Anales del Museo Nacional de México* 6, 481–7.

Gossen, G. H. 1974. *Chamulas in the World of the Sun: time and space in a Maya oral tradition*. Cambridge, Mass.: Harvard University Press.

Guiteras-Holmes, C. 1961. *Perils of the Soul*. Glencoe: Free Press.

Haviland, J. B. 1981. *Sk'op sotz'leb. El tzotzil de San Lorenzo Zinacantán*. Mexico, D.F.: Universidad Nacional Autónoma de México.

Holland, W. R. 1960. Relaciones entre la religión tzotzil contemporánea y la maya antigua. *Anales del Instituto Nacional de Antropología e Historia, México, D.F.* 13, 113–31.

Holland, W. R. 1963. *Medicina maya en los altos de Chiapas: un estudio del cambio socio-cultural*. Mexico, D.F.: Instituto Nacional Indigenista.

Laughlin, R. M. 1975. *The Great Tzotzil Dictionary of San Lorenzo Zinacantan*. Smithsonian Contributions to Anthropology 19, Washington, D.C.: Smithsonian Institution Press.

Lee, T. Jr 1975. *Jmetic Lubton: some modern and pre-hispanic Maya ceremonial customs in the highlands of Chiapas, Mexico*. Papers of the New World Archaeological Foundation 29.

Navarrete, C. & E. Martínez 1977. *Exploraciones arqueológicas en la cueva de los Andasolos, Chiapas*. Mexico: Universidad Autónoma de Chiapas.

Núñez de la Vega, F. 1702. Constituciones Diocesanas del Obispado de Chiapas, hechas y ordenadas por su Senoría Illustriss. el Señor Maestro d. Fr. Francisco Núñez de la Vega, del orden de Predicadores, Obispo de Ciudad Real de Chiappa y Soconusco, del consejo de su Magestad.

Ochiai, K. 1985. *Cuando los santos vienen marchando. Rituales públicos intercomunitarios Tzotziles*. Mexico: Universidad Autónoma de Chiapas.

Sanmiguel, I. 1989. The 'New House Ceremony' among the Tzotzil Maya Indians. *The Teikyo Journal of Comparative Cultures* 1, 133–8.

Sobre ydólatras. Pueblo de Chamula. Año de 1778. Diocesan Historic Archive. San Cristóbal, Mexico.

Vogt, E. Z. 1969. *Zinacantan: a Maya community in the highlands of Chiapas*. Cambridge, Mass.: Belknap Press of Harvard University Press.

14 At the mouth of the obsidian cave: deity and place in Aztec religion

NICHOLAS J. SAUNDERS

Introduction

Sacred places exist in sacred landscapes, alongside, or nested within, secular places and secular landscapes. However, whilst the former is composed of thought, perception and attitude, the latter results from geological processes and, on occasion, human, and possibly animal, activity. Although every sacred landscape is also a physical landscape, not all physical landscapes are sacred, though they retain the potential for becoming so. What confers sacredness is not an array of geographical or geological features *per se*, but rather what a particular culture has decided to make of them. In other words, the ascription of significance to a specific configuration of geographical features is not a self-evident fact conferred by Nature or natural processes, but rather a cultural appraisal (Sauer 1954, pp. 2–3).

Sacred landscapes are a manifestation of world-views which populate a geographical area with a distinctive array of mythical, religious, or spiritual beings or essences. Each culture brings its own ideas to bear on the land it inhabits and, consequently, any analysis of sacred landscapes or the sacredness of place is a part of the analysis of how cultures conceptualize and classify (i.e. bring order to, and make sense of) the natural world.

Attitudes towards landscape and place depend, in part, on culture-specific perceptions of what constitutes the animated natural world. This may include what, in western science, would be classified as 'inanimate' objects, e.g. stones or rocks (Eliade 1974, pp. 47–8; Hallowell 1969, p. 54; Lévi-Strauss 1969, pp. 184–5), mountains (Bastien 1985), or celestial objects (Ruggles & Saunders 1993). Therefore, whilst sacred landscapes or places may be occupied by 'obviously' supernatural spirits, deities, or 'were-animals', as compared with the living humans and animals which inhabit what we would term the real world, both environments are conceived through the lens of classification and are, therefore, cultural constructs.

The significance attached to such constructions, however, is not in any way self-evident; it is culturally established by social agreement and use. For example, correspondences between certain animals and particular physical locations are not inherent qualities, but are relative, variable and culture-dependent (Douglas 1990, p. 26). Putting order into what we call the 'landscape', and designating living matter as 'animal', are cultural decisions, processes whereby a semantic grid is laid down in order for the society to construct its own meaningful universe (e.g. Kus 1983, p. 278). Each culture creates and maintains its own definitions of the natural and supernatural.

In this sense, the way in which a culture looks at, and classifies, the mobile inhabitants of a landscape (whether human or animal) has less to do with what one might call 'objective reality', and more to do with a distinctive cluster of qualities and meanings which are ascribed to them within an emically logical system of classification. In the same manner, the spiritual significance of landscape and place has less to do with geography and geology *per se* than with the architecture of religious thought. This is due, in part, to the fact that the symbolic interpretation of natural facts is carried out within sets of conceptual structures which derive as much from social experience as empirical reality (Crocker 1985, p. 170).

This chapter explores these issues not by an investigation into one specific place, but through a consideration of sacred caves as a locative manifestation of an Aztec deity in late Post-Classic Mexico. It deals with beliefs in caves as entrances to the underworld, as parts of volcanoes which themselves are the source of obsidian, and with obsidian's symbolic associations with the supreme Aztec deity Tezcatlipoca and his zoomorphic *alter ego* – Tepeyollotli – the jaguar 'heart of the mountain'. The aim is not to provide definitive answers to particular questions but rather to illustrate the complexities of belief and action between what, in the western world, would appear to be quite distinct aspects of the social and natural worlds.

The sacred landscape

The physical environment of the Central Highlands of Mexico and, in particular, the unique ecosystem of the Valley of Mexico (Porter Weaver 1981, p. 15) formed part of the framework within which those metaphysical relationships which structured the Aztec world-view would have been created and maintained. The symbolic acquisition of selected features of this landscape was effected by those who, through analogical association, would convert them into metaphorical attributes of a supreme deity.

The Valley of Mexico is the result of volcanic activity; the mountains which enclose it are thus either extinct or dormant volcanoes (Sanders, Parsons & Santley 1979, p. 81). These volcanoes and their lava flows are the source of the volcanic glass, obsidian. The mountain slopes and the flatter land of the valley bottoms are composed of ancient lava flows which have created innumerable subterranean caves (Heyden 1981, p. 3). In many areas of Mesoamerica, mountains were regarded as the abode of spirits and the source of water, moisture and weather, and caves afforded not only shelter and protection, but were seen as entrances to the underworld, and as the places of origin of fertility spirits (Heyden 1981; Taube 1986).

The view from Lake Texcoco, in which the imperial Aztec capital Tenochtitlan was situated, includes, as a prominent feature, the mountainous volcanic landscape, with the snow–capped peaks of individual volcanoes yielding summer meltwater which feeds the Valley of Mexico's extensive lake system (Sanders, Parsons & Santley 1979, pp. 84–5). According to Van Zantwijk (1981, p. 71), mountains were considered by the Aztec to be the original homes of their ancestors, and the places where their spirits and *naguals* (animal spirit familiars) dwelt.

The metaphysical construction of the Aztec world-view, or 'cosmovision' (Broda 1982, p. 81), presumably depended not just on the existence and size of their mountainous environment, but to a considerable degree upon the meteorological features associated with it. Around conspicuous peaks rain-bringing clouds assemble, and clouds and fog fill the steep valleys and canyons of their flanks. Such meteorological phenomena are claimed (Broda 1987, p. 235) to have been symbolically associated by the Aztec with the sacralization of mountains, caves and water, and the rituals which they undertook at such locations. Townsend (1987, p. 373) also draws attention to the symbolic importance to the Aztec of these high peaks where powerful rainstorms form at the onset of the rainy season, and to their abundant springs (many of which emerge from caves) which supply water throughout the year. Sahagun (1950–82, Book 11, p. 247) explicitly points to the Aztec conception of mountains as being in disguise – only on top are they covered with earth and stone; in reality a mountain is like a jar, full of water.

Recently, the archaeological discoveries at the Great Aztec Temple (El Templo Mayor) in Mexico City have been taken as supporting the claim for a symbolic association between mountains, water and caves (Broda 1987). Indeed, Aztec scholars regard El Templo Mayor as an architectural representation of the *atl-tepetl* ('water mountain') (Broda 1987, p. 74; Carrasco 1990, pp. 72–3; Matos Moctezuma 1988, p. 142; Townsend 1987, p. 389). Buried within the temple, or 'mountain', were offerings of several jaguar skulls; one held a flint knife in its mouth (Nagao 1985, p. 117), while others clenched egg-sized jade stones between their fangs (Fig. 14.1). At another location, a complete skeleton of a jaguar lay on top of offerings presumably dedicated to the rain-god Tlaloc (Broda 1987, p. 232; Matos Moctezuma 1988, Fig. v), whose cult activities are documented as having taken place on mountain-tops (Duran 1967, vol. 1, p. 82).

The above archaeological evidence could well support an interpretation which sought symbolically to define Tepeyollotli – the jaguar guise of the Aztec deity Tezcatlipoca – as the heart (i.e. the inside) of mountains, as well as an extension of such symbolism to associate Tepeyollotli with the mountain-top locale of the ethnohistorically attested cult of Tlaloc, whose rituals included human sacrifice (Duran 1967, p. 82; Sahagun 1975, p. 80).

Figure 14.1 Jaguar skull with jade ball in its jaws, from El Tempo Mayor, Mexico City. Found within the temple – itself an architectural representation of the 'water mountain' – this skull may represent the Aztec deity Tezcatlipoca in his jaguar guise as Tepeyollotli, the 'heart of the mountain'. Photo from Matos Moctezuma 1988, courtesy of Thames & Hudson and the Great Temple Project.

A possible ethnographic echo of these beliefs has survived in a remote Aztec-speaking community in the mountains of southwest Mexico. Each May, in the village of Acatlan, there are ceremonies which petition for rain. One day is given over to a pilgrimage to the summit of a local mountain called Cerro Azul ('blue mountain'). Here, according to the participants, resides the jaguar-god of rains who dispenses his largesse in return for the human blood which results from violent fist fights between men dressed in jaguar costumes (Saunders 1984). In prehispanic times, if one can suppose a continuity of practice, such ceremonies would have fallen within the monthly festival dedicated to Tezcatlipoca/Tepeyollotli.

Caves

There is good evidence that the mountainous terrain of the Valley of Mexico was a sacred landscape at least by Aztec times (Broda 1991). It is known that the Aztec regarded caves as entrances to the underworld – a realm of darkness, spirits and death. This is, of course, not to suggest that volcanoes, such as Iztaccihuatl and Popocatapetl, would not have been symbolically significant before this period; they contain innumerable caves which, on ethnohistorical evidence, had long been used for such important rituals as the control of the weather, especially rain (e.g. Heyden 1981, p. 27).

For the Aztec, it appears that caves were also associated with fertility, and particularly with the origins of food and water. Thus, Burgoa (1934, vol. I, p. 341) relates that their deities which controlled water, fruit and seeds lived in caves, and Herrera (1945, vol. IV, p. 166) tells how ceremonial petitions for water for crops also took place in caves. In addition, the Aztec had many myths concerning caves as entrances to the underworld, as places where time and humanity began, and as 'places of emergence' (e.g. Heyden 1981; Taube 1986). In the myth of Chicomoztoc, 'the seven caves' were taken to be the Aztec birthplace, as well as the sacred location of their ancestors (Miller & Taube 1993, p. 60; Townsend 1993, p. 57).

Obsidian: the divine stone

Obsidian has been called the 'steel' of New World prehistory (Cobean, Coe, Perry, Turekian & Kharkar 1971, p. 666) because of its tendency to fracture conchoidally, and thus produce sharp prismatic blades from polyhedral cores. The sixteenth-century Florentine Codex reports that obsidian (*itztli*) was being excavated from mines and used to make implements for sacrificial bloodletting (Sahagun 1950–82, Book 11, p. 227). Obsidian (and the implements manufactured from it) not only possessed utilitarian importance, but also appears to have had a distinct symbolic significance, as it was used to manufacture spearpoints, sword-blades and knives – the *de facto* agents of death and sacrifice (Matos Moctezuma 1978).

A further Aztec use of obsidian was for mirrors. Such mirrors appear to have been more than functional, vested with symbolic and religious significance. They were used for divining, and the Aztec supreme deity, Tezcatlipoca, personified the obsidian mirror (Miller & Taube 1993, p. 125) – the 'lord of the smoking mirror' (Saunders 1990, and see below). In the nine levels of which the Aztec underworld was composed, the Codex Vaticanus (A 3738) lists level iv as the 'obsidian hill', level v as the 'place of obsidian-knife winds', and level viii as the 'obsidian place of the dead'. Similarly, in Caso's listing of the nine Lords of the Night (Caso 1971, p. 336), the god of level ii is Itztli/Tecpatl ('obsidian/flint'), and that of level viii is Tepeyollotli (jaguar, 'heart of the mountain').

Tezcatlipoca/Tepeyollotli: the deity of place

Adopting what might be termed a post-processual symbolic interpretation of the available evidence for Aztec beliefs regarding caves and obsidian, possible symbolic elements come together in the Aztec construction of their supreme deity Tezcatlipoca – the 'lord of the smoking mirror' (*tezcatl*, 'it is a mirror'; *ihpoca*, 'it emits smoke') (Ruiz de Alarcon 1984, p. 235). Tezcatlipoca was the supreme god of the Aztec pantheon (Nicholson 1971, p. 412), and was regarded as omnipotent and omnipresent. By virtue of bestowing wealth, nobility and rulership, Tezcatlipoca was the patron deity of Aztec royalty (Sahagun 1950–82, Book 6, pp. 44–5) and sorcerers (Nicholson 1971, p. 412), and also possessed symbolic associations with obsidian as a stone, and with obsidian mirrors used as divinatory devices. According to Heyden (1991, p. 195), Tezcatlipoca's obsidian mirror was an Aztec metaphor for rulership and power.

In particular, Tezcatlipoca was symbolically associated with 'dark places' and the night and, according to Caso (1958, p. 27), he signified the nocturnal cycle. He brought misfortune, illness, death and destruction (Sahagun 1950–82, Book 3, p. 11) by casting his shadow, and it was he who visited the Aztec with all the evils which could befall 'men' (Sahagun 1950–82, Book 1, p. 5). Tezcatlipoca possessed physical and symbolic associations with obsidian as a dark volcanic glass which emanated from caves.

In the Aztec capital, Tenochtitlan, the god's image was of a lustrous black stone (Duran 1967, vol. I, p. 37), which is generally thought to refer to obsidian (e.g. Heyden 1988, p. 222). The description of this idol was as a shining stone, black as jet, from which sharp blades and knives are fashioned (Duran 1971, p. 98). Sahagun (1950–82, Book 11, pp. 226–7) reinforces this interpretation in his statement that obsidian implements were used in sacrificial bloodletting (p. 227). In Aztec, the term *itztli* not only signifies 'obsidian knife', but was also, itself, a manifestation of Tezcatlipoca himself (Ruiz de Alarcon 1984, p. 229). Apart from establishing the likelihood that Tezcatlipoca's image was of obsidian, this evidence also suggests a possible link with the practice and ideology of blood sacrifice.

Tezcatlipoca's omniscience was due, in part, to his wielding of the magical obsidian mirror (*tezcatl*). With the aid of his mirror, he 'knows everything', he is able to see into the hearts of men (Sahagun 1950–82, Book 3, p. 11). Like the wind he is invisible and, like a shadow, he moves across the land (Sahagun 1950–82, Book 1, p. 5). Already in 1519, Conquistador Diaz del Castillo had remarked on these qualities: omniscience, the associations with obsidian, and the god's jaguar aspect in the guise of Tepeyollotli (Diaz del Castillo 1939, pp. 302–4; and see Saunders 1988).

Whilst Tezcatlipoca clearly had symbolic associations with obsidian and, in general, with dark places, his animal *alter ego* had complementary ones. Tezcatlipoca's transformational manifestation was as Tepeyollotli – the 'heart of the mountain' (*tepetl*, 'mountain'; *yollohtli*, 'heart') (Ruiz de Alarcon 1984, p. 235) – who took the form of a great jaguar. For the Aztecs, like many Pre-Columbian and more recent Amerindian societies, the jaguar was notable for its ritual marking, and the associations between jaguar and royalty, warriors, shamans, spiritual power and mirrors have been explored elsewhere (e.g. Coe 1972; Furst 1968; Saunders 1988, 1990).

According to Jimenez Moreno (1979, p. 28), there is no doubt that Tezcatlipoca was also Tepeyollotli for, in the Codex Telleriano-Remensis, Tezcatlipoca's face is seen emerging from the jaws of a large feline and, in the

Codex Borbonicus (Seler 1904, Fig. 28a), Tepeyollotli appears as a large spotted feline with Tezcatlipoca's 'smoking mirror' symbol attached to his left foot. Furthermore, on the carved-stone 'hackmack box', Klein (1987, p. 334) sees the individual represented as engaged in autosacrificial bloodletting – as Tezcatlipoca, in his guise as Tepeyollotli (identifiable through his large-spotted feline apparel). In Codex Borgia, Tezcatlipoca is seen with his left foot replaced by a 'smoking mirror' device and the head of a jaguar (Fig. 14.2). These iconographic examples support the interpretation of the identification of Tepeyollotli as a manifestation of Tezcatlipoca, and as support for the interpretation of a symbolic association between Tezcatlipoca/Tepeyollotli, and with obsidian mirrors.

In Aztec thought, Tezcatlipoca-as-Tepeyollotli was the Heart of the Mountain, who took jaguar form and inhabited the earth's interior (Benson 1988, p. 165). In this case, the earth's interior could well represent the underworld, one of whose nine levels is controlled by Tepeyollotli himself. It is possible to suggest on the basis of the evidence presented in this chapter that Tepeyollotli, by his very name and nature, embodied the geological source of

Figure 14.2 The Aztec deity Tezcatlipoca, showing his distinctive black face and bands, a flint knife and mirror suspended on his chest, and a foot replaced by a smoking mirror device and either a jaguar's head, or the jaguar head of Tepeyollotli. From the Codex Borbonicus. Drawing: Pauline Stringfellow from Codex Borbonicus, after Seler 1904, Fig. 28a.

Figure 14.3 Chicomoztoc, the mythical cave of origin and 'place of emergence' for the Aztecs, represented as a large, possibly feline, earth monster. From the Codex Duran. Drawing: A. Pina, from Schavelzon 1980.

obsidian – so strongly associated with his 'master', Tezcatlipoca. It is perhaps not irrelevant to speculate that whereas, in Aztec belief, caves gave physical access to the underworld of spirits, mirrors provided metaphysical access to the realm of shadows, and both were symbolically associated with Tezcatlipoca.

The interpretation of the symbolic identification of Tezcatlipoca's manifestation with the jaguar Tepeyollotli is more direct. The heart, or centre, of a mountain is only accessible via a cave opening. Schavelzon (1980, p. 152) is explicit in associating cave entrances with the open jaws of an earth monster and, in particular, with the mouth of a jaguar. Leon-Portilla (1963, p. 41) reports that one of the names for jaguar used by the Aztec was *tecuani* (the 'devourer of people'), and that he was considered an earth monster. Various codex representations portray cave entrances complete with fangs, and one in particular shows Aztec ancestors emerging from what appears to be a large feline mouth (Fig. 14.3).

Thompson (1960, p. 74) relates how Tepeyollotli was regarded by the commentators on the Codex Telleriano-Remensis as the lord of animals, invariably depicted either in physical proximity to a temple, or as part of its structure. He claims, for one example, that a temple had a facade shaped as the open jaws of an earth monster whose features suggested the jaguar. He believed that, in some cases, the earth monster merged with Tezcatlipoca; he also referred to Seler's view that Tezcatlipoca was a god of caves, the interior of the earth, and the manifestation of jaguar.

Tezcatlipoca was the lord of night, the master of the dark realm, and conjuror of shadows – a set of symbols highly suggestive of metaphorical associations between the 'lord of the smoking mirror', obsidian, the darkness of caves and night. Codex representations show him painted black with a blue eye-band. In temples in rural areas, the idol of Tezcatlipoca was made of wood and painted black, as were the bodies of the priests who ministered to the god's image (Heyden 1988, p. 222). The black pitch with which they covered themselves was believed to make them invisible in the night, to give them power to communicate with the deity. Black was Tezcatlipoca's sacred colour and the pitch itself was called Tezcatlipoca's 'divine food' (Heyden 1988, p. 222). It is possible to suggest a symbolic association between the deity, obsidian, caves and the congealed blood which was so thick around the image of Tezcatlipoca in Tenochtitlan in 1519 that the walls and floor of the god's shrine were black (Diaz del Castillo 1976, p. 236).

Conclusions

The realm of ritual and symbolic analysis of past beliefs and practices is a notoriously difficult one. Yet it is not possible to believe that such conceptual activities were not part of the ancient world, least of all amongst the peoples of a complex society such as the Aztec. Attempts to penetrate the symbolisms of past cultures must therefore, by definition, be fraught with problems and unsubstantiable suggestions/insights. Nevertheless, such attempts are necessary if we are not to negate the possible complexities of past lifestyles.

Bearing in mind the origin of obsidian, the use to which obsidian implements were put, its black colour and its designation as the divine substance of Tezcatlipoca (Heyden 1988, p. 222), it is possible to see strong circumstantial evidence that, for the Aztec, obsidian in some way 'represented' the solidified blood-essence of Tezcatlipoca/Tepeyollotli, who, as the jaguar manifestation of Tezcatlipoca, inhabited and symbolized both caves and mountains. Such a symbolic set of equations could give weight to the suggestion that the etymology of Tepeyollotli's name was itself also significant, particularly bearing in mind Heyden's (1981, p. 25) view that obsidian itself was the 'heart of the earth'. Perhaps its incorporation of the word *yollotl* ('heart') – the vital energizing aspect of life – reveals a deeper significance, reflecting the fact that the heart was the most precious offering which the Aztec could make to their deities (Lopez Austin 1973, p. 60). In this sense, Tezcatlipoca, 'the lord of everywhere', was Tepeyollotli, 'the dweller on the threshold of the obsidian cave'.

References

Bastien, J. W. 1985. *Mountain of the Condor*. Prospect Heights: Waveland Press.
Benson, E. P. 1988. The eagle and the jaguar: notes for a bestiary. In *Smoke and Mist: Mesoamerican studies in memory of Thelma D. Sullivan*, J. K. Josserand & K. Dakin (eds), 161–71. Oxford: British Archaeological Reports.

Broda, J. 1982. Astronomy, cosmovision and ideology of prehispanic Mesoamerica. In *Ethnoastronomy and Archaeoastronomy in the American Tropics*, A. F. Aveni & G. Urton (eds), 81–110. New York: New York Academy of Sciences.

Broda, J. 1987. The provenience of the offerings: tribute and *cosmovision*. In *The Aztec Templo Mayor*, E. H. Boone (ed.), 211–56. Washington: Dumbarton Oaks.

Broda, J. 1991. The sacred landscape of Aztec calendar festivals: myth, nature, and society. In *To Change Place: Aztec ceremonial landscapes*, D. Carrasco (ed.), 74–120. Niwot: University of Colorado Press.

Burgoa, F. de. 1934. Geografía descripción de la parte septentrional del polo ártico de America. 2 vols. *Publicaciones del Archivo General de la Nación*, XXV–XXVT. Mexico, D.F.: Talleres Gráficos de la Nación.

Carrasco, D. 1990. *Religions of Mesoamerica*. San Francisco: Harper & Row.

Caso, A. 1958. *The Aztecs: people of the sun*. Norman: University of Oklahoma Press.

Caso, A. 1971. Calendrical systems of central Mexico. In *Handbook of Middle American Indians*, vol. 10, R. Wauchope (ed.), 333–48. Austin: University of Texas Press.

Cobean, R. H., M. D. Coe, E. A. Perry, K. K. Turekian & D. P. Kharkar 1971. Obsidian trade at San Lorenzo Tenochtitlan, Mexico. *Science* 174, 666–71.

Coe, M. D. 1972. Olmec jaguars and Olmec kings. In *Cult of the Feline*, E. P. Benson (ed.), 1–18. Washington: Dumbarton Oaks.

Crocker, J. C. 1985. *Vital Souls: Bororo cosmology, natural symbolism and shamanism*. Tucson: University of Arizona Press.

Diaz del Castillo, B. 1939. *The Discovery and Conquest of Mexico*, G. Garcia (trans. and ed.). London: P. Maudslay.

Diaz del Castillo, B. 1976. *The Conquest of New Spain*. Harmondsworth: Penguin.

Douglas, M. 1990. The pangolin revisited: a new approach to animal symbolism. In *Signifying Animals: human meaning in the natural world*, R. G. Willis (ed.), 25–36. London: Unwin Hyman; Routledge pbk 1994.

Duran, D. 1967. *Historia de las Indias de Nueva España e islas de la Tierra Firme*. 2 vols. A. M. Garibay (ed.), Mexico, D.F.: Editorial Porrua.

Duran, D. 1971. *Book of the Gods and Rites and the Ancient Calendar*, F. Horcasitas & D. Heyden (trans. and eds). Norman: University of Oklahoma Press.

Eliade, M. 1974. *Shamanism: archaic techniques of ecstasy*. New Haven: Princeton University Press.

Furst, P. T. 1968. The Olmec were-jaguar motif in the light of ethnographic reality. In *Conference on the Olmec*, E. P. Benson (ed.), 143–75. Washington: Dumbarton Oaks.

Hallowell, A. I. 1969. Ojibwa ontology, behaviour, and world view. In *Primitive Views of the World*, S. Diamond (ed.), 49–82. New York: Columbia University Press.

Herrera, A. de. 1945. *Historia general de los hechos de los Castellanos en las islas y tierra-firme de el Mar Oceano*, vol. IV. Asunción de Paraguay: Editorial Guarania.

Heyden, D. 1981. Caves, gods, and myths: world-view and planning in Teotihuacan. In *Mesoamerican Sites and World-Views*, E. P. Benson (ed.), 1–40. Washington: Dumbarton Oaks.

Heyden, D. 1988. Black magic: obsidian in symbolism and metaphor. In *Smoke and Mist: Mesoamerican studies in memory of Thelma D. Sullivan*, J. K. Josserand & K. Dakin (eds), 217–36. Oxford: British Archaeological Reports.

Heyden, D. 1991. Dryness before the rains: Toxcatl and Tezcatlipoca. In *To Change Place: Aztec ceremonial landscapes*, D. Carrasco (ed.), 188–204. Niwot: University of Colorado Press.

Jimenez Moreno, W. 1979. De Tezcatlipoca a Huitzilopochtli. *Actes du XLIIe Congrès International des Americanistes* vol. 6, 27–34.

Klein, C. F. 1987. The ideology of autosacrifice at the Templo Mayor. In *The Aztec Templo Mayor*, E. H. Boone (ed.), 293–370. Washington: Dumbarton Oaks.

Kus, S. M. 1983. The social representation of space: dimensioning the cosmological and the quotidean. In *Archaeological Hammers and Theories*, J. A. Moore & A. S. Keene (eds), 278–300. New York: Academic Press.

Leon-Portilla, M. 1963. *Aztec Thought and Culture*. Norman: University of Oklahoma Press.

Lévi-Strauss, C. 1969. *The Savage Mind*. London: Weidenfeld & Nicolson.

Lopez Austin, A. 1973. *Hombre-Dios: religión y política en el mundo Nahuatl*. Mexico, D.F.: UNAM.

Matos Moctezuma, E. 1978. *Muerte a filo de obsidiana: los Nahuas frente a la muerte*. Mexico City: INAH.

Matos Moctezuma, E. 1988. *The Great Temple of the Aztecs*. London: Thames & Hudson.

Miller, M. & K. Taube 1993. *The Gods and Symbols of Ancient Mexico and the Maya*. London: Thames & Hudson.

Nagao, D. 1985. *Mexica Buried Offerings*. Oxford: British Archaeological Reports.

Nicholson, H. B. 1971. Religion in pre-hispanic central Mexico. In *Handbook of Middle American Indians*, vol. 10, Archaeology of Northern Mesoamerica, G. Eckholm & I. Bernal (eds), 395–445. Austin: University of Texas Press.

Porter Weaver, M. 1981. *The Aztecs, Maya, and their Predecessors*. New York: Academic Press.

Ruggles, C. L. N. & N. J. Saunders 1993. The study of cultural astronomy. In *Astronomies and Cultures*, C. L. N. Ruggles & N. J. Saunders (eds), 1–31. Niwot: University of Colorado Press.

Ruiz de Alarcon, H. 1984. *Treatise on the Heathen Superstitions that Live Today among the Indians Native to this New Spain, 1629*, J. R. Andrews & R. Hassig (trans. and eds). Norman: University of Oklahoma Press.

Sahagun, B. de 1950–82. *Florentine Codex: a general history of the things of New Spain*, A. J. O. Anderson & C. E. Dibble (trans. and eds). 12 books in 13 vols. Santa Fe: School of American Research and the University of Utah Press.

Sahagun, B. de 1975. *Historia general de las cosas de Nueva España*, A. M. Garibay (ed.). Mexico, D.F.: Editorial Porrua.

Sanders, W. T., J. R. Parsons & R. S. Santley 1979. *The Basin of Mexico: ecological processes in the evolution of a civilization*. New York: Academic Press.

Sauer, C. O. 1954. *Agricultural Origins and Dispersals*. New York: American Geographical Society.

Saunders, N. J. 1984. Jaguars, rain, and blood: religious symbolism in Acatlan, Guerrero, Mexico. *Cambridge Anthropology* 9, 77–81.

Saunders, N. J. 1988. *Chatoyer*: anthropological reflections on archaeological mirrors. In *Recent Studies in Pre-Columbian Archaeology*, N. J. Saunders & O. de Montmollin (eds), 1–40. Oxford: British Archaeological Reports.

Saunders, N. J. 1990. Tezcatlipoca: jaguar metaphors and the Aztec mirror of nature. In *Signifying Animals: human meaning in the natural world*, R. G. Willis (ed.), 159–77. London: Unwin Hyman; Routledge pbk 1994.

Schavelzon, D. 1980. Temples, caves or monsters? Notes on zoomorphic facades in pre-hispanic architecture. In *Third Palenque Round Table, 1973*, Part 2, M. G. Robertson (ed.), 151–62. Austin: University of Texas Press.

Seler, E. 1904. Ueber Steinkisten, Tepetlacalli, mit Opferdarstellungen und andere ahnliche Monumente. *Gesammelte Abhandlungen zur Amerikanischen Srach-und Altertumskunde* vol. 2, 717–66. Berlin. (1961 edition, Graz: Akademische Druck u. Verlagsanstalt.)

Taube, K. 1986. The Teotihuacan cave of origin: the iconography and architecture of emergence mythology in Mesoamerica and the American Southwest. *RES: Anthropology and Aesthetics* 12, 51–82.

Thompson, J. E. S. 1960. *Maya Hieroglyphic Writing: an introduction*. 2nd edn. Norman:

University of Oklahoma Press.

Townsend, R. 1987. Coronation at Tenochtitlan. In *The Aztec Templo Mayor*, E. H. Boone (ed.), 371–410. Washington: Dumbarton Oaks.

Townsend, R. 1993. *The Aztecs*. London: Thames & Hudson.

Van Zantwijk, R. 1981. The Great Temple of Tenochtitlan: model of Aztec cosmo-vision. In *Mesoamerican Sites and World-Views*, E. P. Benson (ed.), 71–86. Washington: Dumbarton Oaks.

15   Sto:lo sacred ground

Gordon Mohs

The Sto:lo Indians

To:lmels Ye Siyelyolexwa

> You have to be careful with what you tell others, especially things
> which should not be written about. This is spiritual knowledge and
> not meant to be taken away. You take anything away from the
> Great Spirit and you're going to suffer for it. You have to be very
> careful when talking of things of spiritual power, like the winter
> spirit dance . . . because winter dancing is about the most powerful
> thing that ever came to earth. . . . You have to be very careful with
> things to do with the smokehouse and what you say. The same is
> true of these stories. Some people who tell of some stories about
> sacred things are only hurting themselves and those they talk to.
>
> (AC 1986)[1]

> These places are very important for us, those that know about
> them. They are something that is proof of our past. But it seems
> that something that is proof of our past is not as sacred as things
> that are sacred to Europeans.
>
> (EP 1985)

> These places are an affirmation of our spirituality before the white
> man came. . . . I don't mind them [white people] going there to see
> them because it's proof that Xa:ls was here. And that's one thing
> that the white man doesn't believe is that we were spiritual. You
> know, they don't believe it. They figured that when they came and
> found us in our paint and regalia, what we wore for spiritual
> occasions, praying to our Great Spirit, they thought it was all
> Devil's work because it looked strange to them. They didn't under-
> stand that we had our ways.
>
> (TG 1985)

Figure 15.1 Sto:lo 'the river people': fishing in the canyon above Yale.

> These places are special. They were put here for a reason. Xa:ls
> meant for these places to last for all time. They were not meant to
> be destroyed. But white men don't understand this.
>
>   (EP 1985)

> These places are special. But if we don't look after them, our people
> will continue to get harmed.
>
>   (TG 1985)

The Sto:lo are Coast Salish Indians; their language is Halq'emylem. 'Sto:lo'
means 'people of the river' and is a collective name for all Halq'emylem-
speaking people living along the lower 170 km of the Fraser (Sto:lo) River in
southwestern British Columbia, Canada. In general, however, the Sto:lo
name refers to and is used by those groups living along the upper and central
reaches of the Fraser River valley between Fort Langley and Yale. Downriver
groups, notably the Musqueam and Katzie, while considered Sto:lo, are
generally referred to by their tribal names (Duff 1952; Mohs 1990).

Sto:lo traditional lifeways, past and present, have centred on the river and
fishing (Figs 15.1, 15.2). All indications are that these patterns have persisted
for millennia (Mohs 1990).

From a cross-cultural perspective, traditional Sto:lo society was similar to
other cultural groups on the Northwest Coast, despite the fact that they did
not have the rigid ranking structure and/or formalized clan system character-

istic of several of these groups. Their society was complex, as indicated by the presence of social ranking, a highly developed artistic tradition, a weaving complex, monumental architecture (notably, massive residential and ceremonial plank houses), large-scale public works projects (such as fish weirs), centralized forms of redistribution (including the potlatch and trade), an organized spiritual belief system and an elaborate ceremonial complex including: the winter dance ceremonial, the first salmon ceremony, and the *sxw":yxwey* masked-dance ceremonial.

Prior to contact, the upriver Sto:lo tribes occupied and controlled one of the most economically productive regions of the Pacific Northwest. Governing control of lands and resources was the responsibility of individual tribes, primarily through the office, and under the direction of the respected *siy:m* (or chiefs). Accordingly, most social, political, religious and economic functions were under their control. Leadership was largely ascribed by birth and ability, succession generally passing through the male line from father to son.

In the first few decades preceding and following contact, the Sto:lo population was devastated through European-introduced epidemic and endemic diseases (Mohs 1990). Earlier economic patterns underwent a dramatic readjustment and the social order of the times was severely strained. Shortly thereafter, the federal and provincial governments established reserves for the various Sto:lo tribes. Fishing regulations were imposed, traditional religious

Figure 15.2 Fish is a part of everyone's life. A Sto:lo youth learns early how to process fish for wind drying.

practices curtailed, existing forms of native government slowly eroded, and Indian Act regulations imposed (Mohs 1987).

Today, the Sto:lo Indians are situated in a semi-urban to marginally rural cultural landscape; their population numbers approximately 3,500. Politically, the Sto:lo are now organized as bands, some of which correspond to former tribal designations. In total there are 24 bands occupying 83 reserves. For the most part, reserves are small (averaging about 250 acres in size) and are scattered over a large geographical area. The majority of reserves, allotted under the direction of Governor Douglas between 1864 and 1872, were subsequently decreased in size through a series of land appropriations including the allotment of various rights-of-way. The reduction of reserves was done at a time when Indian populations had reached an all-time low. In the central Fraser valley, for example, the reserves of the Chilliwack, Sumas, Nicomen and Matsqui Tribes alone were reduced in size by nearly 35,000 acres (Mohs 1987).

Traditional Sto:lo territory covers an area of approximately 100 sq. km. The main feature of the region is the Fraser River, and with the exception of the Fraser River valley itself, most of the terrain is mountainous. Within this landscape, the Sto:lo have many sacred places: mountains, lakes, bedrock outcroppings, pools, eddies, trees, rocks, hillsides and upland areas.

Today, the region as a whole is characterized by increasing urbanization. In the upper and central reaches of the Fraser valley alone there are now six cities, ten towns and numerous smaller communities, and there is an increasing emphasis on commercial industrialization. Outside the townships, the region is characterized by intensive agriculture. Two major highways, various subsidiary access roads, two national railways, and various 'rights-of-way' including power transmission lines, oil and gas pipelines traverse and dissect traditional Sto:lo territory, connecting the various regional and rural centres with one another. In recent years, recreational developments have also become intense, owing to the proximity of the metropolitan Vancouver population (about 3 million). In brief, commercial, industrial, agricultural, urban, corporate and private development are ever-present and a constant threat to Sto:lo traditional lifeways (Fig. 15.3).

The issue of sacred sites cannot be isolated from a multitude of other modern issues facing the Sto:lo Indians. There is a plethora of social problems (e.g. poverty, unemployment, suicide), further compounded by internal political factionalism and external pressures from local, regional, provincial and federal economic development projects, land-altering activities, and ever-increasing infringements of traditional rights and title. On the political front, settlement of outstanding land claims is a paramount concern, as are projects affecting the aboriginal fishery. In this regard, the river remains a focal point in Sto:lo economic life as well as present-day political struggles. Regular confrontations with Federal Fisheries officers over native fishing rights are a seasonal occurrence and at the centre of numerous legal battles. Industrial pollution, municipal sewage disposal, and encroachments from highways,

Figure 15.3 *Yó:yseqw*, the 'hat rock', a transformer site on the Harrison River; one of many 'stone people' in Sto:lo territory.

railways, pipelines, mining, forestry, dyking and private developments are of utmost concern.

To the Sto:lo, the river and its resources represent tradition itself. The Sto:lo name is taken from the river; its resources have provided sustenance for longer than can be remembered. The river has been a great provider and a source of consolation and much sorrow. The river has been the home and much, much more. It is a living force to which the Sto:lo remain deeply rooted and attached, as they point out:

> The River is our lifeblood. Anything that happens to it is a concern to us.
>
> (AP 1986)

> The river is my friend. The river has never failed me. Every time I needed help, I went down, got my help. . . . Yeah, the river is a great river. I always call it the mighty Fraser River. And that's what I call it when I ask for help from him. And I get my help. That's about the Fraser.
>
> (EP 1985)

Sto:lo heritage – past, present and future – is intimately tied to the river. Not surprisingly, the majority of Sto:lo spiritual sites are in some way connected with the river.

Sto:lo spirituality and mythological base

In much the same way that archaeological sites are perceived as physical evidence tracing the people's presence on the landscape, so too are spiritual sites perceived as ancestral, physical manifestations of Sto:lo spirituality. Both are markers which serve to confirm and validate Sto:lo cultural history (Mohs 1987). However, not just any spot is, was, or can be assigned spiritual status. These landmarks are special places, they colour the landscape, and are rooted in legend and spiritual beliefs.

In the past the Sto:lo had, and have today, an organized spiritual belief system and an elaborate ceremonial complex. Ceremonial activities included: *smíla* dancing in great ceremonial longhouses, first salmon ceremonies, the *sxwó:yxwey* masked–dance, sun ceremonies, and ceremonial burnings (*yéqw*) for the ancestors (*syewá:l*). Over time, a few traditional beliefs and ceremonial practices – such as the once regular sun (*syó:qwem*) ceremonies – have fallen from use. Most, however, have been maintained to the present day, in spite of various negative acculturation processes over the past 150 years.

Spiritual beliefs are centred upon Chíchelh Siyá:m, the Great Spirit, the sun–god and creator of the earth and mankind; the deity Xa:ls, the great creator and transformer; and the tribal ancestors. According to Sto:lo legend, the earth was created by a union of the sun and the moon. Sun was all–powerful and created the first man, the first woman, and a multitude of other animals. During this early epoch, there was little order in the world. There were many evil spirits, people with power, animal people, deformed men and other creatures. Chíchelh Siyá:m was not pleased and sent Xa:ls to earth in order to put things right.

Xa:ls, the son of the sun, was a complex entity. Generally regarded as a singular entity of male gender, Xa:ls is sometimes recognized as a plural entity (Xexa:ls) with a female component. Ethnographic accounts suggest that Xa:ls first appeared at Harrison Lake and travelled throughout the Salishan area in the guise or character of a 'young bear' accompanied by his two 'brothers' and 'sister' (e.g. Boas 1895; Hill–Tout 1902; Jenness 1934/5; Jenness 1955; Teit 1898, 1900, 1909). Xa:ls took on human form following his return from Vancouver Island. In this manner, he travelled up the Fraser River accomplishing many deeds.

An understanding of Xa:ls and his role or place in Sto:lo culture is essential in comprehending the spiritual significance of many sacred sites. For example, the legend of Xa:ls predates the coming of the Europeans and the influence of the Christian missionaries (Mohs 1987). Nevertheless, to many Sto:lo Elders today, Xa:ls is equated with Christ and is revered in the same way that Christ is revered by the non–Indian Christian community:

> Xa:ls is the Little Christ. . . . There was a time when the world was
> a lot different than it is now. Many things were with power; both
> people and animals and other beings. Many people could create
> things their own way. If a man wanted a deer, he could fix it or

wish it; he didn't have to hunt for it. Others could see things before
they happened and others were gifted with the powers of transformation. God didn't like this so he sent Xa:ls, the Little Christ,
down to make things right. Some people were too smart and
abused their power so God send Xa:ls down to destroy those who
were powerful.

(AK 1985)

Xa:ls to me, he's Christ. Today I understand him as Christ . . . and
when he got to Yale and he was teaching the people in each village
as he came along and [was] transforming foods, you know, from
our brothers. In the stories that I could understand from what I hear
long ago, it was always a brother, a grandfather and the female
follows the male afterwards, you see. Not like the way we hear it in
the Bible where they make Adam, and from Adam's ribs they
make the woman. Well, this one is the way I understood it.

(TG 1985)

The role of Xa:ls in Sto:lo cosmology and his place in Sto:lo culture history
cannot be overstated. According to Sto:lo legend, it was Xa:ls who created the
salmon and taught the people how to fish. It was Xa:ls who created the great
cedar and showed the people how to use its various parts and it was he who
inspired Salish weaving. It was Xa:ls who put the world in order, ridding the
land of many evil sorcerers so that the Sto:lo people would have a safe place to
live and it was he who transformed the tribal ancestors. It was Xa:ls who
taught the people prayer and the principles of respect. As Sto:lo Elder AC
relates, these values remain a vital aspect of Sto:lo spiritual teachings:

We have a powerful spiritual life and we worship the Great Spirit.
Our way is the spiritual way, and it's important that we don't
forget this. It's important to respect our old ways and what is
important to us. If we don't, our grandchildren, their grandchildren, the future generations will have no culture. Like this
graveyard here. This graveyard is still our spiritual ground. My
wife is buried here. My Elders are buried here. According to our
tradition, they are not just covered with dirt, put in the ground,
and forgotten. Their feelings, their spiritual feelings, their spirits
are with us for life. So, it's important we remember, our Elders are
not long dead and gone. Their spirits are still here protecting us.
When I was a boy, a young man, I was taught to respect our
spiritual grounds. I couldn't even shoot a grouse near our cemeteries in those days. You weren't allowed to make noise, any noise. If
you did, you'd wake their spirits up. So it's important to respect
our ways, our traditions. Generation to generation has got to learn
now, or we will never learn our culture. It's like cedar trees get
hurt, when you break their branches. So, you have to apologize for

that when you take from it. Then, the cedar tree understands what it is you're going to do. My grandmother used to do that. When she'd take cedar roots for baskets, she'd get up early and thank the tree. These ways are our ways. Indian spirituality is based on respect. Without it we get into trouble. So it's important to identify Indian spirituality for ourselves, to live our life by our spirit, by our spiritual feeling.

(AC 1990)

The river and fishing have also influenced and shaped Sto:lo religious beliefs. Salmon – especially the spring (*Oncorhynchus tshawytscha*) and sockeye salmon (*Oncorhynchus nerka*) – has been the most important resource to the Sto:lo (Duff 1952, p. 62). According to legend, salmon was given to the Sto:lo by Xa:ls, who instructed the people on how to catch, prepare, care for and respect this gift:

Long ago Xa:ls was travelling over this world. He was carrying some little Salmon bones in his hands. He came to a river and dropped in one of the bones. 'You shall become the Humpback and there shall be many of you.' Next Xa:ls came to the great river and travelled far up its course, dropping Salmon bones in many streams and small rivers. 'And you shall be the Sockeye,' he said. He then dropped bones in other lakes and creeks and they became the Suckers, the Trout, and all the other fish.

(adaptation of Thelma Adamson's story,
translated by Amelia Douglas, 1979)

The Sto:lo point out many spiritual places which they say affirm the special relationship between them and the salmon. As noted by Chief Frank Malloway (Yakweakwioose) (Coqualeetza Media Production Centre 1984), the spiritual relationship between people and salmon is reflected in the traditional respect accorded this resource, especially the first salmon ceremonies celebrating the yearly return of the salmon:

A long time ago, the salmon ceremony, the first salmon was taken to the chief of the village. He cooked it, called all of the people together and he divided the salmon; as long as each person in the village got a piece of that salmon. All the bones were picked up, carried back to the river and sent back to the salmon people. We had to do this to please the salmon people that sent their children up to us. If we didn't do this they wouldn't send any more because we didn't respect, we didn't thank them the right way.

(Coqualeetza Media Production Centre 1984, n.p.)

Site classification

To date, the bulk of the current research on Sto:lo sacred sites has focused on documentation of the spiritual values accorded them by the native Elders. In order to gain a greater understanding of these places and their role in native society, site documentation has included the recording of descriptive and locational information, field identification, and the creation of a tribal site registry. So far, 200 sites have been identified.

The Sto:lo do not have a word to describe all sites of spiritual significance. They do have a word, *stl'itl'aqem*, which is used to describe a 'spirited spot' or 'spirited place'. *Stl'itl'aqem* include places or sites which are, in themselves, believed to be spirited or inhabited by supernatural forces, notably sites with resident spirits or beings, transformer sites (see below), and a few other places (MM and ED 1985). There is also a word, *sxwoxwiyam*, used to describe landmarks that have stories or legends attached to them.

For inventory purposes, several 'classes' or 'types' of spiritual sites have been identified, based on interviews with Native Elders. Taken together, these comprise what can be considered Sto:lo sacred grounds or spiritual sites. In the context of this chapter the terms 'sacred ground' and 'spiritual site' are used interchangeably to mean a site or physical locality with which members of a native group have strong spiritual ties or feelings based on traditional beliefs and/or ceremonial usages.

Transformer sites

These are sites that are attributed to or associated with the deeds or actions of Xa:ls and/or other 'transformers'. Transformer legends are powerful stories about places and events held sacred in the hearts and minds of many present–day Sto:lo. Recorded ethnographically at the turn of the century and in the 1940s and 1950s, these legends have been maintained to the present day, demonstrating their importance to the Sto:lo. They are an integral connection to the past, and demonstrate continued maintenance of spiritual beliefs.

According to legend, when Xa:ls travelled through Sto:lo territory putting things in order, he made numerous transformations. The legacy of his deeds and actions are to this day identified with many geographical features in the landscape. To date, about seventy transformer sites have been identified. Most are associated with bedrock outcroppings, prominences, or large boulders, although a few caves, small boulders, river pools and one mountain are also represented. They range in size from 1 metre square to more than 1 km square. Some tend to be rather inconspicuous (Fig. 15.3), and a few have been identified in deep water within the mainstream of the Fraser River.

Transformer sites tend to be found in proximity to ancestral villages and settlements, most of which have been recorded as archaeological sites. In general, it is not so much the physical characteristics of the sites themselves that matter. Rather, it is what each site represents and what individual feelings it evokes. In this regard, the Elders often refer to many of these sites as 'stone people':

> These places [transformer sites], they were people before, our ancestors you know. . . . That's where we lived. That's where our people spent most of their time. All those little rocks that's been changed. That's where we lived at Yale; all along the river. Yeah, there's some at the Hunter, hunting I believe, and the Dog. And there's some old people went squeezing that sockeye oil and they were all gathered around at Hemhemetheqw when they were changed [to stone]. I used to play in them [pitted rocks] at Hemhemetheqw. Do you go to where my grandfather used to fish, Xwelemo'welh? There's three big rocks there. They were old people before. My grandfather told me that there's two old people and a daughter there. I used to avoid them when we go down that way. And I always have a little thing for that. And I make the sign of the cross, you know, when I go by. Don't know why you know. And there's a bear right across from there. That place where the H.'s are fishing. I guess they [Xexa:ls] killed a bear and it's laying on its side. You can just see the hip of the bear, just like a real one there. It's right on top. Right where they tan their fish, changed to stone by Xa:ls.
>
> (AK 1986)

Several sites consist of a number of boulders, which are said to represent groups of individuals who were simultaneously transformed into stone by Xa:ls. Not infrequently, they go unnoticed by archaeologists:

> I can't begin to tell you about the heritage sites you've missed. I can show you a place where Xa:ls transformed a man, woman, girl, boy, and dog into stone right close to Siwash Creek.
>
> (AP 1984)

Th'exelis is the most commonly acknowledged, and one of the most revered, transformer sites among present-day Sto:lo. Simon Fraser (the first white explorer to the region) was taken there by his Sto:lo hosts in 1808 (Mohs 1987, p. 90). The main feature at this site is a number of shallow grooves, some obscured with lichen growth (Fig. 15.4), in a bedrock exposure 15 metres above the Fraser River. Interestingly, Th'exelis was recorded as an archaeological site in 1972, at which time it was described as a petroglyph, and as part of a rock bluff with grooves cut into it for sharpening tools (Ferguson 1972). Th'exelis is one of a handful of transformer sites exhibiting archaeological-type features; other examples include pictograph and petroglyph markings on Harrison Lake and River.

Both the Sto:lo and their Nlaka'pamux neighbours have legends associated with Th'exelis. According to Sto:lo legend, Xa:ls arrived at Yale near the completion of his time on earth. Here he met a formidable opponent,

Kwiyaxtel, a powerful medicine man from Spuzzum with whom he had a duel. In the course of their duel, Xa:ls sat at Th'exelis ('gritting his teeth') and Kwiyaxtel on the opposite side of the river at X̲elhalh ('injured person'). In the ensuing battle, each attempted to transform the other by various means. Gritting his teeth, Xa:ls proceeded to scratch the rock upon which he was sitting with his thumbnail and with each scratch weakened his opponent. Eventually, Kwiyaxtel was defeated and transformed into stone by Xa:ls (AD; AK; AP; EP; TG, pers. comm.)

Many Elders maintain that Th'exelis is where Xa:ls first instructed the people on the methods of catching salmon. According to this legend, Xa:ls was sitting at Th'exelis watching the people across the river trying to catch salmon with their bare hands. As he sat and thought, Xa:ls scratched the rock with his thumbnail. With each new scratch mark, the people gained new knowledge on how to make nets and to catch salmon. The integrity and maintenance of these legends confirm the importance of Th'exelis to modern belief systems. Th'exelis is where Xa:ls left his mark on the earth so that future generations would remember his passing. In context, Th'exelis is an affirmation of Indian spirituality prior to the coming of the Europeans, and also represents a continuity of the present with the past:

When my grandfather used to go up there fishing he'd take me over

Figure 15.4 Sacred 'scratch marks' made by Xa:ls at the site of Thecrlid/Th'exelis ('gritting his teeth'); where Xa:ls taught the people to fish and where he duelled the medicine man Kwiyaxtel.

there and when I turned 13 – I think this was another training that
young people go through – if you want to be strong, you sit there
at 13. So I sat there and I put my feet where his was. Mind you, it
makes you quiver to sit there. Cause maybe the powers are there of
Christ [Xa:ls] himself, being sitting there. Goes through a person
and then makes you feel. . . . I imagine that's the way the longhouse makes you feel too. You know, when they receive the spirit,
you know, they quiver. So that's the way it is up there.

(TG 1985)

Spirit residences

These sites or localities are believed to be spirited or inhabited by supernatural
forces, usually related to particular spirits and/or beings, such as ghosts,
water-babies, Thunderbird, sasquatch, serpent, etc.

Sites with resident spirits or beings are generally much larger in area than
transformer sites, and are distributed more evenly in the landscape. Most are
small upland lakes, although small river pools, stagnant ponds, a few caves,
knolls and rock formations are also represented. Sites of this nature, as well as
all transformer sites, are believed to possess residual power, which can be
drawn upon by those undergoing vision/power quests. To unwary visitors,
effects from these sites can be harmful:

Most of these places don't have power in them but some, like the
'people rocks' do. . . . Xo:li:s is what can happen to you at these
places if you are not careful. . . . You usually have to speak to these
places to let them know that you're not a stranger. Otherwise, the
power in the place may make strange [xo:li:s] upon you.

(EP 1985)

Like when you go by there, if you don't care, they can take your
spirit into them. Whenever they want. You don't know at all . . .
you just get sick. You go [to the] doctor's [but he] doesn't know
anything about it. You just eat and throw up, eat and throw up.
[Your] Spirit is sick.

(AK 1986)

Ceremonial areas

Ceremonial sites are associated with ceremonial functions, formal religious
observances, ceremonial feasts, offerings to the dead, etc. Most are associated
with winter spirit dancing. Primary localities include the sites of many large
cedar longhouses or 'smokehouses' (past and present), ritual bathing-pools
situated along foreshore areas of local creeks, rivers, sloughs and lakes, and
upland training-grounds. There are also sweathouse sites and selected sites
associated with ceremonial burnings. Bathing-pools and isolated training-
areas are particularly important for new dancers undergoing initiation rights
(RM; CJ, pers. comm.).

Figure 15.5 Lhilhetalets ('boiling up from the bottom'), sacred pool of the *sxwó:yxwey*. Note railroad encroachment in foreground.

Traditional landmarks

These sites relate to specific aspects of Sto:lo culture and/or significant cultural historical events. Of particular importance are several sites associated with the origin of the *sxwó:yxwey* mask and the Sto:lo tribal ancestors. One of the more important of these sites is Lhilhetalets, a large, emerald-coloured pool which appears in a dry, side-channel of the Fraser River only during low-water times (Fig. 15.5). Spiritual sites of traditional importance are represented by a variety of features including boulders, caves, cliff faces, pools, and occasionally longhouse sites and pithouse settlements. One example of the latter is the pithouse settlement of Sxwoxwiymelh ('a lot of people died at once'), associated with the smallpox epidemic of 1806.

Questing/power sites

These sites relate to personal vision quests, power quests and puberty rites; some are also repository sites for cedar 'life-poles' and the ceremonial regalia of new dancers (associated with the winter dance ceremonial). Most questing/ power sites are associated with remote areas in the mountains, isolated stretches of the river, caves and transformer sites. The Sto:lo spiritual revival which has occurred in the past thirty years (see Jilek 1982) has seen many of the younger generation undergo extended periods of spiritual training in these areas. New dancers seek out wilderness areas in order to place their training regalia, and also their cedar life-poles, which often involves tying the pole to a young sapling so that life-pole and tree become one with the passage of time (FM, *pers. comm.*). It is generally believed that disturbance, removal or destruction of a life-pole or an initiate's costume can cause severe harm to befall both initiate and/or the responsible party. Thus, repository localities are kept secret.

Legendary and mythological places

These sites are associated with important legends, events and/or personages in Native folklore; they may also be judgement and prediction sites. Sites of legendary and mythological significance vary considerably in nature, form and geographical distribution. Examples include buried villages and several mountain caves associated with the Flood story. One of the better known mythological sites is P'oth'esala ('baby basket rock'), a small island in the Fraser River near American Bar. Formerly, women brought their baby baskets to P'oth'esala after their infants had outgrown them. They were placed in a hollow in the rock, turned to the sun, and left. Sto:lo women were required to make a new basket for each baby in much the same tradition that a new costume is made for each 'new dancer' entering the smokehouse. To do otherwise could cause harm to befall subsequent users. Baby baskets were left here in commemoration of Salmon Woman who, according to legend, was travelling upriver with a message from the salt-water people for the people living upstream. She was travelling with her baby, who was in a *p'oth'es* (baby basket). The *p'oth'es* was heavy and hindered her travel, so on the way Salmon Woman bathed the baby in medicines in order to make it grow fast. At P'oth'esala, the baby finally got big enough to travel without the *p'oth'es*, and it was here that Salmon Woman left it, in a hollow in the rock.

Burials

Burial and mortuary sites include tree burials, box burials, funerary houses, cave burials, and interment sites. Traditionally, tree burials, box burials and funerary houses were most common, but today interment is the most common form of burial.

Among the Sto:lo, human remains are treated with respect, whether they date from recent, historical or prehistoric times. It is generally believed that the handling of human remains can have a potentially harmful effect on the living, notably spirit sickness or spirit loss. The handling of human remains thus requires strict procedures of personal cleansing and protection (MU, pers. comm.). It is also a common belief that the spirits of the dead reside among the living. Although some spirits are thought to offer protection, most are believed to bother, disturb, or generally interfere in the lives of the living. The reasons for this vary (e.g. disturbing human remains through excavation will upset the spirits), but it is often thought that the ancestral spirits are upset by the personal conduct of the person affected. To reconcile and rectify this situation, ceremonial burnings are conducted to appease the spirits. Burnings are also regularly conducted at funerals and on other occasions, such as memorials.

Traditional resource areas

Sites from which materials for ceremonial and spiritual activities are or were obtained are generally small in size and scattered throughout Sto:lo territory. Most common are quarry sites for Indian paint, and there are also crystal quarries. In addition, there are several areas that are important for the collection of medicinal plants (FM, *pers. comm.*).

Other

There are some sites or localities scattered throughout the Sto:lo area which have been identified as spiritually important, but which do not fit into the above categories, e.g. astronomical sites, medicinal pools and springs, etc. A variety of rock formations, ponds, pools and springs are represented. These include *xwith'kw'em* ('sores'), a sacred spring near American Bar noted for its medicinal and spiritual healing properties, and *skwo:wech* ('sturgeon'), a rock at Cheam. Each site is important for a different reason and each has a history associated with it. There are also several pictograph and petroglyph boulders, some of which have been buried so as to reduce the likelihood of their being found (AP; EP; AY, *pers. comm.*).

Individual Elders and band members tend to place greater significance on one or more classes of particular importance to them. For example, spirit dancers might consider certain kinds of site to be of special significance:

> Most important are places associated with our winter dance, places where new dancers go for their training and where we put away our poles, our smokehouses and where we build our sweatlodge sites. And there are other places.
>
> (FM 1990)

A *sxwo:yxwey* dancer would include the origin sites of the ceremonial *sxwo:yxwey* mask. An Elder raised according to traditional beliefs might consider that sites attributed to Xa:ls are the most important; yet others, that burial/mortuary locations are of ultimate significance. Vested interests aside, each class of sites does incorporate cultural/ethnic significance and each may be considered of equal value within an overall ideological context.

There are many Elders who would extend spiritual significance to include old villages, archaeological sites, pictographs and petroglyphs (Fig. 15.6):

> Some places are sacred. You're not supposed to go there and touch anything. Even the lakes way up the mountain . . . and parts of the river. . . . You can't just go there and do as·you like, go swimmin' in it. Those are sacred. Certain things [were] done to it by the old timers. . . . Things that the old timers did years ago, we're not supposed to touch it; even kickwillie houses. And where they were buried. A lot of them died in that place. . . . Chicken pox, small-pox, killed them all off. And they just died there. And we're not supposed to go there and touch them. . . . Like where the people used to live years ago, up Yale. People that are real old are buried there. And the graveyard's still there. And you can't bother them because they're sacred ways. There's a lot of them old graveyards

Figure 15.6 Nlaka'pamux Elder Annie York offering interpretation of petroglyph markings documenting the 'origin' stories to Sto:lo researcher Sonny McHalsie.

up there. Our Great Elders are buried there. . . . People used to
carve on these big rocks. And that's sacred too. You're not supposed to touch them or do anything wrong with them. . . . Cause
it was so sacred, you're not supposed to touch them. Well, that's
native ways, you know.

(JP 1986)

Given that some of the sites identified by JP would be more appropriately
classified as archaeological sites, it is significant that they are valued as spiritual
sites.

Preservation concerns

Sto:lo Tribal Elders and band members who are knowledgeable about spiritual
places are very concerned about their protection and preservation. In the past,
some protection was afforded through silence, i.e. a reluctance to disclose too
much information about the sites, and from occasional more direct practices
such as site burial. These measures appear to have been relatively effective in
ensuring the overall protection and conservation of selected sites – especially
those not found on reserve lands. The tradition of silence is still maintained by
many Sto:lo people who believe that disclosure of information will inevitably
result in the wilful destruction and desecration of these sites:

I'm reluctant to tell you of these spots because the last time, a
loggin' company tried to take the 'head of the dog' and destroyed
the whole thing. . . . You know, I'm a proud man and these places
are sacred to me. I was taught all of this by four Elder Chiefs. If I
tell you about these places and they are recorded, then people will
go there and destroy what is there. So I'm reluctant to tell you.
Enough damage has been done.

(AP 1984)

A reluctance to disclose information has much to do with past attitudes and
activities of mainstream society. Historically, native religious beliefs and
practices in Canada have been discouraged, scorned, ridiculed, even outlawed
(Jilek 1982; UBCIC 1984), and many spiritual places have been defiled, defaced
and destroyed. Between 1884 and 1951, for example, traditional religious
practices, including the Sto:lo winter dance ceremonial, *sxwo:yxwey* dance and
potlatch were prohibited by law and forced to go underground during this
time. While freedom of religious expression is now permitted, the struggle for
acceptance of such traditional practices continues. Confronted with assaults
(perceived, intentional and otherwise) on their spirituality and spiritual places,
it is not surprising that many Native Elders remain silent when questioned
about these matters.

As regional developments have increased in scope and magnitude in recent years, conservation concerns have become more acute. With urbanization, damage to Sto:lo spiritual sites has been extensive. Of 200 spiritual sites identified to date, about 50 sites have been destroyed and 50 damaged or disturbed. Another 25 face ongoing disturbance or potential destruction from development. This represents over 50 per cent of all documented Sto:lo spiritual sites. It is of importance, from a conservation or land claims/Native rights perspective, that the majority of existing sacred sites (about 65 per cent) are not found on reserve lands.

Current and potential impacts are greatest upon sites and areas used for ceremonial/religious purposes. Virtually all sacred training-grounds, ritual bathing sites, and repository locations are affected. For example, several painted dancers have expressed a concern that repository locations for cedar life-poles and training costumes are not safe from development (FM; CJ, *pers. comm.*). Their protection is often at odds with current land-use activities, notably logging operations and recreation. In November 1986 loggers brought a cedar life-pole into the Forestry Office in Agassiz. It was immediately recognized by a Native employee (FD), who informed forestry officials of its significance. Smokehouse leaders were contacted and took charge of the pole. Another incident occurred in 1985, when a hunter brought a life-pole to the Chilliwack Museum. The pole was eventually returned to where it had been found in the Chilliwack River valley (CJ, *pers. comm.*). Such incidents reinforce the fears of Indian dancers regarding the sanctity of their repository locations.

One Sto:lo man (CJ) recently stated that his band (Squiala) has been increasingly restricted from using sacred grounds on Chilliwack Mountain, due to development and settlement of the area by non-Indians. These grounds, which cover an area of about 100 acres, include sites where many dancers (including his grandfather) have placed their life-poles:

> This is where we get our cedar from for the smokehouse, where we get our cedar boughs from, our devils club from. Now we can't go there anymore, can't use that anymore. There's too much development and too many people around. We used to go up Tamihi but too many sports fishermen started coming around and interfering with our sacred ways. Now we go up Chilliwack Lake and Slesse Creek. These areas should be set aside as sacred grounds. We're losing all our sacred grounds.
>
> (CJ 1987)

CJ also said that dancers from his and other bands moved up the Chilliwack River valley to use more remote traditional grounds, but even these have been encroached upon. The beach area and high grounds at the outlet of Chilliwack Lake have since been developed as a park and recreational property, forcing dancers to move progressively further north and east along the lake. CJ believed that soon there would be no place to go, and proposed that further development of Chilliwack Lake and other specified areas be prohibited, and that access to certain areas be restricted to Indians.

The concerns raised by CJ and others demonstrate the need for selected remote areas to be set aside for exclusive use by Indian people, in order that traditional spiritual practices can be maintained without outside interference. A precedent, in this regard, has been set by the State of Washington, where Salishan groups in the northern part of the state have had remote areas on government land set aside for spirit questing purposes (Criska Bierwert, *pers. comm.*, 1987). Failure to address heritage concerns such as these is to deny Native people the freedom and sanctity to pursue traditional religious beliefs and practices.

Management considerations

Damage to spiritual sites has gone largely unnoticed by non-Indians. This is due not only to the nature of these sites, but to a general lack of concern among archaeologists and heritage resource managers. It is compounded by reluctance, on the part of the Indians, to disclose information about these sites, and by a lack of communication between Indians and non-Indians.

Spiritual sites comprise an important part of the Native landscape and are an intimate aspect of Native heritage. Yet our present understanding of these sites is limited, both from a purely scientific point of view and from a resource management perspective. For example, in British Columbia, there are approximately 19,000 heritage sites registered with the Archaeology Branch of the Government of British Columbia, only seven of which are what can be considered sacred sites (John Foster, *pers. comm.*, 1990).

Sacred sites are easily overlooked and often unknowingly damaged or destroyed in the course of development. They do not have the same familiar characteristics as archaeological sites. Generally, there are no artefacts, no cultural markings or cultural alterations, and no distinguishing characteristics. It is only through appropriate investigation and dialogue with Native peoples that archaeologists, anthropologists, heritage resource managers, and the public in general can learn of the existence of sacred sites, and appreciate their value.

In Canada, a poor understanding of spiritual sites stems from a general lack of interaction between Indians and archaeologists and a failure on the part of archaeologists to incorporate native research interests and/or religious concerns into their project designs. Ferguson (1984, p. 225) has suggested that this failure to address native concerns stems from a conflict in value systems; current heritage ethics and values almost exclusively reflect the values and beliefs of Euro-Americans. Dunnell (1984, p. 66) has likewise stated that our professional preoccupation with problem-oriented research strategies has influenced the manner in which evaluations of significance have been made. He suggests that as scientific rationale has developed in the discipline of archaeology, scientific values have replaced humanistic values as the critical or primary factors in making significant evaluations. Trigger (1980, p. 671) contends that a lack of concern for Native interests has dehumanized Indian people and their heritage in favour of scientific research interests.

Archaeologists and heritage resource managers have lobbied hard to convince society that heritage sites are worth protecting, or at least deserving of study, before being obliterated by modern land uses. Thus heritage sites have received a degree of protection only when they have been deemed significant by archaeologists.

Significance

Ethnic or cultural significance is one component of the value given to heritage resources. In British Columbia, the assessment of this aspect has generally been left to the discretion of archaeologists, primarily those involved in heritage impact assessment studies. Archaeologists commonly designate Native burial sites as culturally significant, but few other sites. Thus most sacred sites are not recognized. For example, if the site of Th'exelis were evaluated by archaeologists during a typical survey, it would undoubtedly be written off as an insignificant heritage site. In contrast, there are few heritage sites that the Sto:lo would consider more important. As Trigger (1980) notes, the fact that most decisions about the significance of sites are made by archaeologists means that there is not only bias, but also self-aggrandizement.

From a management perspective, ethnic significance has generally been excluded from heritage resource legislation, policies and programmes. Ethnic values are noticeably absent from the list of criteria of significance recognized under the British Columbia Heritage Conservation Act (1979). Many questions regarding the incorporation of ethnic significance into the evaluation process remain unanswered. How can the significance of a site which lacks archaeological manifestations be verified? Whose role and responsibility is it to provide scientific endorsement and verification of ethnic significance? How does one deal with a site that cannot be excavated, moved, avoided, or developed for tourism? Is designation a matter for archaeologists and heritage resource managers?

Legislation, policies and programmes

Presently, there are no constitutional provisions guaranteeing Indians access to spiritual sites and/or traditional rights of use of their sacred grounds. Existing legislation contains no special provisions affording protection to spiritual sites; they are covered by the same laws that protect archaeological sites, and since few spiritual sites have archaeological manifestations, few are registered. By way of contrast, in the United States, the American Indian Religious Freedom Act (P.L. 95–341) contains provisions affording protection 'to sites considered important in the expression of Native American religious beliefs or lifeways' (Doyel 1982, p. 638). There is no comparable legislation in Canada. American legislation has been further bolstered by recent changes in government policy, such as the requirement of the Bureau of Indian Affairs that developers consult with Native groups prior to the implementation of land modification projects (Doyel 1982, p. 635). The net effect of these measures has been that archaeologists have found it necessary to interact more with Native peoples and to perceive Native traditions and heritage resources within a more humanistic framework (Winter 1980, p. 124). Increasingly, heritage sites and resources are being perceived in terms that are relevant to Native people and evaluated in terms of their potential contribution to ongoing cultural processes. An interesting development, noted by Knudson (1984) and Winter (1980, 1984), is a general trend among resource managers to regard archaeology's scientific orientation as a special interest and not the dominant rationale in cultural heritage resource management.

In British Columbia, in the early 1970s, an attempt was made to accommodate Native interests with the establishment of the Archaeological Sites Advisory Board (ASAB). Two Indians were appointed as board members and several recommendations from the Union of British Columbia Indian Chiefs (UBCIC) were implemented. Two significant policies ensued: (1) permits were granted to archaeologists only if prior permission was acquired from Indian bands, and (2) all recovered artefacts were to be held in trust for Indian bands. However, with the enactment of new heritage legislation in 1979 there was a move away from the earlier initiatives. The ASAB no longer exists and the UBCIC policies which were implemented have since been dropped. Currently, one Indian representative sits as a member of the British Columbia Heritage Trust, the funding arm of British Columbia's Heritage Legislation. The existence of this one position has done little to influence management in addressing Native interests. As noted by Simonsen (1984), less than 4 per cent of all funds allotted by the British Columbia Heritage Trust have gone to Native projects of any kind.

Indians have generally been excluded from heritage resource management decisions, policy development, funding and planning. Present management priorities are directed in response to proposed projects, and are designed to accommodate development. There is little or no long-range heritage planning and no Native input or direction with regard to conservation/preservation efforts, planning, or policing. In short, current policies do not incorporate Indian heritage values or concerns.

In order to rectify the present situation, many Native organizations in Canada have recently hired their own archaeologists, anthropologists, and heritage consultants. Several have initiated their own cultural heritage resource management programmes (Fig. 15.6); a few groups have endorsed policy statements on heritage (Mohs 1987). A major problem is still that most Indian organizations do not have access to funding sources, nor do they have the necessary support from archaeologists and/or management agencies to implement and carry out tribal heritage programmes.

Native options and management alternatives
Taken overall, legislation, policies and programmes in British Columbia and Canada have failed to protect sacred places and to address Native heritage concerns. As a result, the subject of heritage resources has become a matter of political and legal concern to Canada's Native peoples in recent years.

Significantly, the federal government has acknowledged the need to move on this matter. The Federal Task Force on Comprehensive Claims (1985) recommended that specific changes in government policy be made with respect to heritage resources of Native significance. However, despite petitions to both levels of government, there has been little movement on the matter of sacred sites.

The options currently available to Native peoples regarding the protection and conservation of their sacred sites are limited. They are: (1) continuation of a tradition of silence; (2) negotiation with existing provincial and federal governments; (3) legal action; and (4) direct action as a means of protection and conservation. Research among the Sto:lo indicates that the first option has been of limited effectiveness in affording protection and guaranteeing traditional access to sacred grounds. Negotiation with existing provincial and federal governments does not seem a viable alternative, given the limited success rate of negotiations on a plethora of other rights and land claims issues in recent years. Until such time that Native American rights and title are acknowledged by both levels of government, there seems to be little promise of a negotiated solution. Moreover, given the failure of the Meech Lake Accord (June 1990), it is unlikely that government policies and attitudes towards Indian peoples will change in the near future. The legal option may hold some promise as a means of protection and conservation; although there are no special provisions protecting sacred sites under existing legislation, and no *specific* constitutional provisions guaranteeing traditional use rights, the sanctity of sacred grounds and rights of access to them might be upheld if tested in the courts under existing constitutional provisions. Presently, existing aboriginal rights are guaranteed under Section 35 of the Canadian Constitution. However, it would appear that conservation/protection efforts pursued in this manner would be limited by the need to proceed on a case-by-case basis. Another serious limitation of the legal option for Canada's Native peoples is expense – few groups have the capital resources necessary to pursue this option; any existing funds are currently directed to other pressing matters. For many groups, direct action (such as that taken by the Haida Indians in 1988/9 regarding the logging of their traditional lands, or that taken by Quebec Mohawks in the 1990s to prevent a municipal golf course development) may be the only feasible alternative.

In general, there are several additional areas in which action can or should be taken to ensure that spiritual sites have a future. At the most basic of levels, archaeologists and Indians must work together to endorse legislation which better addresses Native needs and heritage concerns, and to ensure that policy changes are implemented which guarantee Indian organizations greater access to funding, a greater role in policy development and planning, and an equal voice in the decision-making process where Native heritage resources are concerned.

Conclusion

The issue of what anthropologists and archaeologists do or do not do, say or do not say, observe or do not observe, record or do not record can become a matter of ideological, political, moral and legal concern when the results affect the cultural integrity and/or rights of those studied. When dealing with a category of phenomena as special as sacred places, archaeologists and anthropologists must be extremely sensitive to how this knowledge is handled, and may be misused, especially in the context of litigation. Native organizations should consider developing and adopting ethical codes as tribal policy prior to information on sacred sites being processed and recorded.

Because of past experience, many Indians still hold rather cynical views with regard to archaeological theories, speculations and postulations. Some Indians and Indian organizations refuse to accept archaeologists' self-proclaimed right to study their cultures, because they consider that archaeologists are often simply concerned with their own academic research interests (Brody 1981, pp. 15–16).

Finally, the words of a young Sto:lo researcher regarding spiritual sites:

> I think they are important for a number of reasons. Lots of people in my generation don't even know they're there. When you learn about them they become important to you. It's like what [Elder] Andy Commodore was saying the other day in the Research Centre: 'Indians are returning back to their spirituality.' This is good because it'll help in pulling our Indian people together. . . . These sites are part of my Indian identity and these sites are an important aspect of our spirituality. I've never related to the non-Indian God. I have only looked to him so as not to take any chances, so to speak. But now I'm beginning to understand God, or the Great Spirit in Indian terms and these sites are an important part of that understanding. These places bind the culture and society which is the same thing. . . .
>
> There's a lot of things that seem to be lost, like my language. And, because of my language, or not knowing it, there's lots I didn't find out. But now I'm beginning to find out. There's lots my dad knew but never told me because it was only talked about in Indian; like all about these places.
>
> (SM 1986)

Without a proper inventory under the direction and control of Native people and without adequate changes in policies, programmes and legislation, it is doubtful that many spiritual sites will survive modern land uses. Whether or not these culturally significant places will be protected is an ethical question.

Note

1 Quotations throughout the text are from oral material given to the author by Sto:lo Elders, who are identified by initials.

Acknowledgements

This chapter is dedicated to the Native Elders who brought this matter to my attention, especially Andy Commodore, Amelia Douglas, Elizabeth Phillips, and in memory of Agnes Kelly.

References

Boas, F. 1895. Indianische Sagen von der Nord-Pacifischen Kuste Amerikas, trans. Dietrich Bertz for the British Columbia Indian Language Project as 'Indian myths and legends from the north Pacific coast of America'. Typescript, 1977.

Brody, H. 1981. *Maps and Dreams*. Ontario: Penguin Books.

Coqualeetza Media Production Centre 1984. *The River is our Home*. Video produced for the Alliance of Tribal Councils, Sardis, B.C.

Doyel, D. E. 1982. Medicine men, ethnic significance, and cultural resource management. *American Antiquity* 47, 634–42.

Duff, W. 1952. *The Upper Stalo Indians of the Fraser Valley, British Columbia*. Victoria, B.C.: British Columbia Provincial Museum.

Dunnell, R. C. 1984. The ethics of archaeological significance decisions. In *Ethics and Values in Archaeology*, E. L. Green (ed.), 62–74. New York & London: Free Press.

Ferguson, G. 1972. British Columbia Archaeological Site Survey Form. Archaeology and Outdoor Recreation Branch, Victoria, B.C.

Ferguson, T. J. 1984. Archaeological ethics and values in a Tribal Cultural Resource Management Program at the Pueblo of Zuni. In *Ethics and Values in Archaeology*, E. L. Green (ed.), 224–35. New York & London: Free Press.

Hill-Tout, C. 1902. Ethnological studies of the Mainland Halkomélem, a division of the Salish of British Columbia. *Report of the British Association for the Advancement of Science* 72, 255–349.

Jenness, D. 1934/5. Coast Salish mythology: Saanich and other Coast Salish myths and notes. Unpublished manuscript no. 1103.6, National Museum of Civilization, Ottawa.

Jenness, D. 1955. *The Faith of a Coast Salish Indian*. Victoria, B.C.: Provincial Museum.

Jilek, W. G. 1982. *Indian Healing: shamanic ceremonialism in the Pacific Northwest today*. Surrey, B.C.: Hancock House.

Knudson, R. 1984. Ethical decision making and participation in the politics of archaeology. In *Ethics and Values in Archaeology*, E. L. Green (ed.), 243–63. New York & London: Free Press.

Mohs, G. 1987. Spiritual sites, ethnic significance and native spirituality: the heritage and heritage sites of the Sto:lo Indians of British Columbia. Unpublished M.A. thesis, Simon Fraser University.

Mohs, G. 1990. The Upper Sto:lo Indians of British Columbia: an ethnoarchaeological review. Report and Legal Opinion, prepared for the Alliance of Tribal Councils and the Sto:lo Tribal Council, February 1990.

Simonsen, B. O. 1984. Open letter to the Chairman and members of the Board of Directors of the B.C. Heritage Trust. *The Midden* 16, 5.

Task Force to Review Comprehensive Claims Policy 1985. Living treaties: lasting agreements. Report of the Task Force to Review Comprehensive Claims Policy, D.I.A.N.D., Ottawa.

Teit, J. 1898. *Traditions of the Thompson River Indians of British Columbia*. Boston: Houghton, Mifflin, & Co.

Teit, J. 1900. The Thompson Indians of British Columbia. In The Jesup North Pacific Expedition, F. Boas (ed.), 163–392. *Memoirs of the American Museum of Natural History*, vol. I, part IV.

Teit, J. 1909. The Shuswap. In The Jesup North Pacific Expedition, F. Boas (ed.), 443–789. *Memoirs of the American Museum of Natural History*, vol. I, part IV.

Trigger, B. G. 1980. Archaeology and the image of the American Indian. *American Antiquity* 45, 662–77.

Union of British Columbia Indian Chiefs 1984. The Indian Nations inquiry into the reasoning behind worldwide philosophies: laws: and international experience on the rights of man. Unpublished manuscript on file at Union of British Columbia Indian Chiefs, Vancouver.

Winter, J. C. 1980. Indian heritage preservation and archaeologists. *American Antiquity* 45, 121–31.

Winter, J. C. 1984. The way to somewhere: ethics in American archaeology. In *Ethics and Values in Archaeology*, E. L. Green (ed.), 36–50. New York & London: Free Press.

16   The spirits of the Chugach people of Alaska are at rest once again

JOHN F. C. JOHNSON

Introduction

The Chugach region, centred in Prince William Sound and the lower Kenai Peninsula, southeast of Anchorage, could be called the melting-pot of early Alaska. All three of the major Alaskan Native peoples – Eskimo, Indian and Aleut – inhabited the region in prehistoric times. The history of the Chugach goes back in time for thousands of years, from the time when the Sound was still largely covered by glaciers from the last ice age.

Between 300 and 400 sites – Native Alaskan villages and fishing camps, rock paintings, trappers' cabins and Russian settlements – mark the rich 4,000 to 5,000-year-old cultural landscape. Most of the sites have been located and recorded in the past twelve years through the systematic survey of the shore-lines and forest fringe. National Register and National Landmark nominations are currently being prepared, although only half the area has so far been surveyed. Oral histories and migration stories have been collected, under the auspices of the Chugach Alaska Corporation (formerly the Chugach Natives Incorporated), from Chugach, Eyak Athabascan and Tlingit people, whose ancestors occupied the area in earlier times. Many of the stories are about families. My own grandmother, Mary Chemovitsky, was born on Nuchek Island, an 800-acre island in Prince William Sound which was once the largest Chugach settlement. The Chugach left the island in 1929, when the last chief – my grandmother's uncle, Peter Chemovitsky – died.

Today, the island is seeing new life, and the Chugach Heritage Foundation has been set up by the Corporation, to preserve, promote and educate the region's Native American population, and help to fund restoration projects. To mask sites from the casual visitor, surface artefacts will be collected and inventoried, and it is planned to recruit villagers as stewards to monitor the sites. Restoration money from the Exxon Valdez oil spill (see overleaf) may be used to build mini cultural centres in the villages, in which the artefacts could be displayed.

The archaeological record of the Chugach region has been subjected to two recent major natural and cultural disasters. In 1964 the Sound was the epicentre of North America's largest recorded earthquake (which threw up, in the process, a large number of prehistoric adzes and stone tools). A tidal wave was set off, lifting one island 40 feet (12 metres), and sinking others some 20 feet (6 metres), and killing many people.

The second disaster was the Exxon Valdez oil spill, which was like a monster eating and destroying everything in its path. It was bad enough to have a black crude oil covering prehistoric villages, burials and subsistence sites, but the aftermath was even worse, when thousands of workers flooded the pristine environment and violated the heart and soul of the Chugach people, and desecrated the burial site of the 1,000-year-old Chugach man.

Chugach man

What happened to the remains of Chugach man is symbolic of the effect the oil spill had, and is having, on the people. He stood 5 feet 3 inches and had no cavities, not unusual for a person between 35 and 40 years old living in the area over 1,000 years ago. He had no contact with the Russians, British, Spanish or Americans who later came looking for riches such as sea otters, furs and gold. When he died, the people of his village honoured him by placing his remains in a cave high above the waters of Knight Island. He was a Chugach man and he rested in peace, undisturbed by the turbulence of the last 2,000 years – until the Exxon Valdez oil spill.

As thick black oil from the Exxon Valdez spread throughout Prince William Sound, so did the thousands of clean-up workers. These workers did more than attempt to clean the beaches. They went upland, often onto Native lands. Historical sites, long protected by the fact that their locations were unrecorded by state or federal bureaucracy, were now being 'rediscovered'. Scores of Exxon workers were trespassing on ancient burial sites, including the one on Knight Island. In fact they did much more than trespass. As a result of their invasion, sacred burials and villages were desecrated by workers trampling over the fragile prehistoric environment.

Reports of finding skeletal remains circulated among workers and, at the request of Exxon's leading archaeologist, Alaska state troopers arrived on the scene to take the remains away. Thus the remains of the Chugach man were torn away from his resting-place – bagged and tagged for observation in the crime laboratory in Anchorage, Alaska. Ten days later, by accident, the Chugach oil spill response team learned of the 'rediscovery'.

No one in the Chugach Corporation was notified. They should have been. Exxon was aware of Chugach's policy on human remains, which states that: 'Upon discovery of any human remains, Chugach is to be notified immediately and the remains are not to be disturbed unless directed by Chugach.'

The Chugach responded in anger. They could not and would not wait any longer for the slow wheels of a blundering bureaucracy to give its blessing to return the remains and to grant permission for a reburial back at the place of their origin. The Chugach Corporation demanded that the remains be turned over immediately to the Chugach people. So it was that two months after the oil spill workers had violated his resting-place, the Chugach man was finally returned to the burial cave by a large delegation of Chugach elders and a Russian Orthodox priest. No outsiders were invited, not the media, not Exxon.

Under federal law, historical sites are protected but in this case, by the time the oil company learned the law, the Chugach man had been disturbed for the first time in many years.

Father Harris of the Russian Orthodox church gave this eulogy prior to re-interring the Chugach man:

> Before we reinter this man back into the earth and bless this coffin and place we must realize that God brought us to this place in the natural beauty of this island. Praying for him, we are asking God to bless all those who have departed this life.
>
> The people of this area were blessed by God to live the Orthodox life. Thus it is appropriate today to celebrate this service. When news came to us that this person's relics were disturbed, we had to do something about it. Chugach and its staff saw to it that an appropriate burial would be made.
>
> This man we are to bury is a representative of all the people of this area, people who lived here for thousands of years. It was God's will that they live a most beautiful life then and it is his will that they live a most beautiful life now.
>
> This wonderful place has been disturbed by that great Exxon Valdez oil spill that has affected all of our lives. We hope and pray that as time goes on that everything that has been disturbed will be restored and that this person who had been reinterred here will be a SYMBOL of this. Although his grave has been disturbed now, he will now be placed back with DIGNITY, with HONOUR and with RESPECT.
>
> By honouring him, we honour everything which God created. We must have respect for every living creature and every blade of grass that we walk on, because God reveals himself in nature and in man. He is the God of the universe.

The burial service was held in a very large, dry cave that was formed by volcanic activity aeons ago (Fig. 16.1). During the service, one could hear Russian Orthodox church songs echoing across the salt waters of Prince William Sound and watch smoke from the incense hovering throughout the cave.

The Chugach man and the Chugach people heaved a sigh of relief as the

Figure 16.1 Burial cave. General view of reburial party. Photo: Chugach Heritage Foundation and John F. C. Johnson.

Figure 16.2 Detail of interior of cave showing reburial. Photo: Chugach Heritage Foundation and John F. C. Johnson.

body was returned to the earth (Fig. 16.2). A small potlatch was held on the beach below the cave where smoked salmon and other foods were consumed.

We thought that the Chugach man and the grave-robbing issue had been laid to rest once and for all – until an Anchorage newspaper reported the following details from a different incident:

$100 Fine For Sound Grave Robber
Brings Criticism From Natives

An oil spill cleanup worker who robbed an ancient native grave in Prince William Sound last summer pleaded no contest to federal charges and was fined $100 last month, angering Chugach Alaska Corporation Natives who say the penalty was too light. The U.S. Forest Service, which prosecuted the case, recommended the sentence and later refused to disclose the name of the grave robber to protect him from unwanted publicity. Eugene F. Wall, 39, also received a suspended $400 fine and a year of information probation from a federal magistrate. Forest Service archaeologist stated: 'The lesson of promoting the respect for human remains would not be served by burning this individual.'

A University of Alaska anthropologist said he turned in Wall, a former student, when Wall shared his finds with him. Wall came to him with the bones and other objects in order to talk about them with him. The anthropologist said: 'I am not sure how much wrong doing he was actually admitting, because he was enjoying the fact that he knew all these secret sites where he could get stuff in Prince William Sound.' Wall brought the skeletal remains to the university and they were subsequently turned over to the Chugach. Wall said that collecting artefacts was widespread on the oil spill cleanup. People would slip off and collect things and in the evening they would compare the bones and artefacts they had found. The Forest Service could have charged Wall under the Archaeological Resource Protection Act, which provides felony sentences for grave-robbing. Instead, he was charged with a misdemeanour under another statute. Chugach Natives were angry because they felt the sentence was too light. The Forest Service's press release pretty much says 'no problem, we won't give you any trouble if you're a grave robber'.

The chief archaeologist for Exxon had attempted to protect archaeological sites from workers by showing them a 14-minute video on the subject, and distributing a memo that outlined criminal penalties. This same archaeologist stated that the Chugach people should reveal the location of all historic sites so that the public can understand them and thus protect them better. Exxon even sent drawings of artefacts to workers in the hope that they could recognize them while cleaning the beach. This experiment, made at the expense of the culture of the Chugach, was a total failure, to say the least.

It gives you a strange feeling; it is as if Native people are not humans – someone can go out and interfere with Native burial sites and receive only a $100 fine. A lot of Chugach people were angry. It was felt that some sort of community service should have been mandated for Wall – like working in a mortuary. If anyone went to the Anchorage town cemetery and dug up some bones, they would certainly get more than a $100 fine. Once again the hearts of the Native people are heavy with sorrow as more remains of honoured ancestors are removed from their hallowed resting-places.

A Native Elder told me:

> I fought all my life to protect the heritage of my people; aren't first Americans' grave sites as worthy of respect as any other? A few archaeologists from Alaska have protested the return of native remains over a thousand years old, saying that they are not native. If this is true than half the hills of Israel are fair game to be dug up and we have another reason to be grateful that Jesus rose from the dead.

Other reburials

The following is another account of a reburial of Chugach remains (reprinted from the Chugach Newsletter):

THE SPIRITS OF THE CHUGACH ARE AT REST ONCE AGAIN!

October 9, 1990 was truly a glorious day. The sky was blue, ocean waters lay calm and mountain goats grazed while the killer whales hunted under the shadows of the mountain peaks of (Ingim–atya) Chenega island. This was the day the Chugach left the material world to arrive at a higher level of spiritual understanding.

Both the young and old mobilized in a fleet of beavers on floats to pay respects and re-inter their prehistoric ancestors in their original resting place after years of desecration by mindless vandals.

The Reverend Archpriest Nicholas Harris of Saint Innocents Russian Orthodox Cathedral and Eyak (Athabaskan) elder Richard Stevens attended to the spiritual needs of this re-interment.

The reburial took place at two prehistoric caves in Prince William Sound. One of the rock shelters near the Columbia Glacier was called 'hidden people in a cave' and at one time contained 23 burials (some of which were mummified). Some were wrapped in sea otter skins with their paddles at their sides while others were dressed in armor and ground hog skins.

The burial cave near Knight Island was reported as containing seven mummies squatting with their backs to the walls. On the cliff walls above their heads were red paintings of men paddling in boats with killer whales in the back ground.

In prehistoric times the Chugach would adze large spruce logs into planks for construction of burial coffins. In 1990, thick cedar plank coffins were made and a Russian Orthodox cross was placed at the grave where massive rock boulders were placed over the coffin.

The desecration of these tombs took place in the name of science, greed and just plain stupidity. Many of these mummified remains were carted off to various museums in California, Washington, Pennsylvania and also to the Smithsonian Institution in the nation's capital.

Good news is slowly emerging out of this gloomy period in the history of mankind. Nearly all of these institutions have agreed to return these bodies back to Chugach. Our advanced civilization is finally realizing that we must have respect for all cultures if we are to truly advance to a higher level of existence. The spirits of both the living and the dead will not rest until these wrongs are corrected. The next reburial is planned for the day we catch the next grave robber in action.

Recently, I have initiated the return of the remains of nearly fifty individuals from the University of Pennsylvania Museum and the Smithsonian Institution. We intend to rebury them in the original locations from which they were taken. In some cases this will mean interpreting and recording what we find after redigging the holes. We had planned to re-inter the remains this summer, but lack of funds for building coffins and re-excavating the sites is impeding our efforts.

The fight for Native rights is an ancient one. We must continue to fight for what is right and what is just. We cannot turn the hands of time back, but we can learn from the past. We should not expect other people to protect our beliefs and interest, for they will not. The fate and survival of a person's culture is in his or her own heart and soul, and if individuals are not prepared to make the time to protect their own culture, they cannot expect others to do so – ask not what your culture can do for you but what you can do for your culture.

17 Waahi tapu: *Maori sacred sites*[1]

HIRINI MATUNGA

Introduction

One of the more vexing issues confronting planners, resource managers, archaeologists and historians in New Zealand is the issue of who owns or guards our past. Similarly vexing is the issue of who then has the right to make decisions about how the past is protected, managed, presented, documented, guarded and ultimately controlled. Whether the 'past' is defined as material culture, artefacts, human remains or physical sites or objects is largely irrelevant. If it is possible to obtain some agreement on who the guardians of the past are, and some acknowledgement made to the ethical, spiritual and cultural obligations that go with this guardianship, the matter of who should then rightfully control or manage 'the past' becomes a political issue.

Maori people are the *tangata whenua* (people of the land, indigenous people) of Aotearoa (New Zealand), having migrated to Aotearoa from Hawaiki over a thousand years ago. There are over fifty *iwi* (tribes) in the country, and prior to the coming of the Pakeha (European) in the early 1800s, they were the *kaitaiki* (guardians) over all natural resources, *whenua* (lands) and *taonga* (treasured possessions), including *waahi tapu* (sacred places) within their *rohe* (territory).

In 1840, the Treaty of Waitangi was signed between numerous *rangatira* (Maori chiefs) and representatives of the Queen of England. There were two versions of the Treaty, an English version and a Maori 'translation'. Most of the *rangatira* who did sign signed the Maori version. The English version ceded sovereignty from the *rangatira* to the Queen of England. The Maori version guaranteed those *rangatira* who signed the Treaty retention of their *tino rangatiratanga* (sovereignty or absolute authority). The aim of the Crown was to legitimize the presence of the English in this country, and take sovereignty, but the aim of the *rangatira* was to ensure retention of their own *iwi* sovereignty.

The Crown did not honour the terms of the Treaty, and there continues to be debate, claim and counterclaim between the Crown and *iwi* as to how the

Treaty should be honoured. In the meantime the majority of natural resources and *taonga*, including *waahi tapu*, have passed out of Maori ownership to private interests and the Crown.

Who owns the past?

This apparently simple question is central to the issue of *waahi tapu* protection, and the many grievances being expressed by *tangata whenua* about the desecration of their sacred sites. It raises, however, a multitude of ethical, spiritual, cultural and political issues.

The past is perceived in different ways by different cultures. Methods of interpreting, recording, managing and protecting the past also differ between cultures. Left in relative isolation, or at least only having gentle contact with neighbouring peoples, and subject only to the natural processes of cultural evolution, the way a culture defines its own reality will remain largely intact, though not unchanging. The way people define their existence, their world-view and creation stories, and how they value, interpret, manage and transmit their past will continue to be handed on from generation to generation.

Experience of colonization around the world has shown that domination by a more powerful culture, which defines its reality in quite different ways, either destroys or at best drives the less powerful culture into a subservient role. What was considered culturally 'valid' can be rendered 'invalid', and the politically weaker are somehow required to modify their reality to fit within the constraints of a new code.

In Aotearoa, as in most colonized countries, the indigenous culture has been the loser, and as a consequence the Maori past is continually being studied and analysed by Pakeha western culture. This has given rise to a number of problems.

First, western culture in Aotearoa continues to define the rules of analysis, to provide the litmus test for what is valid and what is invalid, scientific or primitive, objective or subjective, rational or irrational. For instance, Maori methods for transmitting history are based largely on oral tradition. Western archaeology and historical analysis in New Zealand has tended to view oral tradition and traditional Maori approaches to interpretation of the past as limited in value unless substantiated by scientific analysis – either through archaeology or written history. Evidence from the *matakites* (seers), who use their powers to discern the whereabouts of *waahi tapu* by walking an area of tribal land, even if this is supported by oral evidence from *kaumatua*, is considered by scientific researchers to be invalid unless tested by scientific analysis.

Maori culture has well-defined procedures and rules for dealing with the past. It has its own litmus test for determining validity and invalidity, its own experts for dealing with the *tapu* areas and objects of the tribal past, and it can be dangerous for Maori people who do not follow correct Maori procedures when delving into the past. The fact that western cultures do not acknowledge this reality is evidence of their own limitations in their handling of other peoples' realities, rather than the result of inadequacies inherent in Maori cultural methodology.

Second, a curious amalgam exists in Aotearoa of groups with vested interests in the past. To some, artefacts of the past or land containing *waahi tapu* sites may simply be a tradeable economic commodity. To others the same artefacts and sites may be historical or archaeological curiosities to be analysed and documented. But to the tribe that claims them the artefacts and sites may be sacraments upon which their cultural heritage and spiritual survival depend. It is clear that it is the Maori people who have the most to lose by being denied access to, or control of, the resource called the past, because this past is clearly associated with a culture, an *iwi*, *hapu* and *whanau*.

Third, there are distinct differences in the way Maori and Pakeha people in Aotearoa 'perceive' the past, resulting in a significant disparity in the degree of significance placed on it. To the Maori the future is behind and is unknown. The past is in front and contains within it signposts and messages which give identity, and which enable the community to plot a path into the future with confidence and assurance. In essence, to know where you are going, you have to know from whence you came. Maori people, like many other indigenous people, see themselves as part of a living history, a continuum which reaches back through their *whakapapa* (genealogy), *tupuna* (ancestors) and through time, to the creator. Dotted along the way are events, people, places, objects that create a whole, which is the Maori heritage and identity. Whether the events occurred last year or 300 years ago may be intrinsically irrelevant.

Although the Pakeha conceptualization of their past in Aotearoa may include recognition of the importance of heritage, it lacks the spiritual dimension that makes many sites and objects of the past a fundamental component of Maori spirituality. The past for Maori people is not just a heritage resource. To those Maori immersed in it, it is a spiritual resource, whose 'use' involves prescribed procedures. The past is viewed as part of the 'living present'. This is at odds with the view that there is a firm line between the past and the present, and which often results in the relinquishing of obligations to the past in favour of the present. For Maori, relationships exist through time, from the past to the present and into the future, which must be protected. Furthermore, the Maori past in this country goes back at least 1,000 years, whereas the Pakeha past goes back no more than 200 years. The Maori past exists only in this country, it only has relevance to this land and therefore the Maori people lose everything if their past is not protected.

Waahi tapu

In the Maori creation story humans descended from Papatuanuku (Earth-mother) and Ranginui (Skyfather). The union of Ranginui and Papatuanuku resulted in around seventy male progeny including the *atua* (gods), and

Rangaroa (god of fish), Rongo (god of vegetation and peace), Tumatauenga (god of war), Haumia (god of uncultivated foods), Tawhirimatea (god of winds and weather) and Tane (god of the forest and trees).

Tane, the chief *atua*, represents life, prosperity and light. He made woman from the soil of Hawiki, breathed life into her and called her Hineahuone (earthformed maiden). Tane mated with Hineahuone, and from their union begat Hinetitama and other daughters. These other daughters gave birth to mankind. Tane also mated with his daughter Hinetitama. When she found out Tane was her father, shame and distress caused her to flee to the underworld where she became Hinenuitepo (goddess of death and the underworld). Hineniutepo welcomes all her children who are not immortal.

Maori attitudes to land, natural resources and *waahi tapu* (sacred sites) are based on this close 'kinship' link. Humans are not separate from the environment but are an intimate part of it. Because of this kinship link, humans have a responsibility to safeguard Papatuanuku, Ranginui and natural and physical resources from violation and destruction. When a child is born the *pito* (afterbirth, placenta) is buried under a tree or plant to seal the connection between children/humankind and Papatuanuku. As the children grow up they are taught to care for Papatuanuku and to prevent despoiling and desecration of her resources. Throughout their lives they are taught to be *kaitiaki* of the natural world.

Maori recognize that within Papatuanuku there are *waahi tapu*. These places are sacred either because of events that have taken place there, or because they may be resource sites. The main types of site are listed here to illustrate the wide range of different kinds of sites that exist. They include: places associated with death (e.g. burial-grounds and caves, trees, mudflats); places where people died, and where bodies rested; battlefields; burial places of the placenta; *tuahu* (altars); sources of water for healing and death rites; *ara purahoura* – sacred pathways for messengers; *mauri* stones and trees; carved *poupou* representing ancestors; *pa* sites and *papakainga*; canoe landing sites; sacred mountains, rivers, lakes and springs (and those rivers and mountains named in *whakatauki*); *mahinga kai* (e.g. birding, cultivation, fishing, forest and mineral resource sites); *toko taunga iki* (rocks which identify fishing-grounds); *wahi taonga mahi a ringa* (e.g. resource sites for Maori art resource material, such as *kiekie* (flax), *pounamu*, etc.); confiscated lands; *ara* (e.g. pathways connecting *iwi* areas and resource sites); landscape features which determined *iwi* and *hapu* boundaries; mythological sites; historic sites; and *waahi whakamahara* (sites recognized as memorials to events).

It is important to realize that, unlike Pakeha custom, much of the knowledge handed down by the ancestors about *waahi tapu* is not available to everyone, but is the responsibility of particular individuals, primarily *kaumatua*. The knowledge is special, and may not be understood, valued or respected by others, and if the knowledge is made too freely available the sites may even be desecrated. They are not just places on a map, they have a wealth of 'personal' Maori tribal history associated with them.

It is also true that, although many tribes have retained knowledge of their tribal *waahi tapu*, there may also be 'gaps' in this knowledge. Areas that may have been overlooked or forgotten in modern times are being 'rediscovered' by tribal *tohunga, kaumatua, matakite* and even by archaeologists and historians. The 'pool' of knowledge is thus not 'static' and fixed at any one point in time, but is developing.

Protection and management of *waahi tapu*

The Treaty of Waitangi was an agreement between two sovereign nations, and guaranteed to the Maori people continuing control over their land. It was not signed because of any threat of war, but in the hope of a peaceful, orderly settlement. However, since there were two versions of the Treaty, Pakeha and Maori versions, differences in interpretation inevitably arose. The international *Contra Preferantum* legal rule requires that if such differences arise in interpretation, preference must be given to the indigenous (i.e. Maori) version, but the Government of New Zealand does not recognize this rule.

The three written Articles in the Maori version of the Treaty are quite clear:

Article One: The chiefs gave to Queen Victoria the right to govern;

Article Two: Queen Victoria agreed that the chiefs would retain full possession of their lands, villages and *O ratou taonga katao* (everything which they valued, i.e. lands, forests, fisheries, language, spirituality);

Article Three: Queen Victoria gave all the Maori people of New Zealand the same rights as British subjects.

However, within seven years of the signing of the Treaty the Maori people had become a minority in their own country, and their land has been gradually taken from them. The Maori view is that the Crown has acted in breach of Article Two of the Maori version of the Treaty.

The *waahi tapu*, those parts of the land that are of special significance to the Maoris, have not been recognized by the Pakeha. *Waahi tapu* cannot be forced into preconceived categories of importance, and one group cannot determine what is *waahi tapu* to another. They provide cultural and *iwi* markers which, together with *whakapapa* (genealogy), mark the people with the traditional landscape, providing physical, historical and emotional links to the *tupuna*.

As a result of development, logging and other commercial intrusions, the landscape has changed dramatically over recent years. These gross changes in the physical landscape can be compared to the destruction, in the Pakeha world, of national treasures such as whole museums or art galleries. It is only within very recent times that the number and extent of sacred sites has been fully appreciated by those Crown agencies responsible for the management of areas, for example, such as the Waipoua Forest.

Recently Maoris have participated in archaeological fieldwork, including site survey, mapping, excavation and researching and recording traditional knowledge concerning the *waahi* within different *iwi* domains. Following extensive consultation and discussion, it was resolved that details of the historical, spiritual and emotional significance of *waahi tapu* would be recorded and that knowledge, hitherto withheld, would be imparted. In the past, there has been a reluctance by *tangata whenua* to discuss or divulge traditional information, as it was seen to be one of the very few *taonga* (valuables) not yet plundered by the Pakeha.

Maori have questioned whether the existing historic places administrative structures and legislation afford any real protection for *waahi tapu*, or whether they serve the vested interests of professionals who occupy administrative or scientific positions.

The Historic Places Trust, under the Historic Places Act 1980, is empowered to preserve the historic heritage of New Zealand and uses the NZ Historic Places Board of Trustees to facilitate this. Historic places include sites, buildings or natural objects which are historic through an association with the past, and which provide evidence of any cultural, traditional, aesthetic or other assessment of value of the past. Three types are specified:

> *Archaeological sites:* sites associated with human activity older than 100 years and able, through archaeological investigation, to provide evidence of the exploration, occupation, settlement or development of New Zealand.

> *Historic areas:* areas which contain an interrelated group of prehistoric or historic features which have historical value as a group.

> *Traditional sites:* places or sites that are important by reason of their historical significance or spiritual or emotional association with the Maori people or any section thereof.

There are some concerns about existing legislation as far as the protection of *waahi tapu* is concerned. Traditional sites, which are specifically related to Maori people, are placed in a different category from archaeological sites. An application must be made to the Historic Places Trust to have a traditional site protected and, if the Trust itself is satisfied that it is a traditional site, it assesses its importance, and considers what action (if any) should be taken to protect it. However, there is no guarantee that a non-archaeological site of traditional importance to Maori people will be recognized as such and be afforded protection under the Act.

Archaeological sites, on the other hand, receive automatic protection from the Act, if they are over 100 years old. Archaeological site definition emphasizes the importance of scientific investigation of sites to collecting information concerning the early history of New Zealand. For Maori people, it is the site itself that is important, for cultural and spiritual reasons, and for the associations it may have with past events and *tupuna*. That such sites may not be archaeological is irrelevant.

The present Act and Trust does not recognize, in any meaningful way, that *tangata whenua*, under the Treaty of Waitangi, have the right to control, protect and manage their own heritage and their own sacred sites.

Individual perceptions

In contemporary times Maori people continue to pay the highest respect to their *waahi tapu*. Whether these areas remain in Maori ownership or are now owned by private interests or the government is irrelevant: their value self-evidently remains.

Hariata Gordon has lucidly described Maori views:

> For us the sacred sites are our history books and education processes, necessary for our spiritual existence and survival, for without them we are nothing. They speak to us of another time, another world, the space and its environs within the Universe. Sacred sites are defined as everything, or all those happenings that pertain to the ancestors. These are the *Taonga* – our Treasures.
>
> This concept is the axiom which all tribal structures and their tribal bases are dependent on for the identification of why, when, how, which and, more importantly, who we are as people. A cultural heritage to pass on for the benefit of future generations . . . the treaty of Waitangi . . . guaranteed to the Maori people the power, protection and continuation of their possessions – treasures.
>
> Sacred sites are included in those possessions/treasures, but they are being desecrated and abused by developers for economic development and financial gain, by policy makers and by governments in the name of economic growth, progress and development for the benefit of the nation.
>
> If you can imagine a hill top, with an ancestral burial site on it and my elder and myself, standing beside that burial place, surrounded by bulldozers, machinery, developers and an archaeologist wondering what the hell we were doing there – imagine too the pain, anguish and hurt that we were experiencing as we stand there. These are spiritual pains and values that can not be felt except by those immediately affected.
>
> If you ever visit New Zealand and in particular, Auckland, the largest metropolis in New Zealand, which contained many of our sacred sites, cast your eyes over some of the beautiful and expensive

homes that have been built on those hills. Many have been built on burial sites and ancient ancestral *pa* sites . . . where the tribal chiefs and their people would gather for discussions. Very little of our heritage remains today in the city area that has not been built on for housing, high-rise buildings, roadways etc. and so the struggle for us goes on and on and on.

(Gordon 1991, pp. 48–9)

Alex Nathan similarly presents a personal view:

My *hapu* (subtribe) is called Te Roroa and all of the sites involved are associated with our *tupuna* (ancestors). . . . The relationship that exists between the Maori as *tangata whenua* (people of the land) and the *pakeha* who colonised Aotearoa is one of social, economic and political subjection to majority rule, and our people have harvested the bitter fruits of that tyranny for the past 150 years. . . . In his recent submission on the Historic Places Legislation Review a noted *kaumatua* Reverend Maori Marsden stated, ' . . . of all racial issues that which has to do with *waahi tapu* is the most culturally sensitive, highly emotive and generates more heat than most. . . .' I would like to emphasise that *te tino rangatiratanga* incorporates the authority a tribe has over its natural resources, and their right to determine how these resources should be managed. These resources are more than just the material aspects. They also include the so-called intangible elements of spiritual significance.

There are varying definitions and perceptions of *waahi tapu* in common use by Maori. . . . Any place or feature that holds special significance to a particular *iwi* (tribe) or *hapu* (subtribe) can be *waahi tapu*, but such places may not necessarily be significant to any other group. The existence and history of such sites has been known to our people for many generations and the stories have been retained and recalled in our oral traditions. When exotic re-afforestation began in 1924 the pleas of our *tupuna* (ancestors) to have *waahi tapu* excluded from planting areas were ignored. The legacy of that arrogance is evident today in a highly modified landscape. Within living memory many culturally important landscape features have been destroyed by land development and re-afforestation.

The Waipoua Archaeological Project included direct partici-pation (of *tangata whenua*) in archaeological fieldwork. . . . The work was intended to contribute to . . . the establishment of a partnership between the western scientific approach and traditional knowledge. A few archaeologists . . . had gained our trust and confidence by demonstrating their integrity and sensitivity, and a respect for the *mana* (authority) of the people and our *waahi tapu*. However personal and professional differences between different factions and archaeologists intruded and . . . in the final analysis *tangata whenua* suffered. We have had situations where decisions directly affecting our *waahi tapu* were being made by archaeologists or bureaucrats, who in most cases had no direct intimate knowledge of local situations. There has been no accountability to *tangata whenua* for decisions and actions taken. We have questioned whether the existing (Historic Places Act 1980 and Trust) afford any real protection for our *waahi tapu* or whether they merely serve the vested interests of professionals who occupy administrative or scientific positions in glass towers far removed from the real world.

(Nathan 1991, pp. 50–1)

Conclusion

Returning to the opening question, the issue of 'who owns or is guardian of the past' can be drafted into a statement about cultural and spiritual ownership, guardianship and moral obligation to protect the past.

Maori culture, like all cultures, has its world-view. It is holistic in the sense that it encompasses the metaphysical (spiritual) and physical (natural) world and recognizes the two as part of an interrelated whole. This world-view perceives humans as tracing their *whakapapa* back in the past through their *tupuna* to the creator. Relationships exist between the tribe today and their past, their *tupuna*, the *atua* and the physical 'repositories' of their past, i.e. *waahi tapu*, *urupa* and tribal artefacts. From this world-view (which can and does change over time, but only at the behest of the culture) are derived the ethical principles which maintain the integrity of the culture and its world-view, and serve to ensure that obligations are maintained.

The question posed at the beginning of this article was 'Who owns, or is guardian of our past, our heritage, our *waahi tapu*, our cultural artefacts?' Maori people, and individual *iwi* and *hapu* in this country always have and always will be *kaitiaki* of their past and of their *waahi tapu*, irrespective of the intentions or actions of those who have different perceptions. Within Maori culture there exist intergenerational obligations to the *tupuna*, our ancestors, which must be met and discharged in relation to the past, present and future.

Note

1 This chapter is based on evidence presented by the author to the Waitangi Tribunal in the Te Roroa Claim 1990. It also draws on discussions with Roro Te Puke, Kaumatua (elder), Pita Pou, Te Aue Davis, Hariata Gordon, Naida Pou, Tahu Hikuroa, Alex Nathan, Morrie Love and Mike Barns.

References

Gordon, H. 1991. The significance of *waahi tapu* to the indigenous of Aotearoa. *World Archaeological Bulletin* 5, 48–9.

Nathan, A. 1991. *Waahi tapu* protection and management: case study, Waipoua Forest. *World Archaeological Bulletin* 5, 49–51.

18 Principles and practice of site protection laws in Australia[1]

David Ritchie

Introduction

In the states and territories that comprise the Commonwealth of Australia the need to protect places relating to Aboriginal cultural heritage has long been recognized. The questions 'What is being protected?', 'for whom?' and 'for what purpose?' are still being debated. Early forms of legislation to protect Aboriginal sites were intended to protect 'cultural relics', in particular rock art, burials and artefacts. The value of such sites was conceived of in national and historical terms and contemporary Aboriginal interests were not acknowledged. Paralleling the assimilation policy of the first two decades after the Second World War a number of states sought to protect Aboriginal cultural heritage under general heritage legislation incorporating Aboriginal sites within the regime for the natural heritage and built heritage.

In the 1970s, the Gove Land Rights Case, the Woodward Commission and the subsequent passage of the Commonwealth's *Aboriginal Land Rights (NT) 1976* Act led to the acknowledgement of the continuing importance of traditional sites to Aboriginal people and this basic assumption is reflected in sites laws passed by the South Australian and Northern Territory governments and the Commonwealth's *Aboriginal and Torres Strait Islander Heritage Protection Act, 1984*. In spite of the changes in these jurisdictions, laws for the protection of Aboriginal sites in Queensland, Tasmania, New South Wales and Western Australia are all flawed by their underlying premise that the recording of traditional sites should be based on their treatment as relics of the past and not as places with living cultural value.

Sites which form parts of the Aboriginal cultural heritage fall into two broad overlapping categories. On one hand there are those places which mark the tracks and other actions of the Dreaming Beings who ranged over the earth in the creative period and who, through their actions, gave form and meaning to the landscape. In many cases the features comprising such sites are unmodified geomorphological or 'natural' features such as rocks or trees. The corollary of this is that the significance of such sites may not be assessed by scientific

Figure 18.1 Nugget Majar at a site in the Tabletop Range, Northern Territory. Not all sacred sites are composed of such dramatic features. Photo: D. Ritchie.

enquiry. An explanation of significance lies solely with the Aboriginal custodians of the traditions associated with these sites. In his ethnography of the Pintupi, Myers describes how an outcrop of rock is explained as being the stomach contents of a kangaroo, speared and gutted in the creation period.

> The process by which a story gets attached to an object, is part of the Pintupi habit of mind that looks behind objects to events and sees in objects a sign of something. . . . The landscape itself offers clues about what might have happened. Not only does it reveal something about the invisible, but it offers a link to the invisible forces that created it and whose essence is embodied in it.
>
> (Myers 1986, pp. 66–7)

Of course in many instances the features of such sites may also have been modified by the additions of rock paintings or engravings, stone arrangements or carvings on trees. However, the degree of modification is not necessarily indicative of the significance of the site under Aboriginal tradition. Also in this broad category are places where significant events are remembered to have occurred in the historical period (Fig. 18.1).

The second broad category of sites is of places that have been modified by human occupation. They include sites comprising rock art, burials, stone arrangements, *in situ* artefact assemblages, and of course the deposits associated with sequential human occupation. The nature and extent of such sites can be defined by scientific enquiry and while the significance of such sites under Aboriginal tradition still is a matter for the custodians of those sites, it is usual for the non–Aboriginal community to place a value on such sites on the basis of the scientific or aesthetic consideration relating to the national or international cultural heritage.

As mentioned above, legislation protecting sites was initially aimed at protecting cultural relics that could be positively identified. Definitions of 'relics' usually mentioned rock art, stone artefacts and skeletal material. The definition in the Victorian *Archaeological and Aboriginal Relics Preservation Act 1972* is typical. Under that definition a 'relic includes any Aboriginal deposit, carving, drawing, skeletal remains and anything belonging to the total body of material relating to that past Aboriginal occupation of Australia'. The use of the word 'relic' and use of the past tense in describing Aboriginal occupation of Australia appears to preclude the possibility of continuing significance of any such 'relic' to contemporary Aboriginal people. This particular law is still in force in Victoria and similar terminology is used in other jurisdictions.

The emphasis on the past manifested in such legislation, and which (legitimately) is the focus of archaeological enquiry, has for more than a decade been criticized by Aboriginal people on the grounds that it, by implication, denies the rights of contemporary Aboriginal people to their cultural heritage (see, for example, Langford 1983; and see below).

Categories of legislation protecting Aboriginal sites

For the purpose of comparison it is convenient to categorize site protection legislation in Australia into three main forms, 'relics legislation', 'culture significance legislation' and 'general heritage legislation'.

'Relics legislation' includes laws with the specific object of protecting prehistoric Aboriginal sites or Aboriginal cultural 'relics'. In this category sites are defined in terms of objectively observable relics of past occupation. 'Relics legislation' was enacted in most states in the 1960s and 1970s and six statutes in this category are still in force.

'Cultural significance legislation' is legislation designed to protect sites that are currently important to Aboriginal groups. Such legislation is characterized by an emphasis on the contemporary cultural significance of the site rather than significance as a relic of the past culture. In the Northern Territory such sites are termed 'sacred sites'. In this category protection is extended to sites that are of current cultural significance to Aboriginal groups within the jurisdiction of the legislation. Although this form of legislation is more recent than relics legislation (and see below), there are five statutes in this category currently in force.

'General heritage legislation' takes the form of general laws designed to protect important heritage places without necessarily specifying Aboriginal heritage sites. In this form of legislation significance of a site is assessed against general heritage criteria. The decision to protect a site under the legislation is based on the application of the heritage criteria prescribed in the legislation. There are six examples of this form of legislation currently in force.

Of course, sites which are of significance to Aborigines for cultural, social, religious or historical reasons may also be of significance to other people for other reasons; thus they may be of archaeological significance or of general historical or cultural importance. The various pieces of legislation currently in force throughout the states and territories reflect policies which have placed different emphasis on these values.

In addition, it is important to recognize that, in the context of the Commonwealth, for example, there are a variety of Commonwealth Acts which may be used to protect Aboriginal sites in Australia. This situation exemplifies the complexity of overlapping statutes in the area, particularly when it is remembered that each of the states and territories has its own legislation (see Edwards 1975, Part VI, for a convenient listing of the relevant legislations). Since the 1967 Referendum, the Commonwealth has begun to legislate extensively for Aboriginal, environmental and heritage matters, frequently in reliance upon international treaties to which Australia is a party. Generally speaking, the Commonwealth has stated that this legislation be used where state legislation inadequately or does not effectively protect values of importance to the Commonwealth. Such legislations include: the *Australian Heritage Commission Act, 1975*, which provides that places which meet the criteria of 'National Estate' places, may be placed on the Register of a National Estate (see below), and the *Aboriginal Land Rights (Northern Territory) Act 1976*.

'Sacred sites': Aboriginal beliefs and legal dilemmas

Statutory protection of sites of current cultural significance to Aborigines is more recent than legislation for the protection of sites for their archaeological significance, and was comprehensively discussed for the first time in the *Second Report of the Aboriginal Land Rights Commission* in 1974 where Mr Justice Woodward commented that:

> 517.   In referring to places which are said to be 'sacred' to Aborigines, it is important to remember that no clear dividing line can be drawn between those which are sacred and those which are not. I mean by this that, although some sites clearly fit the description, there will be many others about which different views could be taken.
>
> 521.   Nevertheless such sites must be protected. Too often in the past grave offence has been given and deep hurt caused by their inadvertent or wanton destruction. Because of the Aboriginal's personal identification with this land, such places are even more

important to him than are places of worship to members of other religions. It is hardly necessary to say that all relevant legislation must continue to protect Aboriginal rights of access to sacred sites.

(Woodward 1974, pp. 100–2)

Woodward's recommendation resulted in the adoption, in the *Land Rights Act (NT.)*, of the most all-embracing definition of the Aboriginal site in any jurisdiction. However, in 1985, Woodward reflected that:

Away from land where traditions are still remembered and observed, . . . [Aboriginal sacred sites and places of archaeological importance] have little more significance than historic wrecks or old European graveyards at places of early settlement.

. . . Apart from questions of drafting convenience, I can see no sufficient reason why, once the direct spiritual links are lost, Aboriginal sites should not be protected under the same legislation which preserves other parts of our national heritage because of its history, its beauty, or both. It would, of course, be important for people of Aboriginal descent to be closely involved in the identification and preservation of such sites.

(Woodward 1985, p. 413)

Woodward's opinion, that Aboriginal sites may be protected under the same legislation as protects general cultural heritage, is not shared by many Aboriginal people. They have successfully argued that matters relating to Aboriginal cultural heritage, including the administration of site protection regimes, should be in the hands of the traditional custodians of that heritage – the Aboriginal people (Northern Territory Land Councils 1989, p. 1).

This view is expressed in a document prepared for the Federation of Land Councils in 1983:

Aboriginal people are the only ones who know the location and real significance of sites in this country. They alone are able to determine their sacredness and the area involved in a site necessary for its protection. This is not a matter for negotiation or dispute (Fig. 18.2).

(Toyne & Vachon 1983, p. 1)

Notwithstanding the achievements towards this objective in a number of jurisdictions, in Queensland the only legislation available for the protection of Aboriginal sites is general heritage legislation, which precludes any real control of the administration of the Act by Aboriginal people. The Queensland Act is unique in Australia in that, while it purports to offer protection to Aboriginal sites, it does not mention the word 'Aborigine' in any form. This reflects a deliberate strategy on the part of the Queensland Parliament in order to remove 'The artificial distinction between one group of Queenslanders and another' (Katter 1987, p. 1669). While the Queensland Act may not be a good example by which to judge this type of law, it is conceivable that, following the lead of the Australian Capital Territory (ACT), other jurisdictions may develop this type of legislation rather than legislation targeted specifically at Aboriginal sites. The ACT *Heritage Conservation Act (1991)* is now the only way of protecting Aboriginal sites in that territory.

While the position expressed by the Land Councils (above) is both legitimate and rational from the point of view of Aboriginal custodians, it has been the view of legislators that, in the public interest, determinations of a site's significance by Aboriginal custodians (if sanctioned at all) should be reviewable, particularly where decisions may affect existing property rights.

This concern is expressed by Mr Justice Maurice (former Aboriginal Land Commissioner). He said with regard to the Northern Territory legislation:

> The idea that a person who may have a real interest in gaining access to an area of land is obliged to accept the bald assertion that it is a sacred site or face the prospect of prosecution is not one with which many people would live comfortably.
>
> (Maurice 1985, pp. 84–5)

It could be thought that the criteria by which Aboriginal sites are judged to be worthy of protection would differ from state to state. The approach to protection of sites in the Northern Territory, where 25 per cent of its

Figure 18.2   Tony Luwanpi (left) leads a site mapping expedition in conjunction with the Northern Lands Council and Sacred Sites Authority. Photo: D. Ritchie.

population is Aboriginal and 45 per cent of its area is Aboriginal land, might, then, sensibly differ from other areas where Aboriginal population is smaller and land ownership relatively less, and where Aboriginal tradition is no longer manifested in the maintenance of myth and ritual linking individuals with sites.

However, in 1990, the National Aboriginal Sites Authorities Committee (NASAC), the national body representing the various government authorities charged with the protection of Aboriginal sites, acknowledged that there had, hitherto, been undue emphasis on what they termed 'archaeological sites' and sought to remedy this situation with the following Resolution formulated to highlight the relationship between archaeological sites and traditional sites:

> RESOLVED that NASAC recognises that since its inception it has concentrated, both in representation and focus, on the archaeological importance of Aboriginal and Torres Strait Islander sites. It now recognises that sites have a range of values, including sacred, cultural, research etc. and will in future ensure its representation and discussion reflect these values. In this context, 'Aboriginal site' has a number of meanings including the following:
>
> (a) sites which comprise the objectively observable manifestations of past Aboriginal culture which have a value as the material evidence of the original and ancient occupation of this continent by Aboriginal people. The relative significance of such sites may be accorded on the basis of scientific enquiry and general cultural and historical values. NASAC refers to sites in this category as 'archaeological sites';
>
> (b) sites which are the tangible embodiment of the sacred and secular traditions of the Aboriginal peoples of Australia. Such sites may include sites defined in (a) above. The relative significance of these sites may only be determined by the Aboriginal custodians. NASAC refers to such sites as 'traditional sites'.
>
> (NASAC 1991)

This attempt simultaneously to acknowledge the pre-eminent interest in sites held by Aboriginal people and also the interest of the scientific and wider community has not been endorsed by either the Aboriginal community or the government. There remains a blurring of legislation between 'archaeological relics' and 'sacred sites', and the issue will continue to be confused as long as outdated legislation is used to provide recognition of contemporary Aboriginal interests (and see below).

Site recording, site legislation and site protection

The first legislation concerned with the protection of Aboriginal sites in the
Northern Territory pre-dated 'Land Rights' by twenty years and was contained in the *Police and Police Offences Ordinance (NT) 1954*. Under this
ordinance it was an offence to wilfully or negligently deface, damage and
cover, expose, excavate or otherwise interfere with a place which is, or has
been at any time, used by Australian Aboriginal natives as a ceremonial, burial
or initiation ground. No prosecution was ever authorized under this section.

In 1961 the *Native and Historical Objects Preservation Ordinance (NT) 1955* was
amended to include 'areas' and became known as the *Native and Historical
Objects and Areas Preservation Ordinance (NT) 1955–1961*. This Act extended the
prohibitions of the Police and Police Offences Ordinance by adding the
category of 'prescribed areas' to include land (*only* on unalienated Crown land)
which the Administrator in Council declared to be prescribed or prohibited for
the purposes of the Act.

In the same year the Australian Academy of Science appointed a committee
to examine the position in Australia regarding national parks. Terms of
reference included 'Australian Aboriginal relics *in situ*', resulting in the recommendation that a national Register should be established, aimed at the:

> preservation of all important archaeological sites, as well as
> Aboriginal relics in situ, mythological sites, Aboriginal paintings,
> carvings and excisions in the open or in caves or shelters, stone
> arrangements, rocks and waterholes and so on. The most import-
> ant of these we hope to have declared national or historical
> monuments.
>
> (Berndt 1960, p. 1)

This project was given the support of the Department of the Territories which
requested information 'as early as practicable [on] the place, name, location,
condition, etc., of Aboriginal sites of importance in the Northern territory'
(f. 2, 64/2090). As a result, the Northern Territory administration became a
clearing-house for responses and, as a result, a new criterion of ranking the
importance of sites began to emerge: 'certainly the Northern administration is
aware to the desirability of protecting and preserving Aboriginal treasures and
sites, although in this Territory they are so numerous that only the most
important will probably be considered' (f. 40, 64/2090). Five years later, the
Legislative Council of the Northern Territory was informed by a Select
Committee that, despite a number of incidences of damage protected under
the Act, no offenders had been detected and no charges had ever been laid
(f. 79, 70/5368).

One year later, a newly formed federal statutory body, the Australian
Institute of Aboriginal Studies (AIAS), began to take a special interest in the
preservation of 'our Aboriginal relics', particularly in the Northern Territory:

the attention of the Interim Council has been drawn to the fact that persons who call themselves 'cave sitters' are damaging archaeological material in the nature of floor deposits which contain stone artefacts and other material built up as a result of the occupation of a site by Aboriginal people. . . . We have no objection to cave sitting as a hobby, but object to these individuals disturbing archaeological deposits.

(Trendall 1964)

In 1968 the AIAS convened a conference devoted to discussion of the problems of protecting Aboriginal antiquities in Australia (McCarthy 1970). In 1972 the AIAS again tried to press for positive action, and convened a two-day national seminar. As a result,

The AIAS [was] vested with the responsibility of recording all sites of either traditional or historic importance to the Aboriginal people . . . a committee [was] set up, comprising one nominee from each State Relics Authority and from the Northern Territory Authority responsible for site protection, one fully initiated Aboriginal male, a representative of the Department of Aboriginal Affairs, two social anthropologists and one linguist.

(Australian Institute of Aboriginal Studies 1973, p. 13)

Part of this responsibility was to maintain a 'National Register of Sites . . . correlating all information. Action will be supported to have the relevant sites declared as protected sites under the terms of the particular State legislation' (Australian Institute of Aboriginal Studies 1973, p. 14).

It is interesting to note some parts of the details of the AIAS's 1972 'Instructions for the preparation of a site report':

1 *Name of Site*: Ascertain by questioning and cross-checking the Aboriginal and/or other names for the site.
2 *Address of Owner or Lessee*: Record the names of the Aboriginal owners with tribal and/or totemic affiliations with the site, and all other information regarding control and access.

   Record also the name and address of the property owner or lessee whose consent will be required for the declaration of the site under the appropriate legislation.
3 *Location*: . . .
4 *Definition of Locality*: . . .
5 *Status of Property*: Ascertain whether the area on which the site occurs is freehold property, Crown Land, an Aboriginal reserve, National Park or is held under a mining, pastoral or some other form of lease.
6 *Local Information*: Record any relevant available oral information of an historical nature together with the name and address of informants.

7 *Documentation*: . . .

8 *Definition of Site Categories*:

Category I: Natural Feature: rock outcrops, trees or geological phenomena of significance to Aboriginals.

Category II: Rock Shelters: rock overhangs or caves affording some shelter from the wind and rain.

Category III: Open Sites: shell middens (deposits of shells representing food remains and containing cultural debris, surface scatters of cultural material (i.e. NOT occurring in a rock shelter)), grinding grooves on one or more rocks, rock 'gongs'.

Category IV: Painted Sites: ochre paintings frequently occur in rock shelters or under rock overhangs.

Category V: Engraved Sites: rock surfaces bearing engraved designs.

Category VI: Structures: e.g. arrangements of stones, cairns, hunting hides.

Category VII: Quarries: open workings, dumps, stone quarries, pigments or raw materials quarries.

Category VIII: Fish Traps or Weirs.

Category IX: Exposures: material in river banks, or road cuttings, river deposits, fossil beds.

Category X: Isolated Occurrences: carved trees, rock holes, burials.

9 *Description of Site*: . . .

10 *Significance of Site*: Obtain by careful questioning and cross-checking with informants full details on the significance of each site with particular reference to associated mythology. If possible evaluate the sacredness of the site – whether it is an increase centre, representation of a culture hero, ritual ground, secular site. Note all variations in interpretation and differences of opinion expressed. Record the number of informants interviewed and the status of each, his tribal (and other) name, place of abode, totemic affiliation and relationship to the site.

11 *Status of Site*: Ascertain whether the site is significant to living Aboriginals and the frequency of their visits. Note any evidence of retouching paintings, engravings or reconstruction of stone arrangements.

12 *Condition of Site*: . . .

13 *Recommendations in Respect of Preservation of Site*: . . .

14 *Any other information or comments.*

(Australian Institute of Aboriginal Studies 1973, pp. 14–16)

By 1973, the AIAS was hoping to record some 100 sites each year (Ucko 1974, p. 13). In 1974, the Commonwealth Aboriginal Land Rights Commission made recommendations for the protection of Aboriginal sites and produced guidelines for draft legislation which included the following principles: the creation of a legally recognized register of sites, protective measures such as signs and fences to be erected at the discretion of Aboriginal custodians.

The early 1970s, therefore, saw a somewhat strange mixture of site recording practices and legislation aiming to appreciate the importance of past national heritage, together with some recognition of Aboriginal interest in 'their own' sites. The existing legislation at least provided some protection to places that were investigated scientifically and, as a result of that investigation, were deemed to be part of Australia's cultural heritage, in much the same way as the prehistoric art at Lascaux in France, or the standing stones at Stonehenge in England, are considered to be part of the heritage of France and England and indeed of the world (but see Ucko 1989, p. xiii).

However, by and large, such legislation, while giving protection to certain sites identified by Europeans as particularly significant, neither recognized nor conferred any rights in relation to those sites on behalf of Aboriginal people.

By 1976, the AIAS's 'Sites of Significance' programme was seriously attempting to shift the emphasis away from archaeologically important sites to those sites which continued to be of significance to living Aboriginal people. In addition, the Institute was in the midst of a debate as to whether 'sites of significance' to living Aborigines should be included and, if so, on what criteria, on the newly established 'Register of the National Estate' (*Australian Heritage Commission Act 1975*). Thus, some sites of concern to living Aborigines could gain protection if the sites involved met the conditions of particular statutory definitions. Indeed, some legislations offered high levels of protection to places that had been formally 'gazetted' or 'declared' following an administrative procedure usually designed to allow consideration of the effects of site protection by the executive government. However, the AIAS feared that some sensitive sites could be threatened by such public recording. Indeed, in 1976, it formulated as its top priority 'the recording of sites of significance to Aboriginal people, [only] where the Aboriginal custodians wish such sites to be recorded'.

In the same year, this emphasis on sacred and other sites of significance to living Aboriginal people led the Sites of Significance Committee to stress 'the inadvisability of treating Aboriginal attitudes to land and sites as a concern centred only on individual spot localities rather than as complex and interrelated elements of a culturally significant landscape' (Minute 76/23). Legislation such as the *Northern Territory Land Rights Act* which was at that time before the House, and the South Australian *Aboriginal Heritage Act* both recognized this approach and conferred rights with respect to sites on the traditional Aboriginal custodians of these sites. Aboriginal custodians are given the right to limit access to sites and to determine what appropriate activity can be carried out there and in some cases their right of entry to such sites is also enshrined in the law.

Despite these apparent advances, some members of the archaeological profession were clearly not ready to recognize that previously acceptable ways of ranking and assessing 'archaeological' and other Aboriginal sites had by now become inappropriate. Indeed, even in 1984, some continued to feel able to stand apart from Aboriginal realities – as heritage managers they appeared still to be attempting to carve out for themselves some 'scientific' area of the Aboriginal past:

> The concept of significance is a very broad one. The heritage value of a site encompasses its 'aesthetic, historic, scientific or social significance, or other special value, for future generations as well as for the present community' (Australian Heritage Commission Act 1975, S4(1)). All of these values are at least theoretically taken into account by cultural resource managers in site assessment, listing, and management, but only one aspect of the heritage significance of sites is discussed in this volume. This is their scientific, archaeological, or research value: their potential to answer current or future research problems in the field of human history, or other substantial areas of enquiry.
>
> It is clear that sites have other important values. Many sites have readily apparent public appeal because of their aesthetic or historic value (which may in itself be the result of earlier research). This public appeal however is usually apparent, or tends to demonstrate itself, in contrast to research significance, the assessment of which requires specialist skills and criteria.
>
> All Aboriginal sites in Australia also have significance to Aborigines, which may often override a site's other values. Some sites have particular traditional, historic, or contemporary value to Aborigines. There is often a close relationship, or a potential conflict, between the archaeological research value of a site and its Aboriginal significance . . . but they are different aspects of significance, and require very different approaches.
>
> (Sullivan 1984, p. vi)

'Sacred sites' in Northern Territory legislation

Possibly the most significant development in Northern Territory legislation regarding Aboriginal sites was its adoption of a definition of 'sacred site' in the *Aboriginal Lands and Sacred Sites Bill (NT) 1977* – the first legislation to be drafted under the terms of the *Northern Territory Land Rights Act*. This bill created two categories of sacred sites – those on Aboriginal land and those not on Aboriginal land. The term 'sacred site' was not given a separate definition although it was assumed that the definition in the Commonwealth legislation would apply. For sites on Aboriginal land, an authorized Aborigine, defined as a person who in accordance with Aboriginal tradition might control the entry of persons upon that area of land, might take action to protect a sacred site by either erecting signs and/or requesting that the Administrator make regulations prescribing the area a sacred site and make a complaint to base a prosecution in a Court of Summary Jurisdiction for breaches of the Ordinance. In cases of sites not on Aboriginal land, the authorized Aborigine could only request that the Administrator in Council initiate steps to protect the site.

In the subsequent amended *Aboriginal Sacred Sites (NT) Bill, 1978*, clauses provided clear authority for Aborigines to enter sites and exercise direction over measures for the protection of sites. In addition, the Act established an administrative body of a majority of Aboriginal members nominated by the Land Councils with the powers to appoint staff. This body was charged with the administration of the provision of the Act which, among other things (Toohey 1984, pp. 133–4; Flood 1989, p. 81), gave blanket protection to 'sacred sites' defined as 'a site that is sacred to Aboriginals or is otherwise of significance according to Aboriginal tradition' (a definition clearly derived from Woodward 1974, p. 100). With the new law it became an offence to enter, remain, carry out works on or desecrate a sacred site. The statutory authority made up of Aboriginal nominees of the Land Councils, the definition of sacred site, and the blanket protection afforded to all sites remain features of site protection legislation in the Northern Territory.

The implications and operation of the Sacred Sites legislation throughout the 1980s was poorly understood by sections of the community and there were a number of attempted amendments (Ritchie 1989) by the Northern Territory Parliament to change the Act in response to perceived problems created by its enforcement.

After several failed attempts to weaken the existing sacred sites legislation, the *Aboriginal Sacred Sites Act, 1989* was passed, which provided protection to all sites 'which are sacred to Aboriginals or otherwise of significance'. This blanket protection is increased upon registration by the Aboriginal Areas Protection Authority as the area is then prima facie a site. The Act makes intended work or desecration of a site an offence unless a permit is obtained, and such permits may only be issued if the Aboriginal custodians agree to the work, or the Authority is satisfied that the work can proceed without a 'substantive risk of damage or interference to a sacred site' (Figs 18.3 and 18.4).

Perhaps the most significant addition contained in this Act is the inclusion of clauses requiring the Authority, on request, to undertake surveys to determine the existence of any sacred sites on, or in the vicinity of, proposed capital works (much as had been recommended ten years earlier by Bonner 1977).

It was only in 1991 that the 1960s legislation – which had provided a low level of protection to 'archaeological sites' which were not 'otherwise of significance according to Aboriginal tradition' – was repealed by the *Northern Territory Heritage Conservation Act*. This new legislation provides blanket protection for archaeological sites and objects relating to past Aboriginal occupation. However, if an archaeological site is also of significance according to

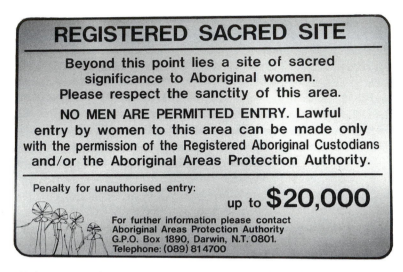

Figure 18.3 Sign used to designate women's sacred sites where access by males is prohibited under Aboriginal tradition. Photo: D. Ritchie.

Aboriginal tradition, then the provisions of the 1989 *Sacred Sites Act* override the later legislation.

Conclusions and some apprehension concerning the future

The considerable and obvious differences in definitions of 'Aboriginal site' in Australian statutes occur because some Acts protect sites which are also 'relics' or heritage areas, others protect sites because of their current significance in Aboriginal tradition. Problems may arise in the future, as one view of Aboriginal traditions holds all land to be significant in one form or another. However, Aboriginal custodians appear to have no difficulty in differentiating between the notion that all land is significant but that certain landscape features are invested with special significance. The policy of most 'cultural significance' legislation, including that operating in the Northern Territory, is to single out such sites of particular significance to Aborigines for protection (Fig. 18.5).

The problem faced by governments is to produce legislation that on the one hand provides the opportunity for the Aboriginal custodians to protect sites, and on the other, provides for persons wishing to utilize the land or resources contained within an area protected by the legislation, a mechanism to have their interests presented to Aboriginal custodians and arbitrated without prejudice.

To achieve the above ends, site protection legislation should take into account the basic principle that: *Aborigines should be given control over the day-to-day functioning of those aspects of the legislation which affect their interest in Aboriginal sites.*

The compilation and dissemination of information relating to the significance of particular sites to outsiders must, to some extent at least, be an
infringement of Aboriginal customary law. Aborigines will embark upon such
a process in the expectation that the sites they are concerned about will receive
protection. The most obvious way for this to be achieved is to create a body to
administer the legislation controlled by Aboriginal custodians and seen to be
independent from direct government or other outside control. Legislation
should respect the right of Aboriginal custodians to retain complete discretion
over the dissemination of information compiled in the course of investigations
about particular sites.

This chapter's analysis of site legislation operating in all jurisdictions within
Australia has revealed that the legislation in many areas has not kept pace with
the political and social changes affecting the rights of Aboriginal people. In
particular, much of the legislation remains substantially unaltered from the
1960s when the value of Aboriginal sites was conceived in national and
historical terms: less than a generation ago Aboriginal culture was still

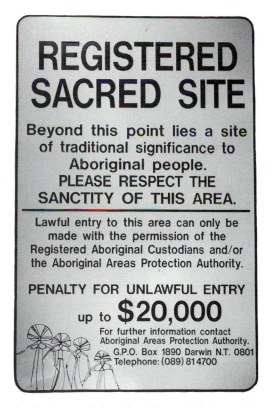

Figure 18.4 Standard sign used by the Aboriginal Areas Protection Authority
where Aboriginal custodians have requested signs on registered sacred sites. Photo:
D. Ritchie.

Figure 18.5 Sacred sites in the sea. The Australian government now acknowledges the existence of sacred sites in coastal waters. Here the Australian Navy assists in the preparation of buoys to be placed by traditional custodians, marking a site off the Arnhem Land coast, Northern Territory. Photo: D. Ritchie.

regarded as a static system of beliefs that either collapsed or became redundant in the face of change.

This situation is in stark contrast to the fact that Aboriginal people have gained considerable recognition both in Australia and internationally, for their special rights which arise from their prior occupation of the land and from their life within it. Legislation in these jurisdictions must reflect the shift in European perception of Aboriginal traditional culture. Aboriginal traditions are now accepted as continually evolving in response to change. Thus, for example Sullivan has recently argued that 'the distinctions between "sacred", "significant" and "prehistoric" sites are no longer applicable or relevant in southeastern Australia, and will not hold' (Sullivan 1986, pp. 154–5).

The recent decision of the High Court in the *Mabo* v. *Queensland* case reinforces the imperative to recognize as a matter of right the interests of Aboriginal people in the features of the landscape which continue to be significant within Aboriginal tradition. By this decision the interests of Aboriginal custodians in a large number of sites have been automatically recognized regardless of any administrative decision of affect of any particular piece of legislation.

J. Brennan observed:

> the common law of Australia rejects the notion that, when the Crown acquired sovereignty over territory which is now part of Australia it thereby acquired the absolute beneficial ownership of the land therein, and accepts that the antecedent rights and interest in land possessed by the indigenous inhabitants of the territory survived the change in sovereignty.
>
> (Brennan 1992, p. 66 aljr 429)

The Mabo judgement changes fundamentally the assumptions on which most, if not all, site protection legislation in Australia has been based. Whereas, prior to Mabo, protection was selectively accorded to particular sites as a result of the operation of various site protection statutes, now, post-Mabo, the pre-existing interest and rights over areas of traditional significance is considered a 'right' at Common Law. Indeed, the operation of certain site protection laws not only may not add anything to these 'rights' but may even potentially lead to the extinguishing of them.

However, Aboriginal groups seeking to establish native title at common law will have to 'substantially maintain' their traditional connections with the land in question. An important way of establishing the continuity of such common law rights is by demonstrating an affiliation to traditional sites on that land.

As a result, site administrators may expect an increase in unease on the part of landowners over the implications of officially acknowledging the existence of sites and Aboriginal traditional attachments to these sites. Any law or administrative process that clearly acknowledges an interest on the part of Aboriginal people to particular areas (Aboriginal sites) is likely to be regarded as an acknowledgement of rights of the same order as those central to an assertion of native title. Those charged with carriage of site protection legislation in Western Australia and the Northern Territory have noted suspicion and even hostility to site recording programmes from interest groups, fearing that their property rights may be impinged upon.

Note

1 This chapter pays particular attention to the Northern Territory which, as a consequence of being effectively a Commonwealth jurisdiction and with Aboriginal people comprising a high proportion of the population, has perhaps the most developed site protection regime in Australia.

References

Australian Institute of Aboriginal Studies 1973. National Register of Aboriginal Sites, *AIAS Newsletter*, 13–16.

Berndt, R. 1960. Survey being carried out by the Anthropological Society of Western Australia: the preservation of Aboriginal sites. Unpublished paper. University of Western Australia.

Bonner, N. 1977. *Report of the Joint Select Committee on Aboriginal Land Rights in the Northern Territory*. Canberra: Australian Government Publishing Service.

Brennan, J. 1992. Reasons for decision *Mabo* v. *Queensland*, 66 aljr 429 (High Court).

Edwards, R. (ed.) 1975. *The Preservation of Australia's Aboriginal Heritage*. Canberra: Australian Institute of Aboriginal Studies.

Flood, J. 1989. 'Tread softly for you tread on my bones': the development of cultural resource management in Australia. In *Archaeological Heritage Management in the Modern World*, H. Cleere (ed.), 79–101. London: Unwin Hyman.

Katter, R. C. 1987. Second recording speech. *Queensland Parliamentary Hansard*, 9 April.

Langford, R. F. 1983. Our heritage – your playground. *Australian Archaeology* 16, 1–6.

McCarthy, F. D. (ed.) 1970. *Aboriginal Antiquities in Australia: their nature and preservation*. Canberra: Australian Institute of Aboriginal Studies.

Maurice, J. 1985. Reasons for decision in Warumungu Land Claim. Unpublished paper.

Myers, F. 1986. *Pintupi Country, Pintupi Self: sentiment, place and politics among Western Desert Aborigines*. Canberra: Australian Institute of Aboriginal Studies.

National Aboriginal Sites Authorities Committee 1991. Resolution 6/1990. Minute of November meeting, Rockhampton, Queensland.

Northern Territory Land Councils 1989. Central and northern Land Councils sacred site position. Paper submitted to Northern Territory Government.

Ritchie, D. 1989. The New NT Sacred Sites Act: a perspective from the Sacred Sites Authority. *Aboriginal Law Bulletin* 2, 11–12.

Sullivan, S. 1984. Introduction. In *Site Surveys and Significance Assessment in Australian Archaeology*, S. Sullivan & S. Bowdler (eds), v–x. Canberra: Australian National University.

Sullivan, S. 1986. The custodianship of Aboriginal sites in southeastern Australia. In *Who Owns the Past?*, I. McBryde (ed.), 139–56. Melbourne: Oxford University Press.

Toohey, J. 1984. *Seven Years On: report by Mr Justice Toohey to the Minister for Aboriginal Affairs on the Aboriginal Land Rights (NT) Act 1976 and related matters*. Canberra: Australian Government Publishing Service.

Toyne, P. & D. Vachon 1983. Sacred sites protection. Discussion paper prepared for Federation of Land Councils.

Trendall 1964. Letter to Minister for Territories, 1 April (file 70/5368). *Native and Historic Objects Journal*.

Ucko, P. J. 1974. Review of A.I.A.S. activities 1973. *AIAS Newsletter* 1, 5–15.

Ucko, P. J. 1989. Foreword. In *Archaeological Heritage Management in the Modern World*, H. F. Cleere (ed.), ix–xiv. London: Unwin Hyman.

Woodward, A. E. 1974. *Second Report of the Aboriginal Land Rights Commission*. Canberra: Australian Government Publishing Service.

Woodward, A. E. 1985. Land rights and land use: a view from the sidelines. *Australian Law Journal* 59, 413.

19 When sacred land is sacred to three tribes: San Juan Paiute sacred sites and the Hopi-Navajo-Paiute suit to partition the Arizona Navajo Reservation

ROBERT FRANKLIN & PAMELA BUNTE

Introduction

On 8 February 1990, Judge Carroll of the US Federal District Court of Phoenix, Arizona, heard the closing arguments in an historic trial to partition the 1934 Act Arizona Navajo Reservation into three reservations. During the three-month-long trial, native and expert witnesses for the three parties to the suit, the Hopi, Navajo and San Juan Paiute Tribes, provided evidence and testimony bearing on each tribe's historic relationship with the land, including sacred sites and areas.

This chapter explores issues of both anthropological analysis and land rights policy. As researchers and expert witnesses for the San Juan Paiutes, our view of the importance of sacred land owes much to our experience of working with Paiutes and coming to understand their concerns. But our intent here is to help pave the way for solutions that can preserve the interests of all three tribes.

Historic background

The roots of the present land dispute can be found in a history of population movements, territorial rearrangements, and long co-occupancy. A close look at this history can show how all three tribes came to have strong spiritual ties to the same land and why they now seem so intransigent and uncompromising in their legal struggle over rights in it.

The San Juan Paiute Tribe of northern Arizona and southern Utah is the easternmost in a continuum of Southern Paiute communities, the western terminus of which is the Chemehuevi Tribe in southeastern California. Figure 19.1 shows the approximate territorial boundaries of the Southern Paiute ethnic group and its constituent communities, including the San Juan, as they existed in the mid-nineteenth century according to Southern Paiute traditions recorded in the 1930s (Kelly 1934, 1964) and largely corroborated by later ethnohistorians and ethnographers (Stewart 1942; Euler 1966; Stoffle & Dobyns 1983; Bunte & Franklin 1987).

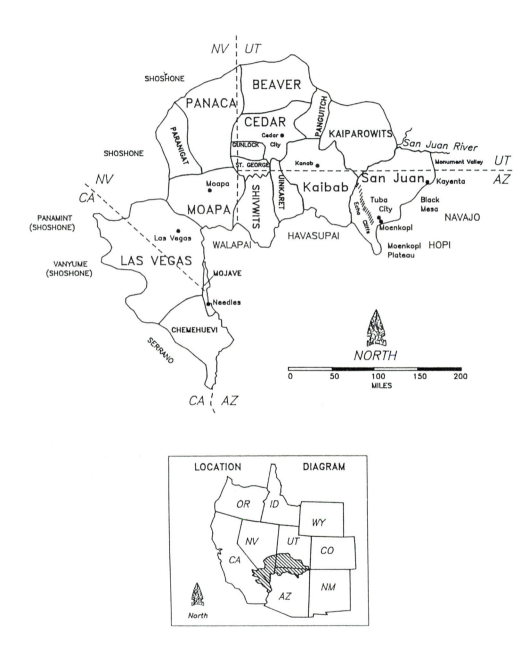

Figure 19.1   Mid-nineteenth century Southern Paiute band territories. Adapted from Kelly 1934.

In the mid–nineteenth century, San Juan Paiute territorial holdings bordered on those of the Hopis at some point between the present-day Hopi villages of Moenkopi and Oraibi. This, however, had come about as the result of a half-century of Paiute expansion southward. According to Hopi oral history (Runke 1914; Hopi Tribe 1939, p. 11; Courlander 1982, pp. 122–4; Adams 1989), the San Juan destroyed the Hopi village of Moenkopi in the 1830s and prevented Hopi reoccupation of it until the 1870s. One hundred years earlier, in the 1770s, the Paiutes' holdings lay some 50 miles north of Moenkopi, although the Hopis and Paiutes were already at war, according to the Franciscan explorers Dominguez, Escalante and Garces (Chavez & Warner 1976, p. 103; Coues 1900, p. 395).

In the 1850s, US Army Captain John G. Walker reported recent Navajo occupation of Black Mesa (Walker 1859), adjacent to both Hopi and Paiute holdings of the period. His Navajo guide further indicated that the Navajos and Paiutes were at war along the edge of the Paiutes' holdings in nearby Marsh Pass. Beginning in the 1860s, the US Army's campaigns against the Navajos began to drive Navajo refugees well into Paiute and Hopi territory (Bartlett 1932; McNitt 1972; Reeve 1974), where many later settled permanently (Henderson 1985).

At the end of the Navajo wars, the Treaty of 1868 granted the Navajo Tribe its first reservation, 3.4 million acres straddling the New Mexico–Arizona territorial line and well to the east of the Hopis and San Juan Paiutes (Fig. 19.2). However, due to their rapidly growing population, which doubled from 10,000 to 20,000 between the 1860s and 1900 (ARCIA 1865–1900; Underhill 1953), Navajos increasingly settled in areas outside the 1868 Treaty reservation. The government dealt with this expansion by creating new reservation lands through a series of presidential executive orders. This reservation expansion took place primarily in northeastern Arizona away from heavy Euroamerican settlement and sanctioned Navajo settlement in lands where Hopis and Paiutes already lived (Fig. 19.2). One executive order, dated 16 December 1882, created the first Hopi reservation. However, since the government either could not or would not prevent Navajo settlement on the 1882 Hopi reservation, for many decades the 1882 reservation was treated as a de facto Navajo–Hopi reservation.

In the 1930s, partly in response to concerns voiced by local Euroamericans, the US Congress sought to consolidate the various executive order areas within permanent reservation boundaries (Hagerman 1932). For the state of Arizona, this was done by Act of Congress on 14 June 1934 (48 Stat. 960). The Act stated that the reservation was to be set aside 'for the benefit of the Navajo and such other Indians as may already be located thereon' (48 Stat. 960, section 1). In so stating, it permanently vested Indian title to this land in all three tribes.

Since the late 1940s, the Hopi Tribe has worked persistently to regain the land which they occupied aboriginally and historically, with the Navajo Tribe struggling just as hard to resist the loss of the lands Navajos had settled on

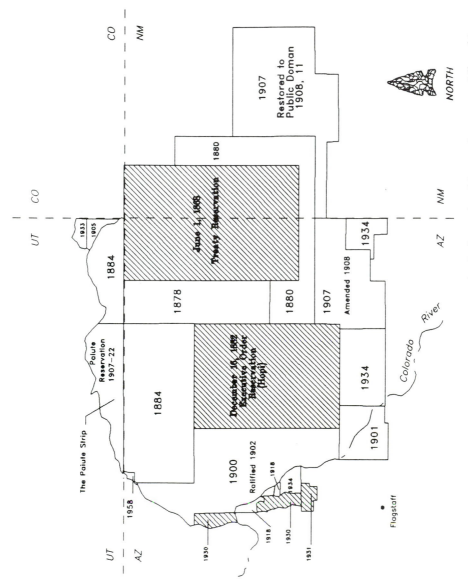

Figure 19.2 Navajo Reservation expansions (the Arizona lands shown in white are those potentially subject to partition).

(Enders 1971; Kammer 1980). Making skilful use of the federal legislative and court systems, the Hopi Tribe was able to sue the Navajo Tribe for its rights to the original 1882 executive order Hopi reservation. Through a 1962 federal court decision, most of the 1882 area became the Hopi–Navajo Joint Use Area, with both tribes receiving joint, but undivided, title to the surface and sub-surface rights there. As a result of a further 1977 decision, surface rights to the Joint Use Area (JUA) were partitioned into separate exclusive Navajo and Hopi reservation areas. Although they received nearly half of the disputed lands in the 1882 area, Navajos continue today to resist relocation from the Hopi-partitioned lands.

The Hopi Tribe also pursued claims to the 1934 Act Arizona reservation outside the 1882 reservation, or JUA, where the Hopi village of Moenkopi, as well as those areas historically and aboriginally occupied by Paiutes, are located. The 22 December 1974 Act of Congress which authorized partition of the 1882 reservation also permitted the Hopi and Navajo Tribes, as well as 'any other tribe of Indians claiming any interest', to sue for partition of the 1934 Act reservation (25 U.S.C. 640d-7). (The areas potentially subject to partition in the 1934 Act area case are shown in white on Fig. 19.2.) Although the Hopi and Navajo Tribes were the original parties to the 1934 Act reser-vation lawsuit, as they had been for the earlier two JUA cases, the San Juan Tribe was able to intervene in the case after the Paiutes discovered in 1982 that their land also was subject to partition by the court, whether or not they were a party to the suit.

Paiute sacred land in the 1934 Act reservation

The same historic circumstances that made conflict over land inevitable also created a bewildering patchwork of interlocking and overlapping tribal claims to land. This is probably more true of sacred sites and areas than of other forms of land use. To establish an initial concrete point of reference, our discussion of sacred land in the 1934 Act area starts with information on San Juan Paiute sacred land, gained during 1934 area claim research (Bunte & Franklin 1989, especially chapter VII).

The San Juan Paiutes' religion and cosmology, like that of other American Indian groups, is intimately connected with the land on which they have lived. Because of its significance as sacred land, the boundaries of traditional San Juan territory (see Fig. 19.1) have remained consistent in the minds of Paiute people since at least the time they were first recorded in the 1930s, long before the present land dispute (Collier 1933–4; Kelly 1934, 1964; Stewart 1942; Bunte & Franklin 1987). In 1933, to give one example, Donald Collier, the son of John Collier, the famous US Indian Affairs Commissioner, recorded these tradi-tional boundaries as given to him by a San Juan living in Paiute Canyon near the Utah–Arizona line: 'The Paiute territory was bounded as follows: the San Juan and Colorado [Rivers] in the north, Oljeto [in Monument Valley] in the east, Black Mesa on the southeast, Tuba City on the south, and Lee's Ferry on the west' (Collier 1933–4, pp. 9–10).

This territory as a whole is made sacred by myth-time events that are said to have taken place there, recounted in the cycle of mythic stories known as 'Coyote tales' or 'winter stories'. The myth-time beings in the stories have the names of animals, Coyote, Wolf, Bear, Rattlesnake and others, but are actually liminal beings, partaking of both the human and the animal and thus more powerful than either. These stories can only be told in the winter, when bears, rattlesnakes and the thunder beings, who might be offended by them, are absent and cannot overhear.

According to the myth that tells the origin of people, Coyote had sex with Ocean Grandmother's daughter. Afterwards, Ocean Grandmother gave him a quiver and told him not to open it. Coyote got curious and opened it anyway. All the peoples of the world emerged from that quiver, running in all directions. The last to emerge were the Paiutes, who remained in *tɨvwipɨ tɨvwitsi toxwoitɨraxuapatakw* 'the very centre of the world' where the sack was brought to its final destination. According to the San Juan Paiute version of this myth as recorded today and in the 1930s (Collier 1933–4, pp. 13–14; Bunte & Franklin 1987, p. 227), the quiver was opened southeast of the Colorado River in San Juan territory, thus underscoring the special character of this land as the Paiutes' sacred homeland.

There are a number of sites within the San Juan Paiutes' traditional territory that are made sacred by legendary events that occurred there in historic times, or by the presence of supernatural beings that dwell in these places. For example, in Pasture Canyon, a site of irrigated Navajo and Hopi fields near the reservation town of Tuba City (see Fig. 19.1), there live *paaɨngapitsing* ('water babies'), water sprites that are dangerous to humans but also beneficial, if left undisturbed, because they control the sources of water. The belief that Water Babies live in water sources is common to the Great Basin peoples (Hultkranz 1986, p. 633; Liljeblad 1986, p. 652).

Many animals are seen as potential or actual spirit guardians for individual ritual practitioners or for the community as a whole. Eagles, for example, have played prominent roles as special guardians for the Paiutes both in legends and in current and past religious belief and ritual practice. One leader and medicine man, who lived in the 1930s, would remove juvenile eaglets from the nest, put strung turquoise beads on their feet, and after certain prayers and rituals let them go. The present tribal leader and other community members continue to pray to eagles and to have eagle dreams in which the 'eagle people', that nest in certain eyries on peaks and cliffs, speak to them and promise to protect the Paiutes. Paiutes strongly believe that eagles should never be killed, and all consider eagle eyries, especially those in the vicinity of Paiute dwellings, to be sacred sites of great importance to the community's well-being.

Paiutes consider the sites of former dwellings and the area surrounding them to be sacred. This is demonstrated by the many rituals that typically take place in and around homes, and the many powerful ritual substances and objects that remain behind when people leave a dwelling to live elsewhere. Examples of practices and beliefs that make homes sacred include prayers to the sun using corn meal of different colours and ashes from inside the home; life-crisis rituals for menarche, first childbirth, and death; health and healing rituals, using sweating as well as plant, animal and mineral medicines; ritual placement of children's umbilical cords, old cradleboards, bark diapers, milk teeth, etc. in specific places in the area surrounding homes; ritual bonfires lit near farming residences in spring and summer to communicate with the thunder beings, or *ungwatowatsing*, 'rain children', and many others.

Among the rituals performed within or near dwellings are the life-crisis rituals performed for a girl's menarche and for a married couple's first childbirth. When a girl has her first period, she is isolated from younger children so that she can undergo a four-day rite of passage. A special structure is built for her or, as is often done nowadays, an existing room or house is set aside. During the four days, she must not touch her hair or face directly, drink cold water, or eat animal foods or salt. She is given a special scratching stick to scratch with and fed corn meal and warm water. Her hair and face are painted with white clay or red ochre, which symbolize in part the power of the sun, and she is directed to run east at dawn and sometimes west at sunset. During the day she is kept busy cutting wood, grinding corn, carrying water, and doing other tasks. Her elder relatives make a special 'hot bed' of buried coals for her to lie on. Medicine plants and red ochre are given to her to promote health and long life. At the end of the four days, she bathes in cold water, is given rabbit's liver to eat, and her old clothes are burnt. Throughout the various events in the ritual, the girl receives special teachings from her elder kinspeople. The first childbirth ceremony follows the menarche ceremony pattern, except that the husband and wife divide certain aspects of the ritual between them. For example, the husband runs to the east and does the wood-cutting and water-fetching. These ceremonies find parallels and variants among many other cultures in western North America (Driver 1941), including the Navajo *kinaalda* ritual (Frisbie 1967; Carmichael 1994). However, the San Juan pattern described above is specific to the Southern Paiutes (Kelly 1964, pp. 96–8; Kelly & Fowler 1986, p. 379). All aspects of the Paiute rituals create places and objects which are imbued with the dangerous and beneficial sacred power associated with human life and reproduction. Thus, among other things, the sites where the burnt clothing and scratching-stick were left and where specific elements of the ritual took place, such as location of the 'hot bed' and the path taken to run to the sunrise or sunset, are all sacred to individuals and families, and to the community at large.

Many other sacred sites and areas are typically or at least occasionally located away from dwelling sites and other areas of most intensive Paiute economic activity. Examples include areas round dance sites, agave-roasting pits, buckskin-processing sites, sites and areas where medicine plants, animals and mineral pigments, such as white clay and red ochre, are gathered, and funerary sites of various types.

San Juan Paiute funerary sites are a good example of sacred sites that are extremely variable in location, since they are dependent on such uncontrollable factors as the season and place of death. As with other Southern Paiutes (Stewart 1942, pp. 312–14; Kelly 1964, p. 95), San Juan Paiutes abandoned or destroyed by fire the house where a person had died, and also their personal belongings, such as clothing, weapons and tools, and horses. Often the corpse and property would be left in the house itself, whether the structure was burnt or not. In this way, many former dwellings are sacred because they are also burial or cremation sites. However, in many cases, the corpse was removed from the house and taken elsewhere to be buried. Also, the deceased's movable property was often taken to one or sometimes several locations away from dwellings to be disposed of ritually by burning, burial, or being hidden in a tree or bush. When they could, San Juan Paiutes would remove a dying person from the family dwelling to be cared for in a small *ramada*, or brush shelter, which had been specially constructed for this purpose as much as a kilometre away and which could later be abandoned or burnt in place of the family's current home. In recent decades, death in the hospital and burial in local cemeteries have become more commonplace. Yet San Juan Paiutes still carry out at least some of the above practices, particularly the disposal of the deceased's property.

Protecting sacred land in the 1934 Act reservation

The 1990 trial to partition the 1934 Act Arizona Navajo Reservation into three reservations is intended as a measure to protect tribal rights in land. Yet, because of a number of factors, partition as a measure to protect sacred land is a problematic solution at best. First, as noted earlier, Indian title was vested in 1934 by the 14 June 1934 Act of Congress. This means that in their efforts to prove title during the recent trial, all three tribes were limited to evidence and testimony relevant to use and occupancy in 1934 only. Sacred sites, such as burials, that were created *after* 1934 were irrelevant, at least at this stage of the partition process. When partition lines are actually drawn in a later stage of the case, the court will almost certainly take into account present use and occupancy as well as 1934 use and occupancy, if only to minimize relocation.

Second, under the 22 December 1974 Act authorizing this intertribal suit, the federal court presently has jurisdiction only over disputed lands in Arizona. The Utah Navajo reservation, as well as the 1868 Navajo Treaty reservation and the 1882 area, or JUA, are excluded from the suit. In Utah, there are many San Juan and Navajo, and some Hopi, sacred sites. Moreover, San Juan in Utah are dealing with many of the same social and economic problems created by Navajo expansion that Hopis and Paiutes have encountered in Arizona.

Finally, in this case, the court is basically limited to an absolute partition of surface rights among the parties as a remedy. Partition can only work well where each tribe's land use is discrete and not coextensive with other tribes' use areas. Some forms of economic activity, notably hunting, plant–gathering and to some extent herding, involve co–occupancy over broad areas by two or three tribes both for 1934 and today, which is likely to make partition in these areas difficult. Far more thorny, however, is the case of sacred land use. According to the information each tribe's expert witnesses have provided (e.g. Ainsworth 1986; Euler 1986; Vannette 1986; Bunte & Franklin 1989), the sacred areas and sites of the three tribes are virtually completely coextensive in the western portion of the 1934 reservation that is the primary focus of the dispute.

The Hopi concept of their sacred land, or Hopi *tusqua*, overlaps the San Juan Paiutes' traditional territory described earlier and also includes much of the rest of the 1934 area and some lands beyond the reservation to the west, south and east (cf. e.g. Euler 1986, pp. 5–6, Map 3). Navajo sacred land, as bounded by the four sacred mountains, including Humphrey Peak near Flagstaff, Arizona, covers most if not all of the Hopi *tusqua* and the San Juan Paiutes' traditional sacred land as well (Vannette 1986, pp. 19–20).

Within these broad boundaries there are many cases of specific sites where sacred use by the three tribes, or two of the three, overlapped and even conflicted in 1934, and still does so today. However the partition is done, each tribe will find some of its sacred sites and areas partitioned into another tribe's reservation. For each of the tribes, this is of course especially likely to happen with sacred sites that are located at a distance from its areas of intensive residential and economic use. What will happen to such sites depends on a number of factors. One factor, perhaps not well known, has already caused problems of limited access to sites and even site desecration, i.e. conflicting religious beliefs concerning the handling and use of sacred sites. Eagles and burials, for example, have already proved problematic for relations between the Paiutes on the one hand, and the Hopis and Navajos on the other.

The Echo Cliffs, north of Tuba City (see Fig. 19.1) form a continuous swathe of sacred sites claimed by all three tribes. Navajos claim the cliffs in part because of mythic visits by the Holy People, some of whom, notably the Wind, still live there (Vannette 1986, p. 34). For Hopis, there are sacred eagle–gathering sites here, claimed by the Bear matriclan (Euler 1986, p. 37; cf. also Ainsworth 1986, pp. 66–8, 211). Paiutes also revere the eagles nesting on the cliffs, which are adjacent to their farms and grazing areas northwest of Tuba City. However, Paiutes have long objected to Hopi eagle–gathering here, both because these are seen as belonging to the local Paiutes and because of the Hopi practice of smothering eagles after the *niman* ceremony (Frigout 1979, p. 572). Historically, individual San Juan have tried to discourage Hopi eagle–gatherers by removing and raising eaglets, or by threatening the gatherers (Bunte & Franklin 1989, pp. 121–2).

During June 1990, the Paiutes prevented a group of Hopis from gathering eagles on the Echo Cliffs in sight of the Paiutes' fields at Willow Springs. Because the two tribes have been on friendly terms despite the lawsuit, representatives of both tribes held a meeting at Moenkopi village the following month in an effort to prevent any bad feelings. The Paiutes asked one of us, Robert Franklin, to attend this meeting. The Hopis also brought along an anthropologist, as well as legal counsel. Although no decision was taken at this meeting, both groups attempted to explain their religious beliefs about eagles and their concepts of kin group and community ownership of eagle eyries. It was clear that the issue of eagle-gathering would not be resolved quickly or without compromises that some members of both groups will find difficult to accept at present.

In traditional Navajo religion, spiritual contamination from the non-Navajo dead, and to a lesser extent from Navajo dead, is believed to cause sickness (Kluckhohn & Leighton 1946, p. 222; Opler 1983, pp. 372–80; Wyman 1983, pp. 539, 541). For this reason, according to Paiute accounts, some Navajos have allegedly desecrated Paiute graves or burned down abandoned Paiute houses when they found them near their own homes. Once during our fieldwork, Paiutes retrieved and reburied the remains of a Paiute man who had allegedly been exhumed by local Navajos for an 'enemyway' curing cere- mony.

Removal or destruction of Paiute burials and grave goods has also allegedly taken place inadvertently for non-religious reasons, for example during road construction and archaeological excavations carried out by the Navajo Tribe and its employees. For example, the Navajo Tribe and the Bureau of Indian Affairs recently resurveyed and widened a reservation road (N-16) which runs very close to several areas of historic Paiute occupation and the sites of several burials. The Navajo Tribe's Cultural Resource Management Program con- ducted a survey of the route (Popelish 1983). Their archaeologists apparently made no contact with Paiutes living in the area and made no mention in their report of Paiute sites, despite a well-established historic record of Paiute occupancy along the survey route. Fortunately, the Paiute community was able to intervene informally with local Navajo officials and thus prevent the destruction of a grave site, but only after the road was already under construc- tion. Partition will probably help to protect many Paiute burials, but many other outlying grave sites will almost certainly be permanently partitioned into Navajo or Hopi land. These and other similarly located sacred sites will require alternative measures to assure their protection.

One alternative solution, which the three tribes may have to turn to in such cases, can be found in the growing body of environmental resource and historic preservation law, particularly laws and regulations which protect Indian religious freedom. The American Indian Religious Freedom Act (AIRFA) of 1978 (92 Stat. 469) was intended to reaffirm Indian peoples' First Amendment rights to freedom of religious belief and practice, and to establish clear policy guidelines for the protection of their religious freedom. Unfortunately, AIRFA has led neither to new regulations or to laws that would clearly delineate federal policy, nor to the establishment of effective consultation procedures between Indian groups and federal and state offices (Ferguson 1983, p. 12). While the possibility that Indian tribes might successfully use AIRFA certainly still exists, other Acts have provided more specific remedies for tribes. The provisions of the Archaeological Resources Protection Act (ARPA) of 1979 (93 Stat. 721), together with the federal regulations that followed it (see especially 43 CFR 7, the sections governing the Department of the Interior and thus Indian Affairs at 7.1 and 7.7), stated that 'federal land managers' – which includes Indian tribal governments on their own federal trust reservation land – are required to notify and consult with Indian tribes when any archaeological work may endanger sites of cultural or religious importance to them. In fact, the ARPA regulations require land managers to identify all such sites, and the tribes that claim them, ahead of time 'so that such information may be on file for land management purposes' (43 CFR 7.7.b.[1]). The Native American Graves Protection and Repatriation Act, PL 101–601, signed into law on 16 November 1990, deals with the repatriation of Native American human remains and cultural artefacts. This Act, although it will apparently not safeguard the sacred sites themselves, may provide a useful framework for the return of Native American human remains and cultural objects to the appropriate tribes (Kintigh 1990). Exactly how useful this law will be for disentangling overlapping tribal claims depends on the specific regulations that are enacted.

Tribes have also used portions of the National Historic Preservation Act to protect sacred sites on reservation land. Specifically, 1980 amendments of the Act ensured Indian tribes the right to work in partnership with the federal government on historic preservation issues, and authorized possible funding for the preservation of their cultural and historic heritage (Suagee & Funk 1990, p. 21). The direction in which historic preservation on Indian land is moving is towards the institution of tribally run historic preservation programmes and the replacement of State Historic Preservation Officers (SHPO) with Tribal Historic Preservation Officers (THPO).

The shift to THPOs, with their focus on their own tribe's historic sites, will certainly be an improvement for tribes in many respects. This will be especially true if, as Suagee & Funk (1990, p. 22) suggest, the tribes begin to 'address the challenge of recognizing the historical significance of non-material culture'. However, since both the tribe (THPO) and the state (SHPO) have important interests in sites outside their own jurisdiction, the potential for friction between them is still quite strong. As Suagee & Funk (1990, p. 22) note, it will be only by co-ordination and co-operation between the SHPO and the THPO that problems will be avoided, and that 'the broader national interest in historic preservation' will be served. In a similar manner, the current trend of replacing SHPOs with THPOs could easily exacerbate problems between tribes, such as access to and respect for sacred sites, rather than solve them, if it is not also accompanied by the will to co-ordinate and to co-operate intertribally.

Under current law, each tribe could at least insist that it was consulted about the disposition of its sacred sites which are located on land partitioned to another tribe. In some cases, notably burials and other funerary sites, each of the three tribes might also be able to threaten the others with legal sanctions in the event that site desecration or hindrance of access occurred on lands partitioned to the other tribes.

The irony of all this is, of course, that such protections should have to be used to protect one Indian tribe from another. Yet, because of current inter-tribal hostility stemming from the lawsuit, intertribal incidents of vandalism and harassment involving sacred sites have already occurred and are likely to continue. In the long run the only secure protection for sacred land will be found not in partition or legal sanctions but in greater mutual respect and tolerance, and continual co-operation and communication among the tribes. This seems to be the road that the Paiutes and Hopis have begun with their meeting on eagle-gathering.

Acknowledgements

This chapter could not have been written without the co-operation, hard work and hospitality of the San Juan Southern Paiute Tribe and the many Paiute consultants that worked with us, whom we wish to acknowledge and thank here. We thank archaeologist Jill Weisbord for her technical assistance during the ethnoarchaeological phase of our land claims research, Elizabeth Wojak for computer-generating our maps, and Daniel Larson and T. J. Ferguson for their information about recent changes in the environment resource and historic preservation laws. We also acknowledge the support given to our field research on Paiute sites by the Native American Rights Fund, Boulder, Colorado. Finally, we wish to state that this chapter has been equally co-authored and that any errors of fact or analysis are our own.

References

Adams, E. C. 1989. Trial testimony. *Sidney* v. *Haskie* v. *James*, Trial Transcript 8, p. 1211.
Ainsworth, A. D. 1986. Hopi use and occupance of the Navajo Indian Reservation defined by the Act of June 14, 1934: a socio-cultural perspective on the uses of natural resources by the Hopi Indians. Expert witness report prepared for Arnold & Porter, Denver, Colorado.
ARCIA 1865–1900. *Annual Report of the Commissioner of Indian Affairs.* Washington, D.C.: US Government Printing Office.
Bartlett, K. 1932. Why the Navahos came to Arizona. *Museum of Northern Arizona Museum Notes* 5, 29–32.
Bunte, P. A. & R. Franklin 1987. *From the Sands to the Mountain: change and persistence in a Southern Paiute Community.* Lincoln, Nebr.: University of Nebraska Press.
Bunte, P. A. & R. Franklin 1989. San Juan Southern Paiute use and occupancy of the June 14, 1934, Act Reservation in 1934 and the period of the 1930s. Expert witness report prepared for Native American Rights Fund, Boulder, Colorado.
Carmichael, D. L. 1994. Places of power: Mescalero Apache sacred sites and sensitive areas. In *Sacred Sites, Sacred Places,* D. L. Carmichael, J. Hubert, B. Reeves & A. Schanche (eds), 89–98. London: Routledge.
Chavez, A. & T. J. Warner (eds) 1976. *The Dominguez-Escalante Journal.* Provo, Utah: Brigham Young University Press.

Collier, D. 1933–34. A survey of the Paiute culture in Paiute Canyon, Arizona, with some notes on the Navaho. MS on file, Native American Rights Fund, Boulder, Colorado.

Coues, E. 1900. *On the Trail of a Spanish Pioneer.* New York: F. P. Harper.

Courlander, H. 1982. *Hopi Voices.* Albuquerque: University of New Mexico Press.

Driver, H. F. 1941. Girl's puberty rites in western North America. *University of California Anthropological Records* 6, 1–90.

Enders, G. W. 1971. An historical analysis of the Navajo–Hopi land disputes, 1882–1970. Unpublished Master's thesis, Brigham Young University.

Euler, R. C. 1966. *Southern Paiute Ethnohistory.* Salt Lake City: University of Utah Press.

Euler, R. C. 1986. Aspects of Hopi land use and occupancy. Expert witness report prepared for Arnold & Porter, Denver, Colorado.

Ferguson, T. J. 1983. The impact of the American Indian Religious Freedom Act: a case study of Zuni Pueblo. *Haliksa'i: U.N.M. Contributions in Anthropology* 2, 1–15.

Frigout, A. 1979. Hopi ceremonial organization. In *Southwest,* A. Ortiz (ed.), 564–76. Handbook of North American Indians, vol. 9. W. G. Sturtevant, general editor. Washington, D.C.: Smithsonian Institution.

Frisbie, C. J. 1967. *Kinaalda: a study of the Navaho Girls' Puberty Ceremony.* Middletown, Conn.: Wesleyan University Press.

Hagerman, H. J. 1932. *Navajo Indian Reservation.* Washington, D.C.: US Government Printing Office.

Henderson, E. 1985. Wealth, status, and change among the Kaibeto Plateau Navajo. Unpublished Ph.D. thesis, University of Arizona.

Hopi Tribe 1939. Information concerning Hopi problems. Hopi report submitted to Charles E. Rachford at Polacca, 4 December 1939. *National Archives and Records Service,* Record Group 75, CCF WNA, File 8970–30, 308. 2.

Hultkranz, A. 1986. Mythology and religious concepts. In *Great Basin,* W. L. d'Azevedo (ed.), 630–40. Handbook of North American Indians, vol. 11, W. G. Sturtevant, general editor. Washington, D.C.: Smithsonian Institution.

Kammer, J. 1980. *The Second Long Walk.* Albuquerque: University of New Mexico Press.

Kelly, I. T. 1934. Southern Paiute bands. *American Anthropologist* 36, 548–61.

Kelly, I. T. 1964. *Southern Paiute Ethnography.* Salt Lake City: University of Utah Press.

Kelly, I. T. & C. S. Fowler 1986. Southern Paiute. In *Great Basin,* W. L. d'Azevedo (ed.), 368–97. Handbook of North American Indians, vol. 11. W. G. Sturtevant, general editor. Washington, D.C.: Smithsonian Institution.

Kintigh, K. 1990. Repatriation bill passes Congress. *Society of American Archaeology Bulletin* 8, 8.

Kluckhohn, C. & D. Leighton 1946. *The Navaho.* Cambridge, Mass.: Harvard University Press.

Liljeblad, S. 1986. Oral tradition: content and style of verbal arts. In *Great Basin,* W. L. d'Azevedo (ed.), 641–59. Handbook of North American Indians, vol. 11. W. G. Sturtevant, general editor. Washington, D.C.: Smithsonian Institution.

McNitt, F. 1972. *The Navajo Wars.* Albuquerque: University of New Mexico Press.

Opler, M. E. 1983. The Apachean culture pattern and its origins. In *Southwest,* A. Ortiz (ed.), 368–92. Handbook of North American Indians, vol. 9. W. G. Sturtevant, general editor. Washington, D.C.: Smithsonian Institution.

Popelish, L. 1983. *An Archaeological Traverse of the Shonto and Rainbow Plateaus, Arizona and Utah: the N-16 road survey.* Window Rock, Arizona: Navajo Nation Cultural Resource Management Program.

Reeve, F. 1974. The Navajo Indians. In *Navajo Indians,* vol. 2. New York & London: Garland Press.

Runke, W. 1914. Letter, October 27, 1914. Federal Archives and Regional Center, Los

Angeles, Record Group 75, Tuba City Superintendent's Letters Sent, Box 3, vol. 80.

Stewart, O. C. 1942. Culture element distributions: XVIII, Ute–Southern Paiute. *University of California Anthropological Records 6.*

Stoffle, R. W. and H. F. Dobyns 1983. *Nꞁvagantꞁ.* Reno: Nevada Office of the Bureau of Land Management.

Suagee, D. B. & K. J. Funk 1990. Reconfiguring the Cultural Mission: tribal historic preservation programs. *Cultural Resource Management Bulletin* 13, 21–4.

Underhill, R. 1953. *Here Come the Navaho!* Washington, D.C.: Bureau of Indian Affairs, Branch of Education.

Vannette, W. M. 1986. Navajo religious use of the 1934 Reservation. Expert witness report prepared for Brown & Bain, P.A., Phoenix, Arizona.

Walker, Capt. J. G. 1859. Letter, September 20, 1859. National Archives and Records Service, Record Group 393, Microfilm Publication 1120, Department of New Mexico, Roll 10, Frames 789–806.

Wyman, Leland C. 1983. Navajo ceremonial system. In *Southwest*, A. Ortiz (ed.), 536–57. Handbook of North American Indians, vol. 9. W. G. Sturtevant, general editor. Washington, D.C.: Smithsonian Institution.

20 Tourism and the Bighorn Medicine Wheel: how multiple use does not work for sacred land sites

NICOLE PRICE

The Bighorn Medicine Wheel (Fig. 20.1) and Medicine Mountain are located in the Big Horn mountains of northwestern Wyoming, 60 miles east of Cody, Wyoming. The wheel sits at 9,750 feet elevation on a rocky ledge. It does not occupy the highest spot on Medicine Mountain – the highest point is the site of an Air Force radar installation.

The ledge containing the Medicine Wheel is part of a barren windswept plateau, accessible for perhaps three months of the year. A stone circle 80 feet across has been placed there, including twenty-eight spokes or lines marked

Figure 20.1 Aerial view of the Bighorn Medicine Wheel. Photo: C. Milne, from *Sacred Earth*, Canada: Penguin Viking Books 1992 and New York: Abraham Books, 1993.

with stones, and six rock cairns: four inside the circle, one in the centre and one outside to the southwest. The central cairn is the oldest part of the feature, and archaeological studies have found that a central hub existed before the circle and spokes were added. There are caves around the area that were used for ceremonial purposes. The feeling of timelessness is always present at Medicine Mountain and hours seem like minutes. There are old trails that come up onto the mountain from both east and west and parts of these old trails are still visible and can be traced and walked. Walking a part of the old trail sends one back into the past; with a little imagination one can feel the walk people would have taken coming here, knowing of the sacrifice they would be making and the hardships to be endured. There are steps cut into the limestone and the trail does not lead right up to the wheel but into what would have been a cave or tunnel that has been filled in with rock by the Forest Service.

History of Native use

The Bighorn Medicine Wheel and Medicine Mountain are sacred land sites and have been for a long time – some of the dating for this site goes back as far as 10,000 years. As different tribes came and went, the one thing that has been a constant is the fact that the Medicine Wheel and Mountain has always been a neutral area for all tribes, and arms were not allowed within this area. While they were there all tribes were friends and not enemies. Tribal Elders talk of enemy tribes camping side by side, while the men were preparing for ceremonies or rituals. At these times much trading of goods and medicines took place.

The Northern Plains tribes were nomadic peoples who travelled over great distances in the course of a year, following the buffalo herds, searching for plants to supplement their diets and to go to places where they could meet other tribes, to exchange medicines and to do trading. The Cheyenne, for instance, travelled from North Dakota all the way to northern Texas.

The tribes were nomadic when the Medicine Wheel and Mountain were first used. Then came the police warfare action of the United States government and Indian reservations were established. The Native Americans became disassociated from the ritual and renewal practices for the Medicine Wheel and Mountain area because they were not allowed to leave the reservations.

However, contemporary use of the Medicine Wheel has continued through the years by a number of tribes: Crow, Northern and Southern Cheyenne, Blackfeet, Shoshone, five bands of Sioux and the Northern and Southern Arapahoe.

Why the Medicine Wheel and Mountain are sacred

Native Americans would only visit sacred sites such as this for a very specific purpose, and only after much preparation had taken place away from the site.

Many offerings would be made, which were purified before the visit even started. Proper respect for the site had to be maintained throughout, and no one would go there just out of curiosity. In fact, Native Americans would only have visited this or any sacred site at times of great tribal need, otherwise they respectfully stayed away. It has been done like this for thousands of years.

The Medicine Wheel and Mountain were and are used as a vision quest area by a number of tribes, and herein lies the great problem in allowing tourism or other types of multiple use of the area. The land base for a sacred site is the home or lodge of the spirit life that dwells within, in this case a mountain. The rulers of the universe reside here, not only the rulers of the physical elements but the spiritual elements as well. It is here where the offerings are taken, and the prayers that go with them are accepted or rejected. It is here that the prayers are answered.

Herein lies the great division between the white, dominant culture and the Native Americans, for the dominant society lives with a commemorative religion, which commemorates a person, place or event in the past. The Native American religion, on the other hand, is one of renewal. Each spring a whole renewal process started again, and each place had a ceremony dedicated to the renewal of the spirit life that was part of an area, be it sky, earth, water, animal or plant.

Because of these cultural differences between the Native Americans and those who dominate planning and legislative organizations, the Elders that work with the Medicine Wheel Alliance have asked many times, 'How do you design plans to protect sacred places when you are dealing with people who have never held anything sacred? People who probe the earth, probe the sky and oceans, tread upon all the earth, touch everything and all without feeling the mother earth under them!'

To Native Americans the highest and best use of land is that which ensures the spiritual harmony of the area, past, present and future. In Montana, Wyoming and South Dakota there are a number of sacred sites: Bighorn Medicine Wheel and Medicine Mountain, Bears Tower (better known to many as Devils Tower), Bear Butte, Black Hills, Sweetgrass Hills, Badger-Two Medicine and Old Man Tree, to name just a few. These are places of great beauty, quiet places – or at least they used to be. As development takes place and people come to the area out of curiosity, they feed upon the spirit of the mountain or area and the spiritual harmony of the land is disrupted. Native Americans believe that this is why they now have the problems of alcoholism, child abuse and diseases of the elderly that they do. They feel that bad things have happened to their peoples because they have not been allowed to come to sacred sites and appease the spirit life of these places.

'Not been allowed' is the key phrase here, because there was a time, from 1880 to 1924, when Indians were not allowed off their reservations. Not until the Native American Religious Freedom Act was passed in 1978 did Native Americans feel they had the right to go onto federal lands and practise their religion. There are still old Shoshone people who do not believe even to this day that they can leave their reservation.

Multiple use and the Forest Service

In the view of the United States Forest Service, 'multiple use' involves the management of all renewable surface resources within the National Forest System so that they are used in the combination that best meets the needs of the American people. Resource conservation is implicit in this, and thus some land will not be exploited for all its possible resources. The intention is that resource management is to be co-ordinated and harmonious, without any impairment of the productivity of the land. Consideration will be given first to the various resource values that exist, even though this may not result in the highest economic or financial returns.

The Forest Service, because of the multiple use mandate, has had to address scenic, historic, wilderness, grazing and water developments. They are now having to address *sacred land sites of the Native American.*

The Forest Service is a formidable agency, started 100 years ago by a group of scientists who were only looking to enhance timber production on forest lands. With the advent of the multiple use concept, a new group of people also wanted access to these spaces. The Forest Service does not have the expertise to deal with all the varied interests that have now sprouted up, especially in the area of sacred land and sites. The difficulty that arises here in relation to sacred land issues is that most federal agencies want these issues debated, whereas the view of the traditional communities is that religious issues should not be debated; such a situation therefore has grave consequences for traditional practitioners when they are asked to do so. The spirit life of a sacred place does have an ecosystem but, unfortunately, as presently administered, there is no place in the multiple use system to access the spiritual quality of the land and its ecosystem.

The Medicine Wheel and Medicine Mountain already support multiple uses. They are used for cattle-grazing, a radar dome, tourism, hunting and snow-mobiling; timbering has been considered, and it will probably be considered again in the future as the Big Horn Forest Service looks for more timber. The land managers need to realize that all the land cannot be used all the time, for all of the multiple uses.

Development plans

In 1988, the Forest Service development plans for the Medicine Wheel included a 2,000 sq. foot information centre right at the Medicine Wheel itself, and a viewing platform at least 90 feet (27 metres) long, wide enough for two wheelchairs side by side, placed adjacent to the Medicine Wheel. Plans also included a new and large environmentally coloured fence around the perimeter, new walking trails to the 'Five Springs overlook' and tipi rings, and interpretive signs to tell people the history of the area. The development proposal also included a new parking lot for thirty cars and two large vehicles. The road up to the wheel was to be widened into a good, two-lane road approaching within 30 feet (9 metres) of the wheel.

All this was planned to take place without any Native American input. According to the then District Ranger, 'We've never seen any Indians up there, so why should they be concerned?' The fact that the Medicine Wheel and Medicine Mountain area is a sacred site was not even considered in these plans or, for that matter, in any other development. Since 1988 the Medicine Wheel Alliance and its affiliated tribes have worked long and hard to get the Native American viewpoint into the working plans for this area. To date, we have gone through a scoping document and Draft Environmental Assessment and are waiting for the Draft Environmental Impact Statement. The Big Horn Forest Service has recently stated that there will not be an information centre right at the Medicine Wheel after all, nor will there be a viewing platform. Beyond that, at this point, we do not know what is in the imminent Draft Environmental Impact Statement.

The highest and best use

The Bighorn Medicine Wheel and Medicine Mountain has always been a very sacred area, used for vision questing or prayer; a place to renew the spirit. Native Americans of today would once again like to see it become just that: a place of spiritual renewal. All they have asked is that at least a 2½-mile radius be established as a preserve of some kind. Sensitive development could include walking trails to the Medicine Wheel and a small information centre, with a replica of the Wheel displayed for the curious, placed at least a mile and a half away from the Wheel itself. Signs should be devised to inform visitors how they should approach the area, what are appropriate offerings, and what the site should be used for.

To traditional Native Americans, Medicine Mountain is the equivalent of a church and therefore should be treated as such. As more and more land is consumed for development of all kinds, places such as these will become increasingly important for the solitude and meditative experiences they can provide to all.

We have created historical and cultural parks which have been turned into recreational developments. When a sacred site is part of a federal, state or local property, it usually becomes the tourist attraction for the area. This may be the reason why Native American Indians are reluctant to discuss or identify areas of importance.

Now, perhaps, we need to think along the lines of sacred land parks; each creating, by its own definition, a space set apart for contemplative uses, to be used in the way that the Peoples originally used them. The Medicine Wheel and Mountain is a place to pray, a place for healing. It is a place for people to 'find' and recreate themselves. Such places should never become commercial ventures.

Postscript

Since this chapter was written a Memorandum of Agreement (MOA) has been drawn up (on 9 June 1993) which initiates implementation of the National Historic Preservation Act (Section 106). The Agreement was signed by the Medicine Wheel Alliance, the Medicine Wheel Coalition for Sacred Sites of North America, Big Horn National Forest, the Advisory Council on Historic Preservation and the Wyoming State Historic Preservation Office. This Agreement mandates a number of temporary measures designed to avoid or minimize damage and deterioration of the Medicine Wheel and Medicine Mountain (Salerno 1993) and also:

> sets aside days for traditional ceremonial use and incorporates traditional practitioners . . . to act in advisory capacity to state and federal agencies of forest management. The MOA will be followed by a Programmatic Agreement, which will provide the basis for the development and implementation of a Historic Properties Management Plan.
>
> (Salerno 1993, n.p.)

The Memorandum of Agreement is only a beginning, and there is still likely to be an uphill struggle ahead, but there is no doubt that it is an important step forward.

Reference

Salerno, S. Medicine Wheel Agreement sets historic precedent for protection of sacred sites. *News from Indian Country* August 1993, n.p.

21 Ninaistákis – the Nitsitapii's sacred mountain: traditional Native religious activities and land use/tourism conflicts

BRIAN REEVES

Introduction

Ninaistákis ('the Chief Mountain'), the sacred mountain of the Nitsitapii (generally referred to by whites as the Blackfoot People), lies half within the Blackfeet Reservation and half within Glacier National Park, Montana.[1] For thousands of years, Ninaistákis has been and continues to be a focus for traditional vision questing and other spiritual activities. The oldest of the medicine pipes was 'visioned' at Ninaistákis, the home of Thunderbird, the most powerful of the 'Up Above People', who gave the Medicine Pipe to the Nitsitapii. The mountain is also an increasingly popular destination for climbers and sightseers who, along with Native people, use an access road constructed in the late 1960s to an exploratory gas well site on the Blackfeet Reservation, providing easy access from a paved highway to within a short distance of the base. Traditional activities are being disrupted by visitors, who are also taking offerings that they find there. Additional visual and spiritual disruptions occur from clear-cut and selective logging of forested slopes licensed by the Blackfeet Tribal Business Council. In September 1991 the Council passed a 'use respect' order restricting vehicle traffic; portions of the mountain above the timber line have also been designated tribal wilderness. Although these are useful first steps, a number of additional proactive measures are required by the National Park Service and the Blackfeet Tribal Business Council, if the spiritual integrity of Ninaistákis is to be maintained in the face of predicted increases in non-traditional Native economic activity, and white tourism activity in the area.

Ninaistákis: the place

Ninaistákis stands at the eastern edge of the Front Range of the northern Rocky Mountains (*mistakis*: 'the backbone') on the border between the Blackfeet Reservation and Glacier National Park on the northern edge of the state of Montana, 7.25 km south of the International Boundary between the United States of America and Canada. North of the boundary lies the province of Alberta and Waterton Lakes National Park (Figs 21.1, 21.2). Together, Waterton and Glacier National Parks form Waterton–Glacier International Peace Park, which attracts over 2 million visitors a year. Both parks are parts of UNESCO Biosphere Reserves, and have been proposed for World Heritage Site status.

Ninaistákis dominates the landscape, standing out to the northeast from the Front Range, and separated from the immediate mountain mass by a linear ridge, on which are situated two small subsidiary spires – Ninaki ('chief woman or chief's wife') and Ninaipoka ('chief's child, papoose') (Figs 21.3–21.8).[2] Chief Mountain and the two small peaks are composed of 1.2-billion-year-old Precambrian limestones, dolomites and quartzites. The older rocks were put in place by the Lewis Overthrust during the creation of the Rocky Mountains some 60 million years ago.[3] Once a solid mountain mass, through time the glaciers, gravity and weather have eroded the limestones and soft underlying siltstones to form the landscape of today.

The northerly cliffs of Ninaistákis are surrounded by boulder fields, debris flows, and ridges of ancient glacial moraines, formed when ice once lapped at the foot of Ninaistákis, 100,000 or more years ago. Springs seeping out along the Lewis Overthrust saturate the underlying clay-rich shales which, as debris flows, carrying boulders fallen from the 160-metre-high cliffs above, move continuously down onto the forest- and grass-covered lower slopes. Older stable sections of the boulder fields and moraines are covered by grassy meadows and flower fields, populated by a large resident community of hoary marmots. Groves of white bark pine occur in sheltered locales along with dwarf birch, willow and other woody shrubs along the spring lines and wetland areas. Vegetation patterning is controlled by slope and exposure. Conifer forests dominated by spruce and fir are found on sheltered slopes, while grasslands dominate the exposed eastern southeastern slopes, swept by westerly winds often gusting in excess of 100 km per hour.

A variety of big game are seasonally present in the vicinity of Ninaistákis. In traditional times mountain bison ranged throughout the grasslands, today frequented by elk and mule deer. Bighorn sheep range along the rocky slopes to the west. The alpine grasslands to the south and west in the headwaters of Lee's Creek are an important summer grizzly bear habitat. Mineral licks in the mudstones along the base of the cliffs are visited by bighorn sheep, mule deer, elk, grizzly and black bear.

Ninaistákis sits on a forested and grass-covered erosional plateau, dissected by tributaries of Lee's Creek and Otatso Creek, streams that empty into the St Mary's River, which heads in the St Mary Lakes, one of the major mountain lake systems in Glacier National Park (Fig. 21.2). The Belly (Mokowans) River valley and its headwater cirque valleys and lakes lie immediately to the west of Ninaistákis. This valley is separated by a large mountain mass containing the highest peak in Waterton–Glacier, Mt Cleveland. The Waterton, Belly

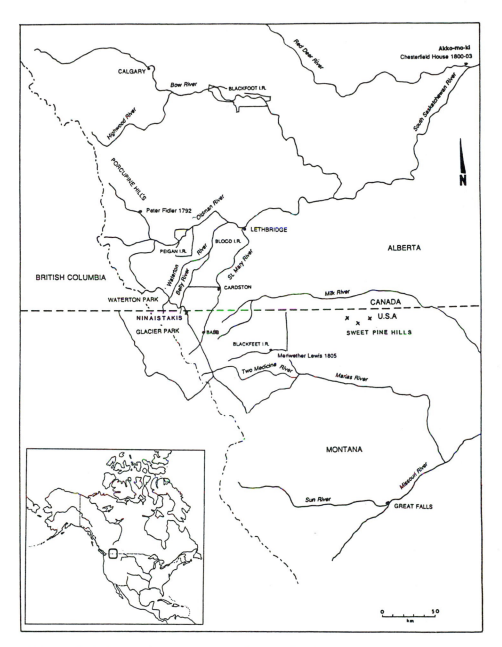

Figure 21.1 Ninaistákis within regional geographical context.

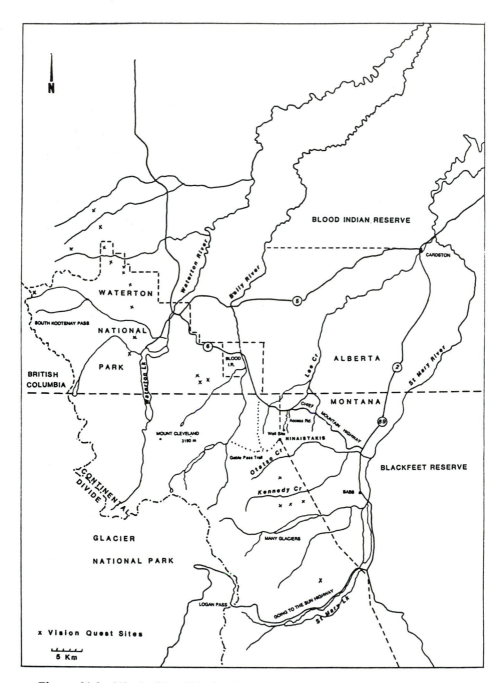

Figure 21.2 Ninaistákis within local geographical context.

Figure 21.3   Ninaistákis: sunrise. Aerial view to the southwest. October 1990.

Figure 21.4   Ninaistákis. View southeast to Ninaistákis from vision quest site on Sofa Mountain in Waterton Lakes National Park, July 1990.

Figure 21.5 Ninaistákis: north face. View from base of boulder field. Piikáni cross in right foreground. September 1991.

Figure 21.6 Ninaistákis: northwest face. View from top of boulder field. Small cairn constructed in August 1984 in foreground. September 1984.

Figure 21.7 Ninaistákis: southeast faces of Ninaistákis, Ninaki and Ninaipoka. View from Chief Mountain Highway. Morning light, September 1991.

Figure 21.8 Ninaistákis: view southwest from summit to Ninaki and Gable Mountain. Otatso valley on left, Belly River valley on right. September 1990.

and St Mary's Rivers are the three principal southern tributaries of the Oldman's River.

Ninaistákis is an ever-changing mountain. As one circumnavigates the mountain, close up or at a distance, its form reveals itself. Viewed from the northwest, it resembles a capped hat or a Piikáni chief's topknot (Fig. 21.4); from the north-northeast it is a massive rectangular wall (Fig. 21.5); while from the southeast it is a more vertical-looking tower resembling a Nitsitapii chief's traditional upright headdress or bonnet (Fig. 21.7). Ninaistákis's south-west side is quite different. Here a multicoloured steep talus slope extends up from the ridge (2,300 metres) at the base to the upper cliff bands, 200 metres below the summit (Fig. 21.8). Viewed from the southwest, the mountain is still rectangular in shape, but gentler in form and texture than the other massive sheer vertical faces.

Although substantial and massive-appearing from a distance, Ninaistákis takes on a totally different aspect to the observer once the summit is reached, at which point it becomes insubstantial. A few metres wide at best along most of the 750-metre-long crest, the summit, sculptured over the hundreds of millennia by water, ice, lightning and gravity, is a castellated walkway of towers, minarets, ridges and platforms, punctuated by cracks and crevices, some over 100 metres deep (Fig. 21.9). Sheer cliffs drop to the base (Fig. 21.10). The spires are home to resident pairs of prairie falcons, ravens, golden eagles and hawks. They are often seen soaring and calling to each other on the rising currents of air. When the wind blows, which it generally does, the 'sound system' tunes up and Ninaistákis, along with its resident beings, begins to sing. Experiencing a thunderstorm or sunrise on the top is a particularly transcendental experience.

Ninaistákis is the most prominent of all peaks along the Front. Standing out in both the first and last light, it can be seen for hundreds of kilometres around, from the highlands southeast of Calgary 190 km to the north, the Sweet Pine Hills 180 km to the east, and the highlands north of Great Falls 160 km to the southeast (Fig. 21.1), as well as from the summits of many nearby and faraway mountain peaks.

Ninaistákis is the sacred mountain of the Nitsitapii.[4] It was, and continues to be, a focus for traditional Nitsitapii spiritual activity. The mountain is also sacred to other neighbouring tribes who frequented these regions before their confinement to reservations in the mid to late 1800s: the Kutenai and Salish Tribes, today resident in western Montana and southeastern British Columbia; the Cree of central Alberta and eastern Montana; and the Atsina and Assiniboine, resident today in eastern Montana.

Figure 21.9   Ninaistákis: northwest summit, view southeast along ridge crest to middle summit. September 1991.

Figure 21.10   Ninaistákis: northwest summit, modern vision quest with offerings in foreground, boulder field at base in midground. View northeast, September 1991.

Ninaistákis: the name

Ninaistákis lies within traditional Piikáni territory which, for at least the last
1,000 years, has centred on the western plains/foothills and adjacent Rocky
Mountains of today's northern Montana and southern Alberta.[5]

The first white man to observe the peak was Peter Fidler, an explorer and fur
trader for the Hudson's Bay Company. In the winter of 1792/3 Fidler travelled
from a Hudson's Bay Company fur post on the North Saskatchewan ('Buckingham House' located 40 km downriver from today's city of Edmonton,
Alberta) to the foothills of southwestern Alberta where he wintered with the
Piikáni, 60 km south of the Bow River and present-day Calgary. In December
of that year, he travelled south along the Old North Trail with Piikáni guides
west of the Porcupine Hills to meet a band of Kutenai on the Oldman River
(Fig. 21.1). Fidler first observed Chief Mountain on 31 December 1792:

> . . . set (sighted) a high cliff on the Eastern edge of the Rocky
> Mountain, S43E, about 25 miles off, called by these Indians (Piik-
> áni) Nin nase tok que or the King & by the Southern Indians (Cree)
> the Governor of the Mountain, being the highest known place they
> know off (*sic*), it Inclines to the East, having a lean that way
> towards the top its elevation above the level of its base I suppose is
> not less than 4000 feet. This I estimate, with the comparison of a
> place I afterwards measured, which does not appear near so high as
> the King.[6]

> (Fidler n.d.)

Information collected by Fidler was used in maps drawn by Aaron
Arrowsmith, a British cartographer, issued in 1795–6. These maps, the first
reasonably accurate maps of the western interior of northern North America,
show Chief Mountain as the principal peak south of the Bow River. During
the winters of 1800–2, Peter Fidler constructed and operated a Hudson's Bay
Post known as 'Chesterfield House' located at the junction of the Red Deer and
South Saskatchewan Rivers (Fig. 21.1), in today's southeastern Alberta. While
he was there, Fidler had a series of maps drawn by Siksika chiefs. One set
drawn by Ak-ko-mo-ki ('Feathers') names the principal rivers and mountains
from the Bow River to the Bighorn. The King is the only mountain shown in
this region of the Rocky Mountains.

The next white man who possibly observed Ninaistákis was Meriwether
Lewis of the Lewis and Clark Expedition, who may have seen it from his
'Camp Disappointment' on Cutbank Creek (Fig. 21.1) on 22 July 1806 during
his return journey from the Pacific. Lewis, however, does not mention the
peak, only noting 'the course of the mountains still continues from S.E. to
N.W. The front rang(e) appears to terminate abruptly about 35 m. to the
N.W. of us' (Thwaites 1904/5, p. 214).[7] The terminal mountain on the range is
Ninaistákis.

Traditional Piikáni territory in today's southern Alberta/northern Montana was not further explored by whites until the 1850s. In 1853, James Doty, a surveyor for the US Pacific Railway Expedition, travelled north along the Front Ranges searching for a railroad pass to the Pacific. On 28 May, Doty entered the St Mary's River valley:

> We obtained a view of the Chief or King mountain, which is a bare rocky peak of a square form standing at a distance of five or six miles from the main chain, . . . so called in honor of Mr. Roan, a gentleman who has been many years in charge of Edmonton House, a Hudson's Bay Company's post on the north fork of the Saskatchewan River.
>
> (Doty 1855, p. 549)

Doty was guided by Hugh Monroe, a white man who had lived with the Piikáni since 1816. Presumably Doty was told this story by Monroe.

Members of the British North American Palliser Expedition of 1856–8 who explored the Western Canadian Interior Plains and Rocky Mountains, examining the suitability of the area for settlement as well as potential railroad passes to the Pacific, also observed Ninaistákis. On 7 August 1858, Captain John Palliser travelled south from his camp on the Bow River to determine the position of the International Boundary. His observation post was on a hill a few miles northeast of Ninaistákis. He observed a glorious sunset behind the mountain (Spry 1968, p. 263). A month later, Lieutenant Thomas Blackiston, returning from the exploration of the South Kootenay Pass, located due west of Ninaistákis in today's Waterton Lakes National Park, camped at Waterton Lake and made a special trip to observe Ninaistákis and the International Boundary line:

> The Chief's Mountain was not visible from the camp, but I obtained a good view of it from a knoll on the prairie about four miles distant, which with my previous bearings enabled me to lay it down, and curious enough, the boundary line passes just over this peculiar shaped mountain, which stands out in the plain like a landmark.
>
> (Spry 1968, p. 579)

The name Chief Mountain is also said to refer to a Nitsitapii legend in which a young chief who was very fond of his wife and baby and reluctant to leave them, left for war and was killed. His body was returned to camp and his wife, crazed with grief, climbed the mountain and threw her baby and herself off

> from that time the towers above the graves was known as Minnow Stahkoo 'the Mountain of the Chief' . . . if you look closely, even today, you can see on the face of the mountain the figure of a woman with a baby in her arms, the wife and child of the Chief.
>
> (Clark 1966, p. 295; see also Holterman 1985, p. 32)[8]

Traditional Nitsitapii religious significance

Although there are other explanations for the origins of the name Ninaistákis, it is the mountain's sacred significance within Nitsitapii (Piikáni) traditional religion as a focal place of sacred power which is reflected in the traditional explanation of the mountain's name and the continuing role of the mountain as a place for sacred religious activities.

Vision questing

Piikáni oral tradition, as told today by the Elders as well as recorded by whites at the turn of the century, speaks of Ninaistákis as a place of great power where particularly powerful and significant visions could be obtained through fasting and prayer (vision questing), a traditional activity which continues today.

A person going to fast and pray often took a buffalo skull up onto the mountain with him, remains of which have been found by climbers over the years. When the mountain was climbed by Henry L. Stimson and William H. Steward III in 1895, Stimson (1895) wrote of their discovery of a buffalo skull on the top. Their guide, 'Billy' or Paiota Satsiko ('Comes-With-Rattles'), told them it had been carried up onto the mountain top for use as a pillow by a man coming to fast and pray for visions. On their return from the climb to the St Mary's Lake, Stimson and Steward told James Willard Schultz, who had a cabin there, of their discovery (Schultz, who had lived with the Piikáni since 1877 (Hanna 1986), became a well-known writer/novelist about them). Schultz was intrigued with this report and curious as to the origin of the skull (there were apparently three in all). In the following winter Schultz asked his close friend and notable Piikáni historian Ahko Pitsu ('Returns-With-Plenty') about the origins of the three skulls, two of which were so old that the black sheaths of the horns had worn away and the sheaths of the other horns had turned from black to yellowish white (Schultz 1962, pp. 320–37).

Ahko Pitsu related to Schultz that an Elder Piikáni friend of his, Miah, had told him many years ago about the skulls on Chief Mountain. Miah had gone on a vision quest to Chief Mountain many years ago, and when he arrived there carrying a buffalo skull for a pillow, he found two skulls on top.

> One of them he said, had been the fasting pillow of that powerful, long-ago warrior, Eagle Head; but none knew who had carried the other skull up there. He had been, of course, some very, very long-ago warrior of our people.
>
> (Schultz 1962, p. 322)

Miah's particular vision quest, according to Schultz's accounting, was to correct his continued string of bad luck in hunting and warfare, which was the result of once not following instructions given to him by his guardian animal received in his vision quest as a youth. Ahko Pitsu recounts Miah's spirit experiences:

So on the next morning we mounted our horses and set out for the mountain, Talks-with-the-Buffalo, my two women, and I. Upon our way to it, I took up the whitened, dry head of a buffalo bull that had been killed in the run of a herd that our hunters had made three summers back. Arrived at the mountain, we rode up the west slope of it as far as our horses could carry us and then, leaving them, climbed up to the summit, arriving there a little after Sun had passed the center of the blue. In a small, level place on the very top of the mountain, we found the buffalo head that Eagle Head had used for a pillow and another head brought up there by some far-back sacred faster of our people.

My women had brought along my bedding, two buffalo robes and a blanket. They went back down the slope, got some pine branches and made a good bed for me, placing the buffalo head at the west end of it so that I could see Sun as he came every morning to travel across the blue. Then Talks-with-the-Buffalo again prayed for me, and, crying, my women joined him in singing some sacred songs. And then they left me. For a little I stood, looking off at our great plain, at our Pine Needles Buttes (Sweetgrass Hills), at our Bear Paw Mountains, much farther to the east. Would I ever camp and hunt among them again? Earnestly I prayed Sun for help, for a good vision, and stretched out upon my couch.

I slept continuously, had no vision on that night. Awoke hungry and thirsty, became more so as the day wore on. For two more nights I lay there, sleeping at times, becoming weak from want of food and water, often praying the Above Ones for help. At last they took pity on me. On my fourth night they gave me a very sacred vision. Came to me a certain animal that frequents the water, all but live in it, and said that he would help me in all of my undertakings and that in return for his help I should do certain things for him in the way of prayers and sacrifices. Oh, how pleased I was. Although so weak that I could hardly stand, still I felt that I had power to do great deeds.

As they had agreed to do, next morning came Talks-with-the-Buffalo and my women to learn how I was getting along, and pleased they were when I told them that, at last, on my fourth night, I had obtained a powerful vision, that a certain water animal was to be my helper.

Then my sits-beside-me-wife asked: 'Tell us, was it one of the long-bodied, short-legged fish eaters, or was it one of the smaller fluffy-furred kind that eats both fish and birds?'

Oh, you woman, Talks-with-the-Buffalo yelled at her, 'Are you crazy that you would have him name his vision animal and so break the power that it has given him?' And he went on scolding her until she cried.

Well, they half carried me down to the horse that they had brought for me to ride, and, oh, how I did drink of the water of the first spring that we came to. And then, in my lodge, how good it was to rest upon my soft couch and eat good meat, and smoke with the many friends who came in to visit with me. I told them about the powerful vision that the Above Ones had given me, there on top of sacred Chief Mountain.

(Schultz 1962, pp. 334–50)

Miah became a very successful war leader, 'eleven enemies I have killed and more than one hundred enemy horses taken, all because of my vision on top of Chief Mountain' (Schultz 1962, p. 337).[9]

Piikáni men went not only to Chief Mountain to obtain visions for success in war but also for success in hunting. Ella Clark (1966, pp. 270–3) transcribed a story told in 1953 by Percy Creighton, a Kainaa Elder, concerning the Two Medicine Lodges on Two Medicine River. Part of the story relates to the husband of the Holy Woman who sponsored the Medicine Lodges; he received instructions in a dream to go to Chief Mountain to fast and pray, as the buffalo had all left and there was not enough to eat. There the Dream Person came to him and showed him where the Buffalo were, far to the east, and where and in what manner the hunters would meet them. The subsequent hunt was successful. According to Creighton, the People

knew there was a person up on Chief Mountain. They call it Chief Mountain because it is an outstanding mountain and because the Dream Person lives up there. That is where the big man of their tribe prayed and fasted.

(Clark 1966, p. 272)

How ancient is this pattern? Vision questing is found in many of the world's Native cultures. Intuitively we know that the first Native peoples to reoccupy this region after the end of the last ice age, some 12,000 or so years ago, would have practised vision questing, an activity which does not necessarily leave any archaeological remains. However, stone structures were often constructed by vision questers in traditional times and are still constructed today. Old structures continue to be used by later seekers as part of the vision quest.

The dream beds or prayer platforms, as they are also called, range from small stone-walled enclosures, large enough for a person to sit or lie in (Figs 21.4, 21.12), to a platform of flat flagstones or a small cairn of a few rocks. Larger cairns are sometimes present. Archaeological studies of Ninaistákis and the surrounding peaks (Dormaar & Reeves 1993) have found the remains of five ancient structures on Chief Mountain (Figs 21.11, 21.12),[10] and over fifty on both the nearby (Fig. 21.4) and distant mountain tops (Fig. 21.2). The structures are consistently associated with and constructed from particular rock formations (black basalts and diorites, red and white quartzites, red argillites, reddish–brown quartzites) which are also the only ones which are

Figure 21.11 Ninaistákis: view west from northwest summit of vision quest site on west buttress. September 1984.

used in sweatlodges. While these rock formations are quite common in the mountains, the structures are only found on those formations in locations from which Ninaistákis or another sacred peak – Sweet Pine Hills – is visible. Structures oriented to Ninaistákis have been found on the mountain tops up to 75 km to the north and south, and 45 km to the west at elevations of up to 3,000 metres on the Continental Divide. Some structures are very heavily encrusted with lichens, suggesting they were constructed thousands of years ago. Others, both on Ninaistákis, and on surrounding mountains, continue to be used and built today. Vision questing on and around Ninaistákis is therefore a very ancient pattern.

Origin of the Long-Time Medicine Pipe

The first medicine pipe, known as the Long-Time Pipe, is currently 'owned' by Elder George Kicking Woman, of the South Piikáni. This pipe is so old that when its origin story was published by Wissler & Duvall (1908, pp. 89–90) no one had any recollection of who made it. Wissler & Duvall (1908, p. 89) noted: 'This pipe must be the real one handed down by Thunder, for all medicine pipes come from Thunder.' Thunder resides up in the high mountains, and it was here in his lodge that the pipe was given to the people. While a specific

Figure 21.12   Ninaistákis: detail of vision quest structure on west buttress. September 1984.

locale for this event is not identified in this or other general origin accounts,[11] Piikáni Elders state that Thunder resides in a cave near the summit of Ninaistákis, a belief of the Piikáni which was first recorded by Walter McClintock (1910, pp. 424–6, 520) from Brings-Down-the-Sun in 1905.[12]

Brings-Down-the-Sun was the Elder spiritual leader of the North Piikáni at the turn of the century. His father, Iron Shirt, a war chief of the Piikáni, also known as Running Wolf, became the owner of the medicine pipe bundle some time in the mid-nineteenth century. It was transferred to him from Wolf Child.

Brings-Down-the-Sun gave McClintock an account of a vision his father had as a young man on Chief Mountain. This vision relates to the origin of the medicine pipe, and in the telling of this vision, Brings-Down-the-Sun transcends Running Wolf's particular vision, recounting the originating vision of the medicine pipe in the 'long ago time':

> I was once camped with my grandfather and father on the Green Banks (St. Mary's River), close to the Rocky Mountains. They were digging out beavers, which were very plentiful. My father went off for a hunt to supply our camp with meat. He followed the

trail of some elk up the side of a steep mountain, until he came to timber-line, where he saw a herd of mountain sheep. He followed them towards Nin-ais-tukku (Chief Mountain). When he drew near the summit, he discovered a dense, foul-smelling smoke rising from a deep pit. He pushed a huge boulder into it to hear it fall. There came back no sound, but a cloud of smoke and gas arose so dense and suffocating that he turned to flee, but it was only to meet a black cloud coming up the mountain side. He was frightened and tried to escape, but suddenly there came a terrible crash, and my father fell to the ground. He beheld a woman standing over him. Her face was painted black and red zig zag streaks like lightning were below her eyes. Behind the woman stood a man holding a large weapon. My father heard the man exclaim impatiently, 'I told you to kill him at once, but you stand there pitying him', he heard the woman chant, 'When it rains the noise of the Thunder is my medicine'. The man also sang and fired his big weapon. The report was like a deafening crash of thunder, and my father beheld lightning coming from the big hole on the mountain top. He knew nothing more, until he found himself lying inside a great cavern. He had no power to speak, neither could he raise his head, but, when he heard a voice saying, 'This is the person who threw the stone down into your fireplace', he realized that he was in the lodge of the Thunder Maker. He heard the beating of a drum and, after the fourth beating, was able to sit up and look around. He was the Thunder Chief, in the form of a huge bird, with his wife and many children around him. All of the children had drums, painted with the green talons of the Thunder-bird and with Thunder-bird beaks, from which issued zig-zag streaks of yellow lightning.

We call the thunder Isis-a-kummi (Thunder-bird). We believe that it is a supernatural person. When he leaves his lodge to go through the heavens with the storm-clouds, he takes the form of a great bird with many colors, like the rainbow, and with long green claws. The lightning is the trail of the Thunder-bird.

Whenever the Thunder Maker smoked his pipe, he blew two whiffs upwards toward the sky, and then two whiffs towards the earth. After each whiff the thunder crashes. Finally the Thunder-bird spoke to my father, saying, 'I am the Thunder Maker and my name is Many Drums (expressive of the sound of rolling thunder). You have witnessed my great power and can now go in safety. When you return to your people, make a pipe just like the one you saw me smoking, and add it to your bundle. Whenever you hear the first thunder rolling in the spring-time, you will know that I have come from my cavern, and that it is time to take out my pipe. If you should ever be caught in the midst of a heavy thunder-storm and feel afraid, pray to me, saying, "Many Drums! pity me, for the sake of your youngest child" and no harm will come to you' (this prayer is often used by the Blackfeet during a dangerous storm). As soon as my father returned, he added to his Medicine bundle a Pipe similar to the one shown to him by the Thunder-bird.

(McClintock 1910, pp. 424–6, 520)

Contemporary religious activity and land use/tourism conflicts

In the late nineteenth century the Nitsitapii were confined to their reservations, and the missionaries and Indian agents forcibly suppressed traditional Nitsitapii culture and religious activities. Many other physically and socially destructive forces were wreaked upon the Nitsitapii by the dominant white majority (Ewers 1958; Harrod 1971; Samek 1986). As a result, traditional religious practices associated with physical visitation to Ninaistákis for vision questing and other visible religious activities decreased markedly.

With the revival of traditional Native religion in recent years, coupled with the passage of the Native American Freedom of Religion Act in 1978, and easy vehicle access to the base of the mountain via an abandoned well site road constructed in the late 1960s, traditional religious activity has considerably increased at Ninaistákis. Today, Ninaistákis serves as a focus not only for traditional vision quests, spiritual renewal and other religious observances by individual Piikáni and Kainaa, but also by members of the Horn Society (Kainaa) and Sun Dancers (Kainaa). Ninaistákis is also part of the Native drug and alcohol abuse rehabilitation programmes operated by the Kainaa. In addition to these Nitsitapii activities, the Cree and other groups gather annually in mid-June at the abandoned well site, to hold group religious activities, involving sweats and the shaking tent ritual.

Ribbon and offering sites occur both in the forests surrounding the well pad, along and adjacent to a trail from the well pad to the base of Ninaistákis, in the forest at the base of the boulder field (Figs 21.13, 21.14), out on the boulder field (Fig. 21.5), along the ridges (Fig. 21.6) and at the base of the talus on the back side of Ninaistákis. On the peak itself, offerings are found in the ancient and modern vision quest structures (Fig. 21.10), as well as in climbers' shelters and other locales.

The ribbon sites typically consist of a series of strips of cloth (generally the five sacred colours – red, yellow, green, blue and white, although red and black, orange and purple also appear) tied to trees, or placed on a boulder and held down by rocks. Sweetgrass and tobacco offerings (plugs, cigarettes, ties, pouches) are associated, as are sometimes freshwater clam shells or sea shells, mirrors, bells, marbles, painted feathers, hair ties and ribbon shirts. Blankets and moccasins may also be offered up. Earth altars and smudges may also be present, as may the pentagonal Piikáni cross (Fig. 21.5) with or without associated offerings. Contemporary ribbon and vision quest sites associated

Figure 21.13   Ribbon site in trees at base of Ninaistákis. View southeast. September 1986.

Figure 21.14   Detail of offerings in ribbon site at base of Ninaistákis. August 1984.

with Ninaistákis are also located on the Blood Indian Timber limit and adjacent slopes in Waterton Lakes National Park.

There has been no obvious evidence of vandalism at offering sites until recently. In the years between 1990 and 1991, offerings were vandalized by visitors to the mountain who did not realize, or chose to ignore the importance of the sites and place to Native people. Conflicts are developing between Native and non-Native use as half is in Glacier National Park and half on the Blackfeet Reservation, and the current access to the trail to the summit is via the well site road on the reservation. In addition, the lower forested slopes on the reservation are being actively logged under licence issued by the Blackfeet Tribal Business Council, an activity which is impairing the visual landscape, increasing soil erosion and degrading the supporting forest ecosystem.

The original Blackfeet Reservation extended to the continental divide. In 1896 the Blackfeet, persuaded by the Bureau of Indian Affairs (see Samek 1986), sold the mountain section of their lands to the US government. The boundary for the ceded strip was surveyed from point to point along the front using many of the mountain peaks as the reference points, with the result that half of Ninaistákis was on the Blackfeet land and half on federal lands administered by the US Forest Service.

In 1910 that part of the ceded strip north of the Marias Pass became part of Glacier National Park. Management and responsibility for that portion of Ninaistákis fell to the National Park Service. Ninaistákis was quite isolated in the early decades of this century. It could only be reached by wagon and horse trails west from the St Mary's valley along the north fork of Kennedy Creek (Otatso Creek), or south along trails from Canada via the forks of Lee's Creek. In the 1920s a horse trail was constructed through Gable Pass (2 km southwest of Ninaistákis) to the Belly River Lakes. This trail provided access for riders who could hike from the trail along game trails to the back of Ninaistákis. This route traverses large boulder fields and unstable slopes along the edges of Ninaistákis and was/is rarely used.

During the early years of Park Service management non-Native visitation to the mountain by casual tourists was restricted to dude ranch rides from the Chief Mountain Dude Ranch located on Kennedy Creek, just above its junction with the St Mary's, parties riding the park trails, and groups riding or using wagons to get access to the Otatso Creek valley, into which a wagon road had been built in the late 1800s. A limited number of park visitors climbed the mountain. In contrast, many residents from Cardston and district visited the mountain. Ninaistákis architecturally resembles the Mormon temple in Cardston (the first and largest Mormon temple outside the United States, built in 1921) and has become a local symbol and, in the minds of some Cardston and District residents, 'their mountain'.[13]

In 1935 the Chief Mountain Highway linking Glacier and Waterton National Parks (Fig. 21.2) was completed, providing the motoring public with outstanding views of Ninaistákis. The Park Service built a connecting link between the Gable Pass Trail and Chief Mountain Highway along Lee Ridge.

This trail was used by hikers and climbers to gain access to Chief Mountain from the Chief Mountain Highway, as were older trails which ran up along the ridges between the forks of Lee's Creek to the base. Visits by the casual tourist were, however, limited, as the trails were not developed or promoted.

A major change in access occurred in the late 1960s, when the Blackfeet Tribal Business Council granted a licence for an exploratory gas well on the north slope of Ninaistákis, 2 km south of the Chief Mountain Highway and at an elevation of 1,900 metres. A road was constructed from the Chief Mountain Highway to the drill site, and a large platform (200 × 200 metres) levelled on the mountain side. The well proved to be dry and the well site was abandoned, but the road remained, providing easy access for trucks and cars from the Chief Mountain Highway (Figs 21.15, 21.16).

The road has become the primary route for access to the base and to the top of Ninaistákis, which is approached by a trail up and over the boulder fields on the west side to the ridge on the backslope, up the steep talus slope, through a crack to the northeast face, and up a series of low cliff bands to the top. This route is a technically easy 2¹/₂-hour ascent. No special equipment is required. I estimate that about 500–1,000 people complete the ascent each year, primarily during the months of July and August. On a fine midsummer weekend, I have counted as many as fifty people in one day climbing the peak.

A much larger number of people (including both non-traditional Natives and whites) make the short and easy hike (20 minutes) from the well site to the base, venturing out onto the boulder field, utilizing both areas for picnics, beer parties and other activities. In all, perhaps 3,000–5,000 people visit the base each year. The result is increased trail erosion and more litter on the trail and in the well site, left by both the non-traditional Natives and whites.[14]

In addition to leaving litter, some visitors have also removed offerings from the ribbon sites immediately adjacent to the trail from the well site, and possibly also from the peak. Objects that have been removed include tobacco pouches, tobacco ties, sweetgrass braids, and possibly shells and marbles (the latter two items missing from ribbon sites next to the boulder field may, however, have been removed by packrats which live in the rocks in the boulder field). It is possible that this vandalism is deliberate, in the sense that the people removing the objects know what their meaning is and why they were placed there, but it is more likely that it is done in ignorance.

Until September 1991, the only sign concerning Ninaistákis was made by the US Park Service and placed by the Blackfoot Tribal Business Council at the trail head above the parking lot, advising hikers of weather hazards on the mountain, and of their personal liability.[15] In September 1991, the Blackfeet Tribal Business Council passed a bylaw restricting vehicle use of the access road and placed a sign advising the reader of the significance of Ninaistákis and the general nature of Native religious activities which take place, and asking that they not disturb the sites or activities. The bylaw was posted both at the entrance to the access road from the Chief Mountain Highway and at the trail head above the well site.[16]

Figure 21.15 Access road to well site on Blackfeet Reservation. View from Chief Mountain Highway. Blackfeet Tribal Business Council closure notice on board. September 1991.

Figure 21.16 Abandoned well site, access road and clear cut. View north from summit of Ninaistákis. September 1991.

Figure 21.17 Abandoned well site pad used as parking lot for access to base of Ninaistákis. August 1990.

Figure 21.18 Clear cut below Ninaistákis view south. August 1990.

The Blackfeet Tribal Business Council has also passed a bylaw designating the boulder field and that portion of the peak within the Reservation as Tribal Wilderness. This is an unsatisfactory measure as the lower forested slopes have been, and continue to be, logged under licence from the Tribal Business Council. Clear cuts from these activities are visible from both the Chief Mountain Highway as well as from the summit of Ninaistákis. Selective logging continues, with attendant soil erosion and visual and physical degradation of the landscape and Ninaistákis's support forest ecosystem (Figs 21.17, 21.18).

The future: problems and solutions

Increasing numbers of Native and non–Native visitors can be expected as the revival of Native religion continues and as more non–Native people, particularly those practising 'New Age' religions, become aware of this sacred mountain – the only one which exists in these latitudes of the Rocky Mountains. Non–Native religious use of Ninaistákis will increase as it has at other sacred Native American sites such as the Bighorn Medicine Wheel. Increased use will attract more tourists.[17] As a result there will be more vandalism, trail erosion and littering.

In order to minimize these harmful effects, non-traditional visitor activities must be regulated, and also the clear cutting and selective logging of the adjacent forests. While the passing of an access bylaw by the Blackfeet Tribal Business Council is an important first step, there are a number of other proactive steps which must be taken. Some are listed below:

1 Ninaistákis should be designated a National Historic Landmark under the National Historic Preservation Act. The area so nominated should be of sufficient size and configuration to ensure protection and conservation of the forested slopes within the Blackfeet Reservation. Once designated, a joint management committee and plan should be developed by the Blackfeet Tribal Business Council and the United States Park Service, to ensure long-term conservation of Ninaistákis and guarantee freedom of use for traditional Native religious practitioners.

    Biophysical and cultural inventories should be made of Ninaistákis, and areas and appropriate uses designated. A proper trail system should be constructed to avoid continued trail erosion and trail braiding.

2 Ninaistákis and a suitable encompassing landscape should be jointly nominated by the Government of the United States, the Blackfeet Tribal Business Council, the Government of Canada, and the Blood Tribal Council for designation as a World Heritage Site under the UNESCO World Heritage Convention. Ninaistákis meets the criteria for nomination as a World Cultural Site. Designation as such would require land use bylaws be established in Glacier National Park, the Blackfeet

Reservation, Waterton Lakes National Park, the Blood Indian Reserve, the Province of Alberta and Municipal District of Cardston to regulate land uses which visually and spiritually impair Ninaistákis and the landscape within which it is set.

3 The National Park Service should encourage hikers to use the existing Gable Pass trail for access to the base of the mountain as the alternate and preferred route to that through the Blackfeet Reservation. The Gable Pass route would not interfere with traditional Native religious activity at the base of the mountain.

   Signs could be placed at the base of the ascent to the peak, informing visitors of the traditional significance of Ninaistákis and the Native religious activities which go on, and ask that they be respectful if they encounter an offering site or a Native person vision questing on the summit.

4 The existing access road on the Blackfeet Reservation should be gated and locked at the Chief Mountain Highway. Use of this road by vehicles should be by special permit only for Native Elders and others with physical impairments. Natives should be encouraged to use traditional methods of transportation to approach Ninaistákis for religious purposes, by walking or riding horses from this gate to the base. Other access roads to the east from the highway should be cut, to ensure that people cannot drive up onto the grassy slopes of the northeast ridges.

5 The Chief Mountain Highway offers outstanding views of Ninaistákis, photographed by thousands of passing tourists each year. There are no developed roadside interpretive exhibits. Such an exhibit should be developed at an existing lay-by, which would interpret Ninaistákis's history and significance. This should be a co-operative effort between the relevant federal, state, and tribal agencies.

The alternative

If logging continues to be permitted and visitor use is unregulated, eventually Ninaistákis will, like other sacred places, become permanently damaged. The Animal Persons and the Dream Persons of this place, among whom is Ksiistsikomiipi'kssi (Thunderbird), the most powerful of all the Up Above People, will leave this place, as they have other sacred Native American places, desecrated by non-traditional Native and white economic and tourism development. No longer will Other-Than-Human-Beings reside in Ninaistákis – the Chief Mountain. No longer will Elders and younger people go up to Ninaistákis to await their visions. No longer will the marmots whistle, the ravens cry, the falcons dive and the eagles soar, nor will real bears (grizzlies) come to sleep in the flower fields. While the wind will still whistle through the spires as it has for millions of years, Ninaistákis will no longer sing, as there will be no one to listen.

Postscript

On 3 July 1992 a major geological event occurred at Ninaistákis. An earthquake measuring 4.5 on the Richter scale shook the mountain, which, combined with very heavy rains, resulted in a major rock fall and mud slide on the
north face. It is the largest of its kind in over 1,000 years. Blackfeet Elders are
of the opinion that this event was the result of inappropriate Native and non-
Native activities taking place at Ninaistákis. The Blackfeet closed the area to all
hikers and non-traditional users. May it remain so.

Notes

1 I have had the extreme good fortune to have grown up in Waterton Park, where I
   seasonally reside. I have observed Ninaistákis from a distance for some 44 of my 51
   years. Since 1984 I have been making regular visits during the summer months to
   observe and document Ninaistákis, its Other-than-Human-Beings, and use by
   Natives and whites. This chapter is drawn from that fieldwork as well as my
   ongoing research in traditional Nitsitapii sacred places/spaces – both documentary
   and working with the Elders and younger traditionalists to better understand and
   protect these special places.
2 The names Ninaki and Ninaipoka, or 'papoose', as shown on the topographic
   maps, were given to these two peaks in the 1920s. They are not original Nitsitapii
   names for these peaks.
3 Chief Mountain is a classic example of a geological klippe (older rocks completely
   surrounded by younger rocks as a result of erosion). It is often illustrated in
   geological texts.
4 The Nitsitapii (generally referred to in the literature as the Blackfoot or Blackfeet)
   are composed of three tribes/nations: the Kainaa (Many Chiefs generally known as
   the Bloods), who reside today on the Blood Reserve in Southern Alberta; the
   Piikáni (Peigan) composed of two divisions – the Aamsskaapipiikani (South Peigan)
   who reside on the Blackfeet Reservation in northern Montana and refer to themselves as the Blackfeet and the Aapatohsipiikani (North Peigan) who reside on the
   Peigan Reserve in southwestern Alberta. The third tribe are the Siksika (Blackfoot)
   who reside on the Blackfoot Reserve on the Bow River southeast of Calgary,
   Alberta.
      Nitsitapii ('real people') is the name traditionally used by Elder members of the
   three tribes to refer to themselves as a collectivity – the three tribes share a common
   language and culture. When white fur traders first encountered the Nitsitapii in the
   late 1700s, they first met the Siksika, whose traditional lands were along the North
   Saskatchewan River in today's provinces of Alberta and Saskatchewan. The traders,
   although they recognized the three tribes, tended to refer to them collectively as the
   Blackfoot or Blackfeet, the name which has come to be generally applied to
   Nitsitapii culture and language. In this chapter, I utilize their traditional names for
   themselves and their tribes. Considerable intermarriage, inter-reserve visiting,
   inter-residential exchange, and common participation in social events and activities
   occur today, as they did in the past among the three tribes. A small but growing
   segment of tribal members is returning to traditional religious practices and
   activities.
      The areas outside the National Parks are grazing leases, ranch and mixed farm
   lands. The closest settlements to Ninaistákis are the community of Babb in
   Montana, and the town of Cardston (4,000 people) in Alberta, settled primarily by

Mormon immigrants from Idaho in the late 1800s. The nearest cities are Lethbridge (70,000) and Calgary (700,000), Alberta, and Great Falls (40,000), Montana.

5   Intensive archaeological research in Waterton Lakes National Park has demonstrated a long and essentially continuous record of Native occupation extending back some 10,000 years (Reeves 1972, 1989). Piikáni and K'Tunaxa (Kutenai) occupation as distinct archaeological cultures can be traced back over 1,000 years within their traditional lands. Nitsitapii oral traditions state that the Nitsitapii originally lived 'west' of the mountains, came to these lands because of famine, and it was here that the three tribes were founded. Archaeological evidence suggests this migration occurred 4,500–5,000 years ago (Reeves n.d.). The majority of focal sacred events relating to the foundations of Nitsitapii religion occurred in this region (Reeves n.d.). These include, in addition to the visioning of the Medicine Pipe at Ninaistákis discussed in this chapter, the visioning of the Beaver Bundle in Waterton Lakes (Reeves, n.d.).

6   Fidler was somewhat off on his measurements. Fidler was 65 miles (104 km) away from Ninaistákis, which is 9,080 feet (2,724 metres) high.

7   Lewis's lack of recognition of Chief Mountain as a distinctive mountain is attributable to the fact that he was not travelling with Native guides, and he himself had no knowledge of Piikáni names for the prominent peaks along the Front, nor had he had any contact with the Piikáni. Presumably he was aware of the place-names on Arrowsmith's maps which the expedition had with them. Arrowsmith's place-names and geography were used in Nicholas King's editions of Lewis and Clark's map – including the name King (see Moulton 1983, Map 123, Lewis and Clark's Map of 1806) and on the Clark map of 1810 (Moulton 1983, Map 125). The weather was very bad and the mountains 'socked in' when Lewis observed the Front. This may be another reason why he did not note Ninaistákis.

8   While it is not uncommon that there is more than one story to account for the name of a place, this particular accounting for Chief Mountain's name is questionable (see also Holterman 1985, p. 32), as it is not reported in the first detailed accounts of Chief Mountain recorded by Stimson (1895) who states it has always been 'The Chief Mountain' (Stimson 1895, p. 220), nor by Schultz (1916, p. 233): 'it can be plainly seen, grim, majestic, a veritable chief of Mountains, and for that reason the Blackfeet so named it in the long ago.' Schultz does not mention this story in his detailed accounting of vision questing on Chief Mountain (Schultz 1962), nor is this account published by Grinnell (1892) or McClintock (1910) in their books dealing with Piikáni oral traditions, nor by Wissler and Duvall (1908) in their monograph on Blackfoot mythology. The earliest published account of this version of the name that I am aware of is M. Holz & K. Bemis (1917).

9   Climbers have found buffalo skulls on the mountains over the years. Some have removed them for souvenirs as recently as the early 1970s. This form of vandalism was first reported in 1913 by Stimson (1949, pp. 66–9), who had returned to climb Ninaistákis for the second time. While riding up Kennedy Creek the day before his ascent, which was to occur almost to the day of his first climb in 1896, he met a couple of young men who were just breaking camp after their climb of Ninaistákis. Stimson told them of his climb and asked if they had seen a buffalo skull on the top. The eldest, a Methodist missionary student who had spent the summer at Fort MacLeod, answered:

> His face sparkled with interest. He said, 'To be sure I have, and I have brought it down. I have it right here', and opening his pack he showed me the same buffalo skull which Indian Billy and James and I had discovered twenty-one years ago. I said to him, 'I wonder if you know that there is a story attached to that old buffalo skull which make it a very interesting relic', and I told him the story. . . . The young man's

face glowed with interest. He said, 'Why no, I never heard that story. If I had, I would never had touched that skull. I should have had too much respect for the old fellow who put it there'. He stopped and hesitated. Then he said, 'I don't want to take away that skull. If it belongs to anyone, it belongs to you for you first discovered it,' and he picked it up and handed it to me. I thanked him and said, 'If you do that, I will take it back tomorrow when we climb the mountain and put it back where the old chief left it' and we shook hands and parted.

The next day we climbed Chief Mountain by the western side and replaced the old Indian's buffalo skull, but this time I took very good care to bury it so deep among the rocks which formed the summit of the mountain that no future tourist is likely to discover and remove it. The spirit of the mountain was as favorable to us as it had been before, and I had again the magnificent view which it commands over the wide green sea of prairie as well as the peaks behind it, and we came back satisfied that the old chief and his totem would sleep in peace hereafter.

At least it was a most astonishing coincidence. As I have said, during that long period of twenty-one years other parties had visited and climbed the mountain, but apparently none of them had seen or tried to remove the little skull. If my niece and I had been ten minutes later in our ride up Kennedy's Creek, the young man who had taken it down would have finished his packing and probably been out of sight and gone, and the skull with him and I should never have heard of it again. But the man who twenty-one years before had first seen the skull, and the man who the day before had just removed it from its resting place, happened to meet in that brief interval and the skull went back to where it belonged.

10 There are also cairns located at various locations around the base of Ninaistákis. Along the spine of the ridge connecting Ninaistákis to Ninaki is a row of some thirteen stone piles, now mostly collapsed. Lichen is well developed on the rocks, suggesting considerable age to their construction. Some are being rebuilt. Cairn rows and isolated cairns of some age as well as modern structures have also been noted on ridges on the northeast and northwest flanks (Fig. 21.6). In August 1990 a small medicine wheel and associated cairn were constructed in the boulder field on the west side.

Modern vision quest structures are also present. One large structure is located on the northwest summit. This structure, now used by Natives, was originally built by white climbers to enable them to overnight on top of the mountain, without fear of rolling off. Other climber's structures and Native-constructed vision quest structures occur on this summit as well (Fig. 21.10) and on a lower buttress (Figs 21.11 & 21.12). A climber's stone shelter is located on the middle summit, adjacent to a USGS geodetic survey bench-mark. It too is used by Native people. This would have been an ideal location for a vision quest structure. It is where Stimson found the buffalo skull in 1896.

11 There are a number of recorded versions of the origin of the medicine pipe. Wissler & Duvall's is the most detailed and is paraphrased by Clark (1966, pp. 273–5). Other accounts include Grinnell's (1892, pp. 113–16) and McClintock's (1910, pp. 253–4, 424–5).

12 Thunderbird's cave is located on the north face of Chief Mountain. It is a deep vertical shaft with a V-shaped entrance, located half-way up the face of an almost sheer vertical cliff.

13 A register is kept on the peak. In September 1991 one entry in it was by a 82-year-old resident of Cardston and District who stated he had made twelve ascents in his

lifetime. Another entry from a younger district resident noted that this was over his twentieth ascent. Regular visitors to Ninaistákis are groups of boy scouts from the Cardston and District Boy Scout Troops, who, as part of their outdoor activity programme, annually ascend to the top, along with other exercises involving wilderness and overnight camps. Cardston is the centre for Mormon settlement in Alberta. The Mormon Temple in Cardston is architecturally sited in relationship to Ninaistákis. A former President of the Mormon Church prophesied some years ago that when the mountain totally collapsed, it would be the time of the Second Coming.

Chief Mountain is featured in the logo of the town of Cardston and used extensively in tourism/business promotion. Local Cardston businesses using the name include Chief Mountain Motors, Chief Mountain Realty, Chief Mountain Gas Co-Op, Chief Mountain Herefords, Chief Mountain Stamp and Coin Co. and Chief Mountain Service and Motel. The local lodge of the Masonic Order is known as the Chief Mountain Lodge.

14 Until recently, traditional ribbon and offering sites have always been clean, the only signs other than offerings being the occasional cigarette butt. Recently this has changed. A group of sites has appeared out in the boulder field in which litter, plastic garbage bags, cardboard cartons, food and beverage containers, Kleenex and soiled toilet paper have been left cast about as well as cached at the base of ribbon and tobacco tie trees (these sites were all destroyed in the landslide of 2 July 1992).

15 The text for this sign reads:

WARNING

SUDDEN, UNPREDICTABLE WEATHER CHANGES IN THE CHIEF MTN AREA FREQUENTLY CAUSE HIKERS AND CLIMBERS TO BECOME LOST. DENSE FOG AND HEAVY SNOW CAN MOVE IN WITHOUT WARNING AND CAUSE DISORIENTATION, LOSS OF ROUTE, SEVERE CHILL AND POSSIBLE DEATH. PLAN AHEAD, BE PREPARED, AND AVOID BEING CHARGED RESCUE COSTS.

16 The text of this notice reads:

NOTICE

The Blackfeet Tribal Business Council, governing body of the Blackfeet Nation, has officially declared the CHIEF MOUNTAIN area as a restricted area for religious and cultural purposes, pursuant to Tribal Resolution #140–82.

CHIEF MOUNTAIN is used by traditional Indian people as a spiritual fasting site & for other spiritual retreats where complete isolation is imperative. Several instances of intrusion by tourists and other curiosity seekers have been reported, in which sacred items and gifts left at this spiritual site have been removed.

The Blackfeet Tribal Business Council, in order to protect the CHIEF MOUNTAIN area from further intrusions, does hereby restrict this area from trespass by motor vehicles and prohibits any individual from intruding upon any spiritual activity or disturbing or removing sacred items. All persons entering the CHIEF MOUNTAIN area shall respect the sacred designation of this area.

VIOLATORS WILL BE PROSECUTED
BY ORDER
THE BLACKFEET TRIBE
OF THE BLACKFEET TRIBAL RESERVATION

17 New regional internationally oriented ecological and cultural tourism initiatives such as the 'Trail of the Great Bear' are predicted to result in a significant increase in tourism in the region, adding to the pressures on Ninaistákis. Ninaistákis will become much better known to the public, as have other sacred mountains of the world. Visitation to sacred sites world-wide is increasing in an exponential manner. Ninaistákis will be no exception to the rule.

Acknowledgements

I should like to acknowledge the good conversations with Elders Joe and Josephine Crowshoe (North Piikáni) and George Kicking Woman (South Piikáni) with respect to Ninaistákis. Curly Bear Wagner, Cultural Officer, Blackfeet Tribe, has assisted me in many ways. Many of the suggestions I make in this chapter for protection of Ninaistákis and traditional Native sites/activities are from Curly Bear, who has been instrumental in getting the Blackfeet Tribal Business Council to pass the resolutions, discussed in this chapter, limiting access to Ninaistákis and protecting certain areas. Thanks to Jack Holterman for providing me with copies of the Stimson materials relating to Ninaistákis. As a newcomer (third generation) to these lands, whose sacred sites of the Abrahamic religious tradition are in faraway lands and hard to relate to (for more than one reason), it is personally very gratifying to come to understand and know that this mountain landscape, one of North America's Last Best Places, is, has been and continues to be, a Native American sacred space. May it be ever so.

References

Clark, E. E. 1966. *Indian Legends from the Northern Rockies*. Oklahoma: University of Oklahoma Press.

Dormaar, J. F. & B. O. K. Reeves 1993. Vision quest sites in the southern Canadian and northern Montana Rockies. In *Kunaitupii: coming together on native sacred sites*, B. O. K. Reeves & M. A. Kennedy (eds), 162–78. Proceedings of the First Joint Meeting of the Alberta and Montana Archaeological Societies, 1990. Calgary, Alberta: Archaeological Society of Alberta.

Doty, J. 1855. Report of Mr. James Doty of a survey from Fort Benton, near the Great Falls of the Missouri, along the eastern base of the Rocky Mountains, to latitude 490 30' N. In *Reports of Explorations and Survey, to Ascertain the Most Practicable and Economical Route for a Railroad from the Mississippi River to the Pacific Ocean*, vol. 1, part 1, 12 vols, 33rd Congress, 2nd Session; House Document no. 91, Serial no. 791. 543–53. Washington, D.C.

Ewers, J. C. 1958. *The Blackfeet: raiders on the northwestern plains*. Norman, Okla.: University of Oklahoma Press.

Fidler, P. n.d. *Journal of a Journey over Land from Buckingham House to the Rocky Mountains in 1792 & 3*. Provincial Archives of Manitoba E.3/2.

Grinnell, G. B. 1892. *Blackfoot Lodge Tales: the story of a prairie people*. New York: Charles Scribner's Sons.

Hanna, W. L. 1986. *The Life and Times of James Willard Schultz (Apikuni)*. Norman, Okla.: University of Oklahoma Press.

Harrod, H. L. 1971. *Mission among the Blackfeet*. Norman, Okla.: University of Oklahoma Press.

Holterman, J. 1985. *Place Names of Glacier/Waterton National Parks*. Glacier Natural History Association, West Glacier.

Holtz, M. E. & K. I. Bemis 1917. *Glacier National Park: its trails and treasures*. New York: George Doran Co.

McClintock, W. 1910. *The Old North Trail: life, legends and religion of the Blackfeet Indians*. London: Macmillan.

Moulton, G. E. (ed.) 1983. *Atlas of the Lewis & Clark Expedition. The Journals of the Lewis and Clark Expedition, Vol. 1*. Lincoln: University of Nebraska Press.

Reeves, B. O. K. 1972. *The Archaeology of Pass Creek Valley, Waterton Lakes National Park*. Canadian Parks Service. National Historic Sites Service, Manuscript Report Series No. 61, Ottawa.

Reeves, B. O. K. 1989. Cultural Resource Management Plan, Waterton Lakes National Park. Report on file, Canadian Park Service, Calgary.

Reeves, B. O. K. n.d. Piikáni sacred geography. Unpublished manuscript.

Samek, H. 1986. *The Blackfoot Confederacy 1880–1920.* Albuquerque: University of New Mexico Press.

Schultz, J. W. 1916. *Blackfeet Tails of Glacier National Park.* Boston: Houghton Mifflin.

Schultz, J. W. 1962. Bison skulls on Chief Mountain. In *Blackfeet and Buffalo: memories of life among the Indians*, K. C. Seele (ed.), 320–37. Norman, Okla.: University of Oklahoma Press.

Spry, I. 1968. *The Papers of the Palliser Expedition 1857–1860.* Toronto: Champlain Society.

Stimson, H. L. 1895. The ascent of Chief Mountain. In *Hunting in Many Lands: the book of the Boone and Crockett Club*, T. Roosevelt & G. B. Grinnell (eds), 220–37. New York: Forest & Stream Publishing Co.

Stimson, H. L. 1949. *My Vacations.* Privately published.

Thwaites, R. G. (ed.) 1904/5 & 1969. *Original Journals of Lewis and Clark*, vol. 5. New York: Reprint by Arno Press.

Wissler, C. & D. C. Duvall 1908. *Mythology of the Blackfoot Indians.* American Museum of Natural History, Anthropological Papers, vol. 2, part 1. New York.

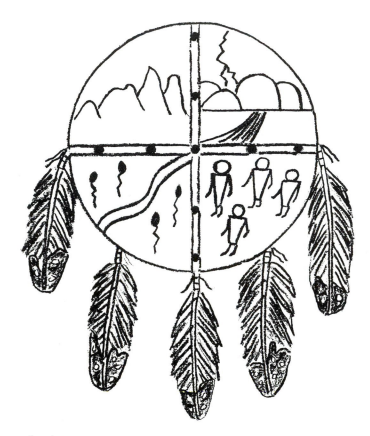

Front cover drawing:
A Blackfeet shield, after Darrell Norman/EE-Nees-Too-Wah-See (Buffalo Body),
Blackfeet artist. In the words of Darrell Norman, 'the circle itself is the circle of life (the
sun) connecting all things, and it is unending. The four sections represent the four
directions of the world (north, south, east and west). The upper left section represents
the earth (mountains); the upper right represents the sky and air (lightning, clouds and
wind); the lower left represents water (a river and the tadpoles which are a symbol of
life in the waters); the lower right represents the people of the world, red, yellow, white
and black, all people inclusive, regardless of colour. The circles inside the cross are
stars. The eagle feathers are instruments of prayer.'

Index*

* Note that numerals in bold indicate pages
with illustrations.